BEYOND CITIZENSHIP

BEYOND CITIZENSHIP

American Identity After Globalization

PETER J. SPIRO

OXFORD
UNIVERSITY PRESS

2008

OXFORD
UNIVERSITY PRESS

Oxford University Press, Inc., publishes works that further
Oxford University's objective of excellence
in research, scholarship, and education.

Oxford   New York
Auckland   Cape Town   Dar es Salaam   Hong Kong   Karachi
Kuala Lumpur   Madrid   Melbourne   Mexico City   Nairobi
New Delhi   Shanghai   Taipei   Toronto

With offices in
Argentina   Austria   Brazil   Chile   Czech Republic   France   Greece
Guatemala   Hungary   Italy   Japan   Poland   Portugal   Singapore
South Korea   Switzerland   Thailand   Turkey   Ukraine   Vietnam

Copyright © 2008 by Oxford University Press, Inc.

Published by Oxford University Press, Inc.
198 Madison Avenue, New York, New York 10016

www.oup.com

Oxford is a registered trademark of Oxford University Press

Library of Congress Cataloging-in-Publication Data
Spiro, Peter J.
Beyond citizenship : American identity after globalization / Peter J. Spiro.
   p. cm.
ISBN 978-0-19-515218-0
1. Citizenship—United States.   2. Naturalization—United States.   3. Dual nationality—United States.
4. Aliens—Legal status, laws, etc.—United States.   5. Equality before the law—United States.   I. Title.
KF4700.S65 2008
342.7308'3—dc22   2007026544

FOR MERIN

ACKNOWLEDGMENTS

THIS BOOK HAS been a long time in the making. I started research on the project as an Individual Project Fellow with the Open Society Institute in 1998–99, to which I am grateful for a generous grant.

I'm also grateful to my colleagues in the field of immigration and citizenship law and theory. The immigration law crowd is particularly congenial, and I feel fortunate to be a part of it. Among those with whom I have had useful exchanges on the subjects addressed in this book are David Abraham, Alex Aleinikoff, Rainer Bauböck, Joseph Carens, John Fonte, Kevin Johnson, Steve Legomsky, David Martin, Hiroshi Motomura, Gerry Neuman, Michael Olivas, Noah Pickus, Peter Schuck, and Rogers Smith. I have been especially fortunate to have the insight and friendship of Linda Bosniak, whose sympathetic hearing for my sometimes controversial positions has been informative and reassuring. Chapters of the book were presented at workshops at Rutgers University, Princeton University, and Florida State University Law School. The book also greatly benefited from the suggestions of Dedi Felman and David McBride, my editors at Oxford University Press.

Above all, I'm grateful to my wife, Merin, and my children, Liana and Julian, for their patience and love.

CONTENTS

Introduction   3

1   Born American   9

2   Made American   33

3   Not Only American   59

4   Take It or Leave It American   81

5   American Defined   109

6   Beyond American   137

Conclusion   159

Notes   165

Selected Bibliography   179

Index   183

BEYOND CITIZENSHIP

Introduction

THE 2001 INAUGURAL address of George W. Bush was not particularly memorable or rhetorically elegant, and it will no doubt be forgotten to history. But the speech was a paragon of America's citizenship discourse. Delivered by a conservative politician, it betrayed the universalism of the American liberal tradition. At the core of this tradition is the notion, to use the Bush articulation, that "America has never been united by blood or birth or soil." On the contrary, according to Bush and consistent with the tradition, "we are bound by ideals that move us beyond our backgrounds" and "lift us above our interests." Among the "grandest" of these ideals, he intoned, "is an unfolding American promise: that everyone belongs, that everyone deserves a chance, that no insignificant person was ever born."

But of course not everyone belongs. Some people, namely, the members of the American community, are more significant than others. The speech betrayed another premise of the modern national political imagination, the premise of a bounded national community and a distinct American mission. When Bush spoke of "our work, our unity" as being the "serious work of leaders and citizens in every generation," he was not looking to all humanity. And if "Americans in need are not strangers, they are citizens," then by implication at least there is some group of people that are strangers and not citizens, differentiated from those who are American, and thus not necessarily as worthy of our attention.

This book examines the lines that mark the boundaries of the human community, the lines that divide Americans from others. The objective is an old one: to isolate the qualities that have defined what it means to be American. The approach differs from others in the sense that it doesn't take the national community as insulated; rather, it uses those boundaries as a tool for illuminating the nature of the community. *Before one asks what it means to be an American, one must ask who is an American.* Unlike other treatments of American national character, it takes the legal status of citizenship as a mirror of the community. In this view, nothing is more constitutive of the community than its membership practices.

The Bush address skipped between universalist and particularist versions of citizenship, just as both strands of citizenship figure centrally in everyday American political vocabulary. They have been able to coexist comfortably, at least until the end of the twentieth century, in a world marked by the segmentation of national communities along economic, social, political, and cultural dimensions effectively coinciding with national territorial boundaries. In a world in which physical location situated individuals along these dimensions of life, the universalism of citizenship talk was bounded by the frontier and the differences that lay beyond. It was easy, for instance, to speak of a nation defined by constitutional values at a time when those values were themselves particular to Americans and American space. Even if being American was no more than a matter of subscribing to a set of political ideals, in a nondemocratic world those ideals distinguished Americans from others and could be effectively assimilated only on American soil. In that world, particularism was implied even in universalist conceptions of citizenship. "We are all Americans" would be taken to mean those individuals set off from the rest of humanity above all by location, and then by all the traits, above all political, that were associated with the place. American universalism, in other words, was aspiration, not description.

That is changing in the face of globalization as the importance of space and territorial boundaries declines. American universalism may be achieving its ambitions, as defining elements of American identity are now global in their reach. Constitutional democracy is no longer distinctively American; democratic governance may not be universal among states, but its range has expanded dramatically. American-generated culture is globally pervasive, and the engines of a global market economy are at least of American origin. At the same time, the rest of the world has insinuated itself into American space, with a wave of immigrants (legal and otherwise) that may sustain homeland ties in a way that assimilationist predecessors did not. In both directions, the territory of America—in the sense of human community—no longer so clearly coincides with its physical boundaries.

These developments require a different starting point in the running debate about what defines this American community. This book attempts to situate American citizenship against a changed global backdrop. Citizenship can no longer be addressed in comfortable isolation. Citizenship is ultimately about difference; it is a relative quantity, not an absolute one. As the context absorbs and infiltrates the features of American identity, that difference will fade. It will be difficult to sustain a robust sense of national community in the face of this penetration.

I note here at the outset that although I hope this book will be useful to academics in and outside of my own field—that of law—it is written for the general reader. (For those interested in more detailed scholarly accounts of the various elements of citizenship law and theory addressed here, I suggest consulting works listed in the selected bibliography.) Citizenship law is something that should be in all of our sights as we confront the changing nature of national identity and other communal attachments in globalization's wake. It supplies a tight focal point for understanding the meanings of "we." Citizenship law dwells outside the national political consciousness, even when immigration is centered among public policy concerns, but it is not obscure.

On the contrary, citizenship law supplies a lens of singular clarity through which to consider the place of American national community going forward. Citizenship law is about membership—who gets it and what it gets you. But citizenship status cannot perpetuate communal solidarities all by itself; one cannot generate feelings of trust and support by issuing passports to some individuals and not to others. For the most part, citizenship law will track the social facts of community membership. Citizenship law, in other words, maps the boundaries of community.

These rules tell us a lot about the terms of American identity. Territorial presence is a central criterion in the acquisition of citizenship, most obviously with respect to almost all individuals born in the United States (regardless of parental status), but also in the naturalization regime. That demonstrates the importance of location and shared space to the American experience, compounded by the absence of other strong identity markers. Additional naturalization requirements highlight other key elements of the national character. New citizens must demonstrate facility in English, powerfully testifying to the community's linguistic identity. Applicants must also pass a test on the principles of U.S. government and American history, an exercise which—in theory, if not reality—would attest to a common national data set.

The historical bearings are also instructive. Citizenship-for-life can now descend through U.S. citizen parents to children who never set foot on American soil, a sign of erosion in the territorial premise. Where dual nationality was at one time not merely disfavored but reviled as a moral abomination, today it is completely tolerated under U.S. practice, suggesting a less jealous—and less distinctive—nature of the affiliation. The rights and obligations attendant to citizenship have also attenuated over the course of American history. Citizenship both demands and privileges less than it once did. The declining legal significance of the status betrays and reinforces the waning intensity of bonds among members.

Using citizenship practices as an optic, this book tests the leading theories of American nationhood and finds them lacking. Citizenship law proves the ultimate unsustainability of a strong national community, as globalization undercuts community boundaries. That conclusion is offered primarily as a descriptive one, but it has important normative implications. If the state no longer dominates identity, it will inevitably lose ground as a location of governance. That also explains the political unpalatability of my thesis across the ideological spectrum. Conservatives transparently center the state as the keeper of social order and national security. But most American progressives are also nationalists, seeing the state as the guardian of liberty and a primary agent of redistribution. Both orientations, in other words, take the state as a given, as a natural object of faith, even reverence, and "citizenship" is something that they can agree on as a paramount institutional virtue. To suggest the decline of membership in the state—and by extension the decline of the state itself—takes the rug from underneath this consensus position. It requires remapping the contours of human community. If the state falls from its pedestal among forms of human association, we will have to rethink approaches to governance. The shift renders obsolete the very notion of "policy." This conclusion is unlikely to make anyone very happy, invested as we are in basic structures of the status quo, especially we Americans who as a group have recently prospered in a state-oriented world. What lies beyond is conceptually challenging, perhaps even slightly scary.

This book might well have appeared with the title *The End of Citizenship*. Citizenship is a historically contingent institution, a modern phenomenon that is not inherent to social existence. Humankind existed for millennia without states and without citizenship, and there will come a day when we once again live without them. That day remains far off. The state will persist as the most important actor in international affairs and as a central location of identity. But the present circumstances and the nascent features of a transnational institutional order suggest shifting powers and associations, ones not rooted in the state. The shift may be tectonic—slow and not easily detected but also broad and irreversible.

On this front as it has been on others, the United States may be at the edge of change. American identity has always been ahead of its time. American identity has been more fragile than other national identities, which have been moored in commonalities beyond the state: in ethnicity, religion, language, and histories far more ancient. American identity has also been more adaptable to a world in which those moorings have been shaken, as territorial intermingling precludes the possibility of spatial homogeneity. That has been America's success—to marry the contours of identity to place. It may also be its decline. As America's universalist aspirations are realized on a global basis, detached from place, the identity begins to lose its defining features, and no other proxy appears to fill the gap. As that distinctiveness erodes, so, too, will the salience of citizenship in the United States. All of this we can see in the law, as now set against the backdrop of globalization.

By no means do I intend to celebrate the trajectory charted in this book. America has been a great project, among the greatest in the span of human history. Whatever follows is unlikely, at least in the short term, to match that greatness. The opening of the next era will be marked by instability, fragmentation, and conflict. With the end of citizenship we are hardly witnessing the end of history. No universal community, no world citizenship will take its place. Of course, the hegemony of states has also been characterized by instability, fragmentation, conflict, and collective wrongdoing, in which the American state has sometimes been complicit. It is thus important not to romanticize either the state as an institution or the United States as it apotheosis, for that system of organizing human affairs has also been flawed. As we think about the possible shape of things to come, perhaps the best we can hope for is that the lessons and virtues of citizenship be carried forward to new forms of association. That project is a challenging one, to say the least. The sooner it is undertaken, the more likely that scholars and others will be able to confront the terms of the reordering and, if only marginally, work to correct its own structures of injustice.

1

Born American

MOST AMERICAN CITIZENS have come to their status unthinkingly. For most, it's not something that has to be studied for; there's no application process; it's nothing by way of an achievement. They acquire citizenship by accident of birthplace. If you're born in U.S. territory, you are a U.S. citizen, no other questions asked. It doesn't matter who your parents are or why they are here. They may be here illegally, or for a year or two on business, or even here only for the purpose of giving birth to you; in any case, you will enjoy birthright citizenship, yours to keep on a guaranteed-for-life basis.

Long at the core of citizenship law has been the nearly absolute rule that any individual born in the territorial United States is irrevocably a U.S. citizen. This is a matter of constitutional practice and understanding. Recent proposals to scale back birthright citizenship, which flopped even in the intensely anti-immigrant context of the mid-1990s, demonstrate that this rule is here to stay. Lamented as it may be among restrictionists and nativists, accident of birth is the cornerstone of U.S. citizenship law.

This expansive territorial conception of citizenship is rooted in controversy relating not to immigration but rather to race. One can trace the Civil War to a citizenship problem and the *Dred Scott* decision, which denied citizenship to free blacks born in the antebellum United States. Reversing *Dred Scott*, the Fourteenth Amendment enshrined a birthright citizenship principle under which all individuals born in the United States are citizens thereof. The rule was incidentally instrumental in ensuring the full legal assimilation of massive immigrant communities arriving in the late nineteenth and early twentieth centuries. And it made sense in a world in which the fact of birth in U.S. territory was likely to coincide with actual subsequent assimilation into the American community.

In the face of globalization, however, that assimilation assumption seems less powerful. Increased global mobility and the sustainability of distant ties are rendering place of birth an attenuated marker of life trajectory. A child born in America may well leave America in childhood, or she may grow up with a primary attachment to some other community. The fact of birthplace becomes a happenstance, and persons sharing birthplace in the United States may in fact share little else. A citizenship based on birthplace neither creates nor evidences any necessary bonds among its holders.

Birth citizenship based on parentage where birth occurs outside U.S. territory further demonstrates the thinness of American citizenship and the lack of any alternative to territorial determination. Those children born to a U.S. citizen temporarily abroad are extended citizenship at birth, but citizenship only descends where a citizen parent has resided in the United States before the child's birth. Birth citizenship by parentage thus works from a territorial premise as well. On the one hand, the American approach to citizenship has been more restrictive than that of countries in which ethnic identification coincides with nationality; those states often recognize a citizenship tie on the basis of blood alone. On the other hand, global mobility may have enlarged the numbers of American citizens born and residing abroad who maintain no affective, sentimental tie to the United States, who are American by virtue of a parent's short stay in the United States.

These birthright citizenship rules govern how the American community does and does not replicate itself, how it carries itself forward by the march of generations. They will not be framed more restrictively. Their tenuousness highlights the eroding foundation of the national community, and the implausibility of its being recemented.

THE ROOTS OF A TERRITORIAL CITIZENSHIP

Through history, all nations have provided for the automatic conferral of birth citizenship to some class of persons by way of ensuring perpetuation of the community. Birth citizenship has been granted either on the basis of parentage (known as the rule of *jus sanguinis*, the right of the blood) or place of birth (*jus soli*, or right of the soil). In the ancient world, birth citizenship was extended only on the parentage criterion. In Greece and Rome children enjoyed citizenship at birth only where at least one of their parents was a citizen (at some points, both parents had to be citizens for the status to pass to their children). It could have been no other way in societies in which slavery and other forms of status subordination were accepted conventions, for the population of slaves and other noncitizens needed to be maintained along with that of the citizenry. Even with the abolishment of slavery, however, the rule of jus sanguinis still persisted into the modern era in civil law countries, such as Germany and France.

By contrast, the rule of jus soli was established early on under the English common law. In the 1608 decision in *Calvin's Case*, Sir Edward Coke held that a child automatically and indissolubly became a subject of the sovereign into whose protection he was born. This conclusion was wrested from the medieval system of hierarchical status and reciprocal obligation; the child enjoyed protection of the sovereign, in return for which "Ligeance or obedience of the subject to the Sovereign [was] due by the law of nature."[1] Although the theory did not hinge on a territorial principle, as a practical matter it rendered the place of birth determinative for purposes of nationality; in the overwhelming majority of cases, a child would enjoy the protection of the sovereign in whose territory he was born and thus be deemed a subject of that sovereign. Subject, but not a citizen—for the world of *Calvin's Case* was still one in which the individual had no legal rights against the sovereign. The common law system was nonetheless inclusive, certainly in contrast to the classical approach, for one enjoyed at least a basic membership in the sovereign's community by virtue of his status as subject and the sovereign's obligation to protect him.

The common law rule moved with the colonists to the New World and was adopted by the new republic, if only as applied to whites and as a matter of custom rather than codified law. Indeed, the Constitution makes no provision for the determination of citizenship; beyond affording Congress the power to adopt standards for naturalization,[2] it sets no criteria for the bestowal of citizenship at birth. The first Congress soon extended birth citizenship to the children of American citizen fathers born abroad, thus adopting a limited form of jus sanguinis.[3] With respect to territorial citizenship, however, it, too, was silent.

And for obvious reasons. The issue of birth citizenship stood at the core of the race controversy that the Framers could not resolve. The South, of course, would not have accepted an absolute rule of jus soli, for that would have meant citizenship for the children of slaves—an expropriation of property, in the plantation view. But the South could not abide national citizenship even of free blacks and their offspring. On the one hand, slaveholding interests saw free blacks as subversive of the institution and as instruments and instigators of slave revolt. Many slave states had what were considered necessary protective measures constraining the activities of free blacks sojourning in their jurisdictions, in some cases barring their entry altogether.[4] Such laws would have been clearly unconstitutional had free blacks enjoyed the status of national citizens. On the other hand, antislavery forces would themselves have rejected a rule of jus soli excluding blacks. Although jus soli was uncontested as a matter of practice with respect to whites (most important, with respect to the children of immigrants, who often could not claim citizenship through parentage),[5] in the face of the race question it did not lend itself to political resolution.

But the courts could not duck the issue, and the matter came to a head in the Supreme Court's infamous decision in *Dred Scott v. Sandford*. Scott claimed that he became a free man when his owner transported him into jurisdictions in which slavery was prohibited. For the Court to hear that claim, however, it first had to find that if free, Scott would qualify as a citizen, for the federal courts had the power to hear claims of citizens only. The Court concluded that blacks, even free blacks, could not hold citizenship in the nation. Chief Justice Roger Taney's opinion followed a faulty logic in which the various disabilities suffered by blacks even in nonslave states were taken to evidence a lack of citizenship status.[6] But whatever the flaws of the judgment, birth citizenship was qualified on the basis of race.

Dred Scott was one of the primary sparks of the Civil War, and among the major accomplishments of the immediate aftermath was its direct reversal. Effective in 1868, section one of the Fourteenth Amendment— the so-called Citizenship Clause—provided that "all persons born or naturalized in the United States, and subject to the jurisdiction thereof, are citizens of the United States and the State wherein they reside." Codifying the common law rule, the provision adopted a territorial basis for birth citizenship, under which place of birth became the determinant of citizenship status at birth. In keeping with its clear intent to reverse *Dred Scott*, thereafter blacks[7] born in the United States enjoyed a constitutionally protected right to national citizenship. With respect to most others, the territorial basis for birth citizenship was now settled.

The Fourteenth Amendment did leave room for ambiguity with respect to three significant groups, however. First were the children of Asian immigrants who were themselves barred from citizenship under racially qualified naturalization measures (which persisted in some form until 1952). Could a child be deemed a citizen at birth even if her parent could never be one? In its 1898 decision in *Wong Kim Ark*, the Supreme Court found such individuals entitled to citizenship under the Fourteenth Amendment, concluding that the amendment was not meant in any way to vitiate the common law rule and spotlighting a specific purpose on the part of its sponsors to include the children of such Asian immigrants.[8] "[I]n clear words and in manifest intent," the Court concluded, the amendment was intended to extend citizenship to such children born in the territory of the United States, "of whatever race or color."

Second was the question of how the Citizenship Clause applied to Native Americans. In this context the qualifying phrase "subject to the jurisdiction thereof" created the ambiguity. In *Elk v. Wilkins*, the Court found Indians not constitutionally entitled to birth citizenship.[9] The Court characterized Indians as owing "immediate allegiance to their several tribes," and thus they "were not part of the people of the United States." Congress, however, subsequently extended birth citizenship to Native Americans by statute in 1887 to those not living on tribal lands and in 1924 to all Native Americans.[10] Similar statutory grants of birth citizenship have been extended to those born in Puerto Rico, Guam, and (with the exception of American Samoa) all other U.S. territories. As a matter of personal status, individuals acquiring citizenship through these statutory provisions and not under the Fourteenth Amendment aren't disadvantaged in any real way. (Those who live in Puerto Rico don't have a vote in federal elections, but that's on the basis of residence, not place of birth—if I were to move there, I would lose my vote even though I was born in Boston.) No effort has been made to reverse these extensions of birth citizenship, at least not by anyone outside the communities affected.[11]

BIRTHRIGHT CITIZENSHIP, HERE TO STAY

Finally, there has been the question of how the Citizenship Clause applies to the children of undocumented aliens (that is, noncitizens present in the United States in violation of immigration laws, "illegal aliens," in the popular discourse). The Supreme Court has never definitively resolved the issue. Instead, the citizenship of such individuals has been assumed for legal and other purposes. It is reflected in the fact that one need only prove birth in the United States, and not the lawful immigration status of one's parents, to claim citizenship for such purposes as passport issuance.

This assumption has been vigorously challenged, on both the scholarly and political fronts. In an important 1985 book, *Citizenship Without Consent*, Yale professors Peter Schuck and Rogers Smith questioned the application of the Citizenship Clause to the children of undocumented aliens.[12] Schuck and Smith set forth a consent-based theory of citizenship, under which membership in the nation should be a matter of choice for both the individual and the community. As a historical matter, they argued that the consent premise best explains the early story of citizenship law (for good or ill, for it was on a consent basis that one could rationalize the result in *Dred Scott*). They also situated the "subject to the jurisdiction" condition of the Fourteenth Amendment in a consensualist tradition. On that reading, Schuck and Smith asserted, the Citizenship Clause is more appropriately read to exclude the children of undocumented aliens. The consent principle dictates denial, they argued, because the parents of such children are territorially present in defiance of the will of the community.

Schuck and Smith argued that birth citizenship for such individuals is not only optional as a constitutional matter but also possibly unwise as a policy one. Extending birth citizenship regardless of parental immigration status creates an incentive for illegal immigration, which in turn undermines popular support for a generous regime for legal immigration. Moreover, the incentives to secure legal status in the United States (and for undocumented alien parents to bootstrap on the citizen status of their children) has been magnified by the growth of the welfare state. At the same time, Schuck and Smith observed, the children of undocumented aliens don't really need U.S. citizenship, because they almost always will be born with (on a jus sanguinis basis) the citizenship of their parents and will thus avoid statelessness. "The crucial fact is that admission to the American political community is and, under any imaginable circumstances, will remain a zero-sum game—a situation in which aliens must compete against one another for the very limited number of available admission slots," they conclude, "and it is not at all obvious that illegal aliens are the ones who should win it."

Although the book ultimately did not call for scaling back birthright citizenship, it drew a vigorously critical response in the academic world.[13] Some policy makers, meanwhile, were receptive to the suggestion. The early 1990s saw the rise of intense anti-immigrant sentiment, at least in certain areas of the country. In 1994, California voters resoundingly approved Proposition 187, a ballot measure that would have denied undocumented immigrants almost all public benefits, including primary and secondary education. Although Proposition 187 was immediately blocked in federal court (and much later faced a quiet death there, as the anti-immigrant fever in California subsided), a 1996 tightening of federal immigration control measures vindicated the new intolerance of illegal immigration. Several resolutions were introduced in Congress to amend the Constitution to limit citizenship at birth to the children of legal residents only.[14] "Given the outcry against illegal aliens," as Gerald Neuman observed, "it would be surprising if someone had not proposed denying citizenship to their children."[15]

What is surprising is how little headway these proposals made, even in so hostile a historical context. The proposals were consistently criticized in the press, and at no point did they appear to command significant popular support.[16] No birthright citizenship amendment was voted out of committee, much less approved by the Congress and submitted to the states. In short, denying birth citizenship to the children of undocumented aliens emerged as a nonstarter. That experience demonstrates just how entrenched the territorial premise for birth citizenship is by way of a constitutional norm. If one of the most strident anti-alien fevers in American history could not come close to dislodging the strict rule of jus soli, nothing will. More recent efforts to revive restrictive birthright citizenship proposals will no doubt suffer the same fate. As a constitutional and policy debate, this one is over. Into the future, anyone born on U.S. soil will qualify as an American citizen by that fact alone.

EXPLAINING THE TERRITORIAL PREMISE

As a historical matter, at least, territorially determined citizenship made sense. The place of blacks aside, it guaranteed the growth of the citizenry in the early Republic and the manpower required to support the nation's defense. (Before the end of the nineteenth century, immigration controls were limited to measures undertaken by individual states to deny entry to paupers and other undesirables;[17] it is difficult to speak of undocumented aliens against that legal landscape.) Expansive territorial birth citizenship has also reaped significant administrative savings. To claim citizenship, one need prove only one's place of birth in the United States, a fact usually settled with relative ease. By contrast, if citizenship depended on a parent's citizenship or lawful immigration status, individual citizenship cases would often pose tough evidentiary calls. For an immigration bureaucracy already taxed far beyond its capabilities, the additional proof requirement could result in an administrative debacle.[18]

Far more compelling has been the human rights rationale for an expansively defined birth citizenship. The strict rule of jus soli has ensured that any deprivations visited on undocumented aliens will not give rise to a hereditary underclass, that in effect any caste created by operation of the immigration laws will not last any longer than a single generation. Undocumented status may bring with it a variety of legally sanctioned disabilities, most notably the continuing potential insecurity that comes with the possibility of deportation. This insecurity can make illegal aliens vulnerable to exploitation by others (in the labor context, for instance, where although they technically enjoy the protection of the law, they may be unlikely to seek vindication under it as a practical matter). They are also ineligible for most public benefits. It has amounted to something of a shadow existence. For that to be visited on an intergenerational basis would present serious justice concerns. The prospect of forcibly returning a person to a "homeland" to which she has never been, for instance, seems more like banishment than deportation.

But the human rights argument may not be one about citizenship so much as it is about legal residency status. Affording the children of undocumented aliens some sort of permanent residence status could satisfy the objection.[19] As legal residents, the next generation could come out of the shadows into which their parents may have been forced. One could provide that noncitizens born in the United States be immunized from deportation, even if they engaged in criminal behavior that would otherwise make them deportable. As legal residents they would enjoy almost all the rights (save some rights of political participation) enjoyed by the citizenry. They could also be given a right to apply for naturalization, perhaps at the age of majority, if habitually resident in the country following birth there.

But even if the law had nearly equalized the rights of the children of undocumented aliens, there would have remained a powerful urge to extend citizenship to them at birth. That urge is more about community than about rights. Persons born in the United States, regardless of parentage, in many cases could be expected to make their lives in the country, to become members of the national community as a matter of fact. It is part of the American experience that most immigrants who came here, settled here; with the exception of Mexican aliens in the Southwest, the concept of the guest worker (so prominent, even if unrealistically, in the European context) is unknown, even antithetical, to the American tradition. It has also been part of that tradition—an ethos, really—that immigrants will assimilate into the national community. New immigrant communities in the second and succeeding generations have become more like their neighbors than their cousins back home.

This was true, of course, before the imposition of significant immigration controls, and explains why birth citizenship has uncontroversially been extended to the children of legal immigrants. (This is best illustrated by the case of nineteenth- and early twentieth-century Asian immigrants, who were themselves ineligible to naturalize even as *Wong Kim Ark* found their children to be citizens automatically.) But it has also been the case more recently, in the context of illegal immigration, that illegal immigrants do often stay, despite the status (often leading remarkably normal lives, even against the threat of deportation), and often are able to eventually regularize their status to that of legal residents and, finally, as citizens. The children of these immigrants have been as likely, as a matter of social existence, to be a part of the community as have the children of legal immigrants. They learn the language, they go to school here, they marry and work; they have become Americans.

The law of birth citizenship has reflected that fact. Given that the children of immigrants—legal and illegal—have become members of the community, it would deeply offend liberal values not to afford them full status equality. These values are entrenched as a constitutional norm, indeed of Western democracy in general. As Michael Walzer has observed, modern liberal democracy cannot comprehend the classical institution of the metic, the hereditary status above slave but below citizen.[20] It is not only progressivism that supports equal legal membership for those who are members in fact. It is an understanding that pervades the political spectrum. Status equality among community members is a trumping proposition; it can be contested in its application, but the premise stands undisputed.

Illuminating this perspective are recent events in Germany, where citizenship law issues have been the focus of major national debates, much more so than in the United States. It had long been the case that children born in German territory to non-Germans were not extended citizenship at birth, although they were granted all other rights of legal residence (including the substantial benefits of the German welfare state). This regime resulted in successive generations of noncitizens, especially from Turkey, so that birth citizenship was denied even the child of the parent born and thereafter resident in Germany. In the face of sustained protests from the Turkish community, the regime proved unsustainable, and in 2000 the German citizenship law was amended to grant birth citizenship to the children of immigrants who have been resident in Germany for eight years or longer.[21]

Because those born in Germany had been afforded nearly equal legal status even as noncitizens, developments there cannot be fully explained from a rights perspective. The reform movement was, rather, driven by the old policy's failure to recognize the multigenerational Turkish inhabitants as the members of the community that they believed themselves to have become. This also explains heated German opposition to reform, on the view that the German-born Turks were (on the contrary) in fact not a part of the German community, nor likely to integrate into it simply by virtue of their birth and subsequent territorial residence. The Turks had come to Germany as guest workers; there had been no intention of assimilation, and assimilation was retarded, but to some degree nonetheless inevitable. Germany had been the last Western stronghold of jus sanguinis; its recent recognition of the territorial premise demonstrates that far from being uniquely American, it may now represent an emerging international norm.

In the United States, by contrast, the fact and tradition of assimilation established the territorial premise early on as a bulwark of citizenship law. That tradition explains the extension of membership to those already a part of the community by birth and residence thereafter. This community lens gives the lie to the standard policy arguments against birthright citizenship. The marginal additional incentive for illegal immigration has paled against the danger of intergenerational caste. Unlike immigration, citizenship is not a zero-sum proposition, a question of who would be granted one of a limited number of admission slots. The fact that the birthright citizenship amendments of the 1990s could find no coattails on successful contemporaneous anti-immigration initiatives demonstrates that this was ultimately not an immigration issue at all. The American system would not tolerate a subordinated group in its communal midst. Hence the durability of birth citizenship based on place of birth.

HAPPENSTANCE AMERICANS

Focused on the subordination of undocumented aliens and their children, the birthright citizenship debate has appropriately reaffirmed the territorial premise. But the birthplace metric has implications beyond that particular debate. Insofar as place of birth once largely coincided with subsequent community identity, it was a practical surrogate for measuring actual community membership. Birthplace presented a clear-cut criterion on which to peg the ultimate (but less determinable) objective of the citizenship decision—to mark the boundaries of the human community. To the extent that place of birth no longer represents an accurate predictor of life associations, continued use of the territorial premise will create a disconnect between the legal and actual boundaries of the national community. At the same time, there are no serviceable alternatives to the birthplace criterion. As globalization diminishes the significance of territory, the significance of American citizenship will diminish with it.

As a community marker, the territorial premise has always been over-inclusive. That is, there have been persons who have secured citizenship under it who have no affective tie to the American community, persons who, although born in the United States, have not in the end become American in any sociocultural sense. In the face of limited mobility and the assimilationist tradition, however, this group of citizens has never been proportionally large. Moreover, in an international context in which multiple nationality was highly disfavored (as I will describe in chapter 3), those who through accident of birthplace were extended U.S. citizenship would often have renounced or forfeited it by actively engaging as citizens of the other country of genuine affiliation. A child born in the United States to early nineteenth-century Italian immigrants who later moved to Italy in the vast majority of cases would have lost his birthright American citizenship in the course of being an Italian in Italy. In this context, birthplace was a good proxy for lifetime community attachment.

But the match between birthplace and ultimate community affiliation is waning. Two facets of globalization are at work here: increased mobility and the maturation of sustainable transnational networks. Both are consequential for the territorial premise. Greater global mobility means that fewer individuals will end up making their lives in the countries in which they were born. Transnational networks will afford individuals the possibility of maintaining attachment to communities other than the one identified with the territory in which they reside.

These developments raise the U.S. profile of two prototype groups, temporary immigrants and members of the new diasporas.[22] The phenomenon of "return" migration is historically well established; even in an era of plodding and relatively expensive steamship travel, in the massive wave of immigration at the turn of the nineteenth to twentieth centuries, as many as a quarter of all immigrants ended up returning home.[23] The possibilities for return (and now "circular") migration have been enhanced with globalization, and many aliens who come to the United States will remain here on a temporary basis only. Numbers are hard to come by, insofar as "the bulk of our international migration data collection, much of our empirical knowledge and theory is anchored in a permanent settlement migration paradigm," but according to one recent study, "international circular migration is occurring on an unprecedentedly large scale, involving a greater cross-section of groups and taking a wider variety of forms than ever before."[24] Return migration implicates birth citizenship where temporary immigrants have children during their stay in the United States and take them home thereafter.

Every class of immigrant will be represented among return migrants. Among them are the growing numbers of legal nonimmigrants, that is, aliens who are legally admitted for (in most cases) a limited period of time only. The number of nonimmigrants entering the United States has almost doubled since 1990, the intervening reversal of 9/11 notwithstanding. Although few visitors on tourist or six-month business visas are likely to give birth in that authorized period, a small but increasing number of pregnant women travel to the United States with the objective of securing birth citizenship for their children (a phenenom now common enough to have a name—"birth tourism"), which is not inconsistent with the terms of short-term entry.[25] More significant are increasing numbers of longer term nonimmigrants. Holders of the category of employment visa preferred by professionals—the so-called H-1B, of which more than 750,000 have been issued, 2000–2005—are eligible to stay for up to six years. Visas for business executives temporarily relocated to the United States (the L visa) has also tripled since 1994 (about 120,000 were issued in 2004); so-called exchange visitors (J visa holders), which covers a grab-bag of educated workers and students, are now numbering more than 275,000 annually.[26] Extrapolating from estimates of the number of foreign-born naturalized citizens and undocumented aliens, it appears that there are at least 1.5 million noncitizens present in the United States as legal nonimmigrants.[27] The group is one that is constantly cycling through as some depart and others arrive, so the cumulative numbers are significant. Some visa holders will adjust their status to that of permanent residents and thereafter naturalize, and children born here may in that case affiliate to the community. But many others will transfer out to their countries of origin as a matter of course.

To this group one must add temporary illegal immigrants, that is, those who enter or remain in the country in violation of the immigration laws but who do not permanently resettle here. Of the estimated more than 12 million undocumented aliens now present in the United States, many will return to their homelands after stays of years rather than decades. By one estimate, for example, every year one in three undocumented aliens from Mexico will return there; "[o]f all Mexicans who have ever migrated to the United States...the vast majority currently live in Mexico."[28] Finally, temporary immigrants also include nontrivial numbers of naturalized American citizens and green card holders who subsequently return permanently to their homeland. Of the total population of foreign born people who entered the country before 1980, according to the Census Bureau, more than 10 percent left during the decade 1980–1990 alone.[29]

For such temporary immigrants, the possibility of childbearing in the United States is not at all remote. Children born during the sojourn in the United States will take U.S. citizenship with them, even though they mature as something other than Americans. Prevailing tolerance of multiple nationality and the insubstantial burdens of citizenship will give them little cause to renounce the status. This class of citizens has no tie to the United States other than place of birth and a limited residency during childhood; their parents are not American citizens and they do not reside in the United States. One notable example (although most will be obscure): Yaser Hamdi, apprehended on the battlefield in Afghanistan and detained at Guantanamo Bay until it was discovered that he had been born in Louisiana during his father's short stint as an oil worker there. Hamdi had maintained no connection to the United States since early childhood, and didn't even know he was a citizen, and yet no one challenged his status as such. As global mobility increases, this group of happenstance Americans will surely grow.

DIASPORA TIES

Children born to members of strong diasporic communities present a more subtle, and perhaps more speculative, dilution of the birthplace metric. In this case, the child may well remain territorially present into maturity. The possibility, however, is that territorial presence will no longer result in the development of affective ties, as attachments are directed to a homeland or other transnational community. This proposition still faces the test of time; whether the children of recent immigrant waves from such countries as Mexico, India, the Philippines, and the Dominican Republic sustain a primary identity with their homelands or transfer it to the United States is an open question. But globalization makes possible the intergenerational maintenance of nonterritorial ties; it has provided tools for perpetuating such communities. As anthropologist Arjun Appadurai notes, "[f]or every nation-state that has exported significant numbers of its populations to the United States...there is now a delocalized transnation."[30]

The population of Mexican-born residents in the United States now exceeds 10 million; almost one in ten Mexicans now lives north of the border. Those from such other diaspora homelands as Korea, India, China, and the Philippines all exceed 1 million each. Most of the top twenty countries from which legal immigrants now hail are counted among those whose emigrant communities maintain strong homeland ties, also including Cuba, El Salvador, Colombia, and Haiti, this in a context in which some 62 million residents are either foreign born or the children of at least one foreign parent.[31] These numbers may give the lie to the American tradition of immigrant assimilation. If so, the fact of birth in the United States will not necessarily equate with an attachment to the American community, which will itself be further atomized by the presence of those who anchor their social, cultural, and even political commitments in other lands.

Children of temporary immigrants and diasporic immigrants, rather than those of undocumented aliens, present the best case against an expansive territorially based birth citizenship. Legal nonimmigrants would have offered up a poster child for a birthright citizenship amendment, if only the politics would have allowed. The normative case for affording citizenship for life to the child of, say, a professional in the high-tech industry just because she was lucky enough to be born during Mommy's three-year stint in California seems weak. In the absence of jus soli, if Mommy ended up staying put, the child could naturalize with the parent or on her own. As for those who return home, granting citizenship serves no apparent purpose. Indeed, in such other common law countries as Great Britain and Australia that otherwise apply jus soli, birth citizenship is denied to the children of nonimmigrants.

As for those born in diasporic communities, the probability of alternative nationality, deployed by Schuck and Smith with respect to undocumented aliens, might support an argument against birth citizenship (framed as a discrete entitlement beyond rights of residency). Here again the fact of birthplace may not be predictive of later community attachment. Members of diasporas are more likely to subsequently move to their parents' homeland. Those who do remain in the United States may pursue their entire lives within their diasporic communities, defined not by geography but by social ties, even if they episodically venture into the larger national community otherwise defined. The dramatically reduced costs of travel and communication make the sustaining of diaspora ties more likely; one can stay in active touch with one's roots more easily than was possible in the past, and not just in the detached community of émigrés. It has become increasingly common for immigrants to send their American-born children back home for schooling; more than 10,000 mostly New York–area Dominican American youth are enrolled in Dominican Republic schools, for example.[32] Distinctive transnational cultural practices are persisting in the American-born generations, as with the return of Indian Americans to India for arranged marriages.[33] These trends point to the possible persistence of segmented identities.

With respect to the children of those individuals whose primary attachment is to another polity, a respectable abstract argument could be made against the grant of citizenship based on place of birth. This is not to say that the argument against birth citizenship for the children of nonimmigrants and members of diasporic communities is the better one. With respect to diasporic communities, implementation problems would be insurmountable. At one time, the citizenship status of the parent might have supplied a benchmark by which to determine such membership; those who failed to naturalize could have been presumed to belong to an alternate polity, and their children could have been denied birth citizenship, where immigrants who naturalized would be presumed assimilated for such purposes. But such a jus sanguinis approach is no longer available now that multiple nationality is usually an option. Immigrants can acquire citizenship in their new place of residence while retaining their original (and affective) citizenship, and they might well naturalize for no other purpose than to ensure their children's citizenship in their place of birth. No other practicable criterion presents itself for determining whether a child is born into a diasporic community.

As for the children of legal nonimmigrants, denying birth citizenship could be effected (as British and other approaches demonstrate) by extending the child the same status as the parent at time of birth. Those whose parents end up staying in the United States would have their status derivatively adjusted with that of their parents, so that when their parents became permanent residents and then citizens, they would as well, as is now true for children born to nonimmigrants before admission to United States. But that limitation on birth citizenship wouldn't be worth the trouble. As already noted, the administrative convenience of the expansive rule of jus soli has been considerable. To impose even a minor (and normatively unobjectionable) qualification would eliminate that convenience, insofar as thereafter all persons claiming citizenship would need proffer not just place of birth but also parental immigration status at the time of birth. Even as the number of nonimmigrants grows, and with it the number of persons born to nonimmigrants who depart in childhood, this cost hardly seems worth any benefit derived from making the boundaries of the citizenry better reflect the boundaries of the community.

In any case, with respect to both diasporic communities and nonimmigrants, the prospects of limiting birth citizenship are nil. That birth citizenship in neither group excited any political opposition with the introduction of birthright citizenship amendments focusing on undocumented aliens (although at least one version would have denied birth citizenship to children of nonimmigrants[34]) demonstrates as much. These individuals will continue to obtain citizenship at birth. This has long been the case, but globalization changes the magnitude of application, for there are many more who become Americans notwithstanding a lack of future attachment to America. One can no longer assume birth in the

United States to result in a subsequent bond. Territorial presence is now more transient than that.

AN AMERICAN BLOODLINE?

From the earliest days of the republic, birth citizenship has also been extended to individuals born outside the United States on the basis of parentage. All nations provide for citizenship based on parentage. That makes sense: there are some cases in which birth outside of the country is irrelevant, and attachments to the country of parental citizenship are clear. The best example is the flip side of the nonimmigrant example—American parents who bear a child abroad during a temporary absence. The place of birth in that instance has nothing to do with community attachment. The child is obviously not a foreigner, and it would serve little purpose to impose naturalization requirements on her.

But American adoption of the rule of jus sanguinis has been qualified by the territorial premise. Blood descent has always been limited in the absence of sustained territorial presence. As a historical matter, this facet of citizenship law has pointed to the lack of an American ethnicity and protected against individuals claiming membership outside the United States through ancestry only. As a contemporary matter, however, the territorial contingency is less effective at policing against such claims, even where individuals have no real tie to the national community.

Some countries allow citizenship to descend through several generations born and residing in another country. In one extreme case, Germany recognized a latent citizenship in ethnic German communities that had left German territories centuries ago for Eastern Europe and Central Asia. Several European countries, including Ireland, Greece, and Italy, extend citizenship to any person enjoying one grandparent citizen, even if the intermediate generation—the person's parent—had never set foot in the country. Countries with such liberal descent mechanisms are ones with a strong ethnic definition, countries that are as much about blood as they are about place or history (although they are about that, too).

The law of U.S. citizenship, by contrast, has never admitted a bloodline community. The first statutory provision made for those born abroad, enacted in 1790, granted citizenship to the foreign-born children of U.S. citizen fathers.[35] (It was not until 1934 that the same privilege was extended to the children of U.S. citizen mothers.[36]) But that measure also provided that "the right of citizenship shall not descend to persons whose fathers have never been resident in the United States." The nationality laws were subsequently refined to distinguish between cases in which both parents are citizens and those in which one is a citizen and one a foreigner. In the former case, the child is a citizen at birth if either parent has resided in the United States at any time.

In the latter, it was at one time required that the citizen parent have resided for at least ten years in the United States (five after attaining the age of fourteen) before the child's birth for the citizenship to descend, and then the child herself was required to spend at least five years in the United States before the age of twenty-eight to maintain the status.[37] To take one historical example: Aldo Bellei was born in 1939 in Italy to an Italian father and a U.S. citizen mother who had been born and lived in the United States for more than twenty years. Bellei's birth citizenship was retracted, however, when he turned twenty-eight, having spent less than two years on U.S. soil. The Supreme Court upheld his expatriation in a 1972 decision, finding residency for the foreign-born citizen an appropriate "talisman of dedicated attachment."[38]

The law at issue in *Bellei* was subsequently softened to require parental presence of five years (two following the age of fourteen) and to eliminate any subsequent presence requirement on the part of the child. Thus, today, U.S. citizenship extends to a child whose parent was herself born abroad, so long as the parent resided in the United States for at least five years before the child's birth.[39] The child is herself subject to no residency requirement. It is possible to be an American citizen for one's entire life without ever setting foot in the United States.

That said, the historical logic behind these requirements plainly echoes the territorial premise. Citizenship by descent is recognized, but only where the parent has kept up the territorial connection. The parent who has resided in the United States is sufficiently a part of the American community to transmit that identity to her children. (Under the prior law, that wasn't enough: the child herself had to confirm membership by coming to America.) In the past, this regime has largely reflected and maintained the boundaries of actual community. Think of the person born in another country with an American citizen grandparent, whose parents never lived in the United States. That person would have had little in common with Americans back home. Compare the reverse situation of a person born in the United States with Irish, Italian, or Greek ancestry; the relative place of pedigree is clear. There is no American bloodline. The law of U.S. citizenship continues to demonstrate the lack of an American ethnicity.

But contingent as it is on the territorial premise, citizenship by parentage has arguably grown more overinclusive, as has citizenship on the basis of birthplace. In the world before globalization, a residency period on the part of a parent (certainly at the previously required duration of ten years, in cases where only one parent was a citizen) was probably meaningful in terms of evidencing a continuing attachment to the United States, and the likelihood of transmitting that attachment to a child (certainly, again, insofar as the child herself then faced a required residence to maintain citizenship extended at birth). Under the current provision, and in the face of greater mobility, it is less clear that the law marks any meaningful boundary. What of the child with one parent who is a citizen and has spent five years in the United States? Many of the global elites now come to the United States for college education and early professional experience for that period of time, yet that presence would confirm no strong American identity. The relatively relaxed residency requirement for citizenship by descent may give rise to something of an American diaspora, at least as a legal matter, at the same time as American identity seems no more capable of bloodline descent than in the past. United States passports will come to be held by another growing group of individuals who are effectively foreigners.

The numbers of such individuals is presumably small, at least in the short term and relative to the numbers of such "foreigners" who secure citizenship by place of birth. It is also the case that many who enjoy citizenship at birth by reason of descent are in fact American in some other sense of the word, which militates against a raised threshold for acquiring the status. But there remains the prospect of a group of citizens who share no bond with other citizens other than in the status. The rules for citizenship by descent thus also contribute to a less meaningful delimitation of the national community.

(NON)MEMBERS BEYOND

The overinclusiveness of birth citizenship's territorial premise is increasingly coupled with an underinclusiveness. Just as the fact of territorial presence may no longer represent affective ties to the community, the fact of territorial absence may no longer represent the lack of such ties. By any social, economic, or political definition of national community, many born and living abroad, with no tie of ancestry, are members of it as a matter of fact if not as a matter of law. A citizenship premised on territorial definitions of community takes no account of them, and no other mechanism appears that can.

Consider border regions, especially communities along the U.S.–Mexico border. There one finds municipalities that bridge the national boundary running between them.[40] The border notwithstanding, such adjacent cities as El Paso and Ciudad Juárez, San Diego and Tijuana, and Laredo and Nuevo Laredo comprise unitary metropolitan complexes. Individuals cross the border to work, shop, and go to school; own property on both sides; and have families that span the divide. Socially and economically the two sides are integrated. What is of political interest to those on one side of the border is of interest to those on the other side. The Mexican resident of Ciudad Juarez has a significant interest in decision making by municipal authorities in El Paso, the state legislature in Austin, and the federal government in Washington. She will likely be affected by environmental, labor, fiscal, law enforcement, and education policy at all three levels, in addition, most obviously, to immigration and associated border control measures set by the federal government.

The fact of integrated border communities is reflected in various legal regimes. Municipal authorities establish various joint policy-making structures, and may for some purposes eliminate distinctions based on place of residence. Under Texas law, Mexican residents are eligible for in-state tuition rates at state universities located in border counties.[41] Federal immigration law provides for the border crossing cards critical to cross-boundary interaction in border zones, good only for day travel within twenty-five miles of the border.

Why not extend citizenship to include such populations? Even as a theoretical matter—as a thought experiment—the very notion might seem silly. Those who are born on the other side of the border are Mexican, not American, represented by and having allegiance to the Mexican authorities, not American ones, facts citizenship law sensibly reflects. But these are constructions, not facts. That individuals born on the Mexican side of the border have interests in Mexican governance issues does not exclude the possibility of an interest in American policy making. To the extent that they are integrated into communities that are in significant part comprised of U.S. citizens and U.S. territory, one might venture the label "American" as a nonstatus description. If the person born and living in Ciudad Juárez is part of a community including El Paso, is not that person in some sense American? Shouldn't formal status designations reflect that membership? From a justice perspective, one can attack the question as one of account-ability. To the extent that the Ciudad Juárez resident has integral interests in U.S. decision making, he should enjoy a voice in those processes. Those interests in many cases will be much more significant than the citizen's interest, especially where the citizen has garnered the status in the absence of any real tie to America.

But citizenship law does not and cannot account for those who are on the other side. A person born in Ciudad Juárez to Mexican citizen parents is not a U.S. citizen at birth (nor will his birth there help qualify him in any way for subsequent acquisition of the status). Nor could the law be reformulated in any practicable way to extend citizenship at birth to per-sons in border regions. The challenge would defy both the jus soli and jus sanguinis approaches to birth citizenship; it would go against all citizenship traditions. It would also challenge entrenched notions of international law; to designate those outside one's territory with no parental tie as citizens would be taken as an affront to the other country's sovereignty (as surely it would be taken by Mexico, though not necessarily with good cause). Finally, such a regime, however delimited, would have greater problems of overinclusiveness than the existing territorial regime. No better line would offer itself by way of substitute for the border itself. Including some strip of borderland would inevitably include many whose affective and other attachments are firmly rooted on the other side.

Much the same can be said of communities beyond the territorial space of the border. As Ronnie Lipschutz observes, "borderlands are no longer restricted to border areas; they can be anywhere."[42] On the one hand, diasporic communities suggest the overinclusiveness of the birth citizen-ship regime, insofar as it extends territorial citizenship to persons whose hearts lie elsewhere. On the other hand, however, it may also suggest its underinclusiveness. A key feature of recent diasporic migrations is that those who stay behind maintain their attachment to those who leave and come to have a significant stake in the fortunes of the external citizen in his new place of residence and/or nationality. Often, these communities are bridged by families, sometimes nuclear ones. Thus, communities in such countries as El Salvador, the Dominican Republic, or the Philippines may have intimate continuing social, economic, and political ties to communities established in the United States. In some countries, the largest source of foreign exchange is remittances from immigrants to the United States; some local homeland communities depend on external citizens to fund such basic public works as schools and roads. In that sense, again, the boundaries of human community transcend territorial ones, in a way that citizenship cannot process. The important, direct interests that homeland individuals have in U.S. conditions find no reflection in any legal regime. The membership of homeland diasporas would be even less amenable to recognition in the birth citizenship regime than that of border communities; there is no way a law could intelligibly distinguish between different degrees of connection.

And so today we find some born within the national territory who come to citizenship notwithstanding the lack of other substantial connection, and some born outside the territory who do not enjoy the status notwithstanding a clear stake in the community. The territorial premise is challenged from both directions. It is no longer clear who belongs and who does not belong.

THE FEEDBACK LOOP OF DILUTED TIES

Whether by place or parentage, birth citizenship thus includes an increasing number of individuals who in the end have no sentimental tie to the United States and excludes an increasing number who do. Yet the extension of birth citizenship seems to provoke little condemnation outside the context of illegal immigration, to which the issue has only a tenuous relation. No one in the border zones or elsewhere outside the territorial United States is clamoring for the status. The absence of such controversy further evidences the declining importance of citizenship itself and of the national community. If citizenship were a valuable commodity, and if it reflected and maintained a strong communal bond, then one would witness a much broader attack on expansive birth citizenship, against its extension to the children of nonimmigrants and others who are perceived not to maintain an American identity.

I will explore in chapter 4 the shrinking category of rights that specifically attach to citizenship, from the perspective of the would-be citizen. Becoming a citizen entitles one to little more than the right to vote, eligibility for some public benefits programs, and freedom from any threat of deportation. From the perspective of the existing community, the absence of significant citizen-specific benefits lowers the cost of granting citizenship. Deeming someone a citizen at birth does not impose much burden on society. There is thus little reason to oppose an overinclusive approach, even though many who garner the status share little commonality with existing citizens. This is true also with respect to the grant of citizenship after birth, that is, through naturalization, and to the toleration of multiple nationality; in both instances, citizenship's lack of consequence has smoothed the way to greater liberality.

But as with easy naturalization and tolerance of dual citizenship, an expansive birth citizenship policy reinforces that lack of consequence. To the extent that citizenship as a legal status no longer reflects distinctive communal bonds, the less meaning will attach to the category. A citizenship that denotes nothing more than place of birth or parental status will not bear the burdens of redistributive sacrifice. I will not fight for someone who shares membership merely because his parents were passing through when he was born, nor will I be inclined to share my paycheck with him. Ditto for someone who was born and has lived abroad all her life and happens to have had one American parent who spent five years in the United States.

For most citizens whose parents were not passing through, in one respect or another, place of birth and/or parentage do continue to represent some affective tie. But the trend away from a strong definition of national community seems clear, and it is self-reinforcing. The larger the group of happenstance citizens, the less likely the status will be consequential, which renders existing citizens more accepting of expansive admission criteria and the addition of nominal members, which in turn entrenches the lack of consequence. Indeed, this proposition offers an explanation for the general decline in governmental authority. As members come to perceive a thinner connection with other members of the polity, they will recapture powers previously delegated to the government as the polity's agent, and as that happens they will care less about who is granted membership in the first place.

Some would launch from these observations into calls for more restrictive birth citizenship and other citizenship policies, by way of injecting the status with restored meaning. But any such effort will fail. There is no realistic alternative standard for the grant of birth citizenship; in the American context, deprived of the bloodline alternative, the territorial premise has proved an imperative. Until recently, it performed well as an organizing principle for the extension of birth citizenship, the mechanism by which most individuals come to the status. Territory has been consequential; for these purposes, more specifically, national delimitations of territory have been consequential. It mattered where one was born. Of course, even in a globalized world, space and presence still make a difference; on average, a person born in Indiana is more likely than a person born in Bangalore to be in some ways distinctively American, however that identity continues to be defined. To that extent, the territorial premise in this way holds true; citizenship law continues coherently to reflect actual community lines.

But in fact physical location, especially at one point in time in any person's life (even the point of time at birth), is less defining of identity than it once was. The person born in Bangalore may have uncles and cousins in the United States and parents who travel there often, end up working for Microsoft (while remaining in India), and follow American political and cultural developments. The person born in Indiana may have parents who are there temporarily, may have no other familial connections in the United States, may not speak English, and are otherwise detached from the dominant culture. And that is the hard pairing. On average, the person born in Vancouver would more likely follow the life trajectory of an American—as popularly conceived—than of the person born in the multiethnic new immigrant borough of Queens.

Of course the juxtapositions provoke questions about what exactly it means to be an American, questions further illuminated by the contours of naturalization law, to which I turn next. But the answer cannot simply be: to be born in America is to be American. And yet that is the answer that citizenship law supplies. In other days, that answer worked insofar as being born in America came bundled with other characteristics that, one way or another, were associated with the national identity. Today, place of birth is becoming increasingly detached from identity, even as the law remains unchanged. The disjunction between the legal and actual boundaries of the national community is itself consequential; insofar as the two do not coincide, the coherence of the community dissipates. At the same time, no fix is available. This is not a context in which policy elites can offer a solution, for the change runs much deeper than any set of national leaders can channel. To be born American no longer makes you one. That further fogs a national identity that is already elusive.

2

Made American

JUST AS ALL nations extend citizenship to some individuals at birth, they all provide for the acquisition of citizenship thereafter through naturalization. As with birth citizenship, rules relating to naturalization open a window on the meaning of national identity. Indeed, naturalization offers a more refined decoding of the elements of that identity. Where birth citizenship is about projecting life trajectories, naturalization can be more precisely tailored to define individual qualifications. Where birth citizenship is a matter of designation, naturalization presents the possibility of attainment. One can aspire to become a citizen through naturalization, and perhaps it can be said that the nation's aspirations are reflected in its naturalization regime.

As a reflection of community boundaries, naturalization further evidences the diminishing force of American national identity in the face of globalization. This conclusion holds whether one subscribes to a cultural definition of American nationhood or a political one. For starters, naturalization is also grounded in the territorial premise in the form of durational residency requirements. Because that premise is undermined by mobility and dense transnational networks, the naturalization regime becomes less capable of molding or instantiating something distinctively American. Likewise with requirements relating to knowledge of English and the principles of American government, history, and culture, which knowledge is now in some sense universal. In that respect, naturalization becomes overinclusive of meaningful community.

It is also underinclusive. To the extent that for some individuals naturalization requirements pose a barrier to citizenship, they may not bother to undertake the process; for many, the status offers little benefit. Yet these individuals may in all other respects comprise members of the community. The result, again, is a citizenry that no longer coincides with any organic association and works against the possibility of maintaining one.

Naturalization was an anomaly in the classical and early modern periods. In ancient Greece and Rome, the citizenry was an aristocracy of sorts, with a limited number enjoying full rights of political participation beside a horde that did not. Naturalization was used as a reward, to both individuals and whole communities. Citizenship might be conferred on an individual for great acts in the service of the community. In its decline, the Roman Empire used the mass conferral of citizenship on allied powers as an instrument of policy.[1] As nationality emerged as an important institution during the Renaissance period (in the form of the sovereign-subject relationship), naturalization presented a challenge to the belief in natural order and hierarchies. *Calvin's Case* bound individuals to sovereigns as children to parents. Although naturalization was possible in early modern England, it was exceptional, granted only by special act of Parliament.[2] The very term evidences the difficulty of reconciling naturalization with the rigid, immutable, and divinely mandated social order of the day; the change in status made one "natural," implying something on the order of rebirth.

WHAT IT TAKES TO BECOME AN AMERICAN

The first country of immigration, the United States was also the first country in which naturalization was put to common use. But naturalization has never simply been for the asking, as the conventional wisdom would have it. Although American naturalization standards have always been low relative to those imposed by other countries, historian Philip Gleason stretched the case by supposing that "the universalist ideological character of American nationality meant that it was open to anyone who willed to become an American."[3] As an initial matter, naturalization was qualified in racial terms until the middle of the twentieth century. The original naturalization statute, enacted in 1790 as one of the first orders of business for the new Congress, provided for the naturalization of "free white persons" only.[4] In the Civil War's wake, blacks were made eligible, but through the middle of the twentieth century immigrants of other races—Asian, most notably, broadly defined to include South Asians and even some Middle Easterners—faced a bar to citizenship regardless of length of residence. It was not until 1952 that the last such restrictions, against those of Japanese origin, were removed. In these restrictions on naturalization, one finds a reflection of the nation's racial self-definition.[5] For those who faced such bars, citizenship was hardly a question of will; it remained unattainable by law.

Other requirements have qualified eligibility for naturalization. From the beginning, naturalization has been conditioned on a period of residence in the United States. The 1790 measure set the bar at two years. That was raised to five years in 1795; except for a brief interval during which the period was raised to fourteen years (under the notorious Alien and Sedition Acts of 1798), it has remained at five years ever since. Also since the Founding period, naturalization applicants have been required to take an oath in support of the Constitution and to demonstrate that they are persons of good moral character. In the face of massive immigration from Eastern and Southern Europe, in 1906 Congress required that new citizens have an ability to speak English. As a matter of judicial practice (the courts were largely responsible for administering naturalization during the first half of the twentieth century), applicants were also required to demonstrate an understanding of American history and government (the so-called civics requirement), a requirement codified in 1952. The 1952 act also added the ability to read and write English as a condition. Naturalization provisions have imposed ideological exclusions; even today, membership in the Communist Party renders an alien ineligible for citizenship. In most cases applicants must pay application and fingerprinting fees totaling more than $600.

Naturalization has never been and is still not today merely for the asking. The thresholds do, however, show signs of being relaxed, in both law and practice, at least relative to mid-twentieth-century standards. The residency requirement has been reduced with respect to various applicants, most notably spouses of U.S. citizens. Other statutory measures exempt many applicants from the language and civics requirements, based on age, length of residence, and physical or mental impairment (broadly defined in practice). Those subject to the civics requirement face a test that requires nothing more than memorization. The language requirement has been clarified to require only facility in simple English, and examiners are generous in finding it satisfied. With the end of the cold war, ideological restrictions implicate a tiny number of cases. Even the oath requirement, long standing as an absolute (if in most cases easily satisfied) condition to naturalization, is now waivable where the applicant cannot for mental reasons understand its nature.[6] Perhaps the most serious obstacles to naturalization are the fear of tests that uneducated would-be applicants often harbor, the maze of the immigration bureaucracy, and a fee that represents a hefty bite out of many immigrant wallets.

Some nationalists highlight the relaxation of these requirements as part of the "dumbing down" of American citizenship and demand the imposition of tougher standards for naturalization.[7] As with controversies relating to birth citizenship, however, these developments cannot be reversed by the policy makers. They reflect an inexorable erosion of the national community against the backdrop of a world that has been largely Americanized. The old thresholds to membership can no longer be justified where in a sense everyone has already met them. They are artifacts of a world in which America was different, and adjustment was required. Today, naturalization requirements are alternatively an instrument of exclusion for the unlucky few who are unable to navigate them and a deterrent to others willing to contribute to the project, but not at any cost. Formal membership in the American community is increasingly a take-it-or-leave-it proposition. That proves a depletion of affective intensity. It also demonstrates the harm that naturalization barriers pose to the perpetuation of the community, even as a diminished quantity. Nationalists should be bemoaning the maintenance of existing naturalization requirements, not calling for their supplementation.

Not that the elimination of naturalization requirements would revive the nation to its former glories. On the contrary, pressure to lower these barriers evidences the dwindling bargaining power of the state. Citizenship no longer presents a seller's market, in which the existing community could expect to extract substantial commitments from prospective members as the price of admission. This is reflected in the relaxation of naturalization conditions that has already occurred. As in the context of birth citizenship, however, that relaxation contributes to the further dissipation of community, as individuals with little in the way of real ties to the community become formal members thereof. The circle becomes unbreakable. Raising naturalization barriers will only turn dedicated would-be members away.

Lowering them allows in proverbial interlopers and itinerants, persons nurturing no sentimental attachment to other members.

These observations hold true however one defines the American community. To the extent America is defined in a sociocultural sense, it is now the case that most immigrants come to the United States with some familiarity of its social ways and cultural icons, at the same time that they are enabled to sustain a homeland orientation after arrival. To the extent that America is defined as a constitutional community, it is now the case that most immigrants come to the United States with some familiarity of American-style democracy. In either case, the incentive formally to join the American community has diminished. At the same time that most immigrants will have partially integrated an American identity, even before their arrival in the United States, many will find no need or inclination to adopt America as their primary association.

BEING THERE

Residency has been a requirement for naturalization since the Founding. Current law mandates a five-year period of residency as a permanent resident alien in most cases, including physical presence for at least half that period with no interruption of longer than a year.[8] The durational residency requirement is the most unbending of all qualifications for naturalization; although there are reductions in the required duration for some categories of applicants, there are no waivers from applicable thresholds based on disability or humanitarian considerations. Residency requirements may be passively satisfied (that is, it takes no special ability to meet them), but naturalization will not be granted before they have been fulfilled.

Durational residency requirements present another deployment of the territorial premise. As with the birth citizenship regime—under which most individuals garner citizenship by virtue of where they were born— the naturalization regime makes an assumption about physical presence, namely, that by being present, one will become a member of the national community as a matter of fact and assimilate whatever characteristics make up the national identity.

Naturalization is thus mostly about being there. Reductions of the standard five-year requirement demonstrate the assumptions behind the residency condition. For spouses of U.S. citizens, the threshold is reduced to three years, on the theory that exposure to national values and customs in the household accelerates their assimilation. In the case of spouses of government officials posted abroad, spouses of American missionaries, and employees of certain U.S. corporations, the residency period is eliminated. These exceptions remove any disadvantage to working abroad in the national interest and are (perhaps) further explained by the hyper-Americanized qualities of these communities, notwithstanding their location outside of U.S. territory.[9] In times of peace, one year's honorable service in the U.S. armed forces qualifies an alien for naturalization; during periods of military hostilities, including now the post-9/11 period, an alien becomes eligible on enlistment and need not return to the United States even to undertake the naturalization oath, an exceptional regime under which citizenship becomes the reward and the incentive for service.[10]

These reductions and exceptions evidence some watering down of the residency predicate, especially as coupled with the lower physical presence thresholds—even in the ordinary case, an alien need be in the United States for only two and a half years before becoming eligible for naturalization, and only a year and a half for the alien spouses of U.S. citizens. But the fact that some period of residency is required in almost all cases demonstrates its continuing centrality. As a historical matter, it has been the orienting point for the naturalization regime.

In the past, at least, the territorial premise of the naturalization regime proved a useful and necessary measure of membership. One could assume that presence in the United States would (on average) impart to an individual the distinctive qualities of American life in all its elements, cultural, historical, social, and political. Better than any test of specific knowledge, one could be expected to absorb, through the contacts of everyday life, what it has been to be American. Through employment, civic association, education, and the media, one would have come to understand the American identity and become a part of it. The presence benchmark has skirted the challenge of more precisely defining what being American entails. Whatever it is, you have been expected to discover, learn, and incorporate it. The residency requirement may have been necessary in the sense that, historically, there has been no other way really to learn what it means to be American other than being there. Before cultural and political globalization, America would have been a truly alien quantity for most immigrants, and assimilation could work only from a baseline of presence and the passage of time.

Of course, some immigrants have historically managed to insulate themselves from America, however defined. One might take the immigrant woman from Eastern or Southern Europe who never entered the workforce, did not learn English, and maintained a social network wholly within her immigrant community. That person would not have incorporated the core elements of the American identity and yet would (at least until 1906, when an understanding of English first became a condition to naturalization) have been eligible to naturalize. In this respect the regime's reliance on presence as an indicator of membership has always been inexact and overinclusive. But tolerably so; on average, presence would correlate with assimilation, especially as buttressed after 1906 with the English-language requirement and in the face of powerful social pressures on immigrants to assimilate. Satisfying the durational residency requirement would also show a commitment to remain in the United States; those who had been resident for five years could be expected to remain for life, to become permanent members of the community.

As in the context of birth citizenship, however, the logic of the territorial premise has eroded in the face of globalization and the diminishing significance of space. One can now be here, and not be here. The tendency to overinclusiveness may thus be more pronounced. Diasporic immigrants are in a better position to insulate themselves from what goes on around them, should they so choose. This capacity is clear in the larger, geographically concentrated immigrant communities, within which individuals can lead their entire lives. Such immigrants might as well be back home for purposes of assimilating the American identity. They are, in effect, in a different part of their homeland, one that happens to be physically located in the United States. Washington Heights becomes a district of the Dominican Republic, New York's Chinatown East a slice of Fujian province, Miami's Little Havana a part of Cuba, and so on. Other immigrants, meanwhile, are bucking traditional patterns by aggregating in prosperous suburbs as a matter of choice rather than market necessity. "For some, the ethnic neighborhood is a starting point; for others, it may be a favored destination."[11]

The phenomenon is not restricted to large cities. Immigrant communities in smaller towns often represent only a particular area of the country from which they come, the result of chain immigration patterns (family members following relatives following neighbors) and leading to strange pairings of small middle American towns and obscure foreign ones. Villages in Jalisco, for example, have effectively been bisected to such American communities as East Point, Georgia; Turner, Maine; and Juneau, Alaska.[12] The physical juxtaposition with other groups results in exposure that would not come in its absence (and of course goes in both directions, so that immigrant customs are absorbed by the indigenous population). But the homeland link can be maintained today as not before, and the result must be a lesser degree of assimilation through duration of residence.

The result, again, is the greater possibility of citizenship divorced from true affiliation with the national community. One can satisfy the residency requirement without necessarily becoming any more American than before one's arrival. As with the birthplace metric, residency has become a less reliable indicator of present or future membership. Increased mobility also reduces the likelihood that physical presence for now translates into presence and commitment for the long haul. The disconnect between the citizenry and the actual community further erodes, and the less meaningful both become.

EVERYONE AN AMERICAN, NO ONE AN AMERICAN

Place of birth cannot prove membership, nor can a period of residence after birth. Whatever it means to be American, being there by itself does not suffice. Unlike in the birth citizenship context, however, where there's no viable alternative for the territorial premise, the naturalization regime can and does otherwise attempt to measure newcomer membership in the community. Here citizenship law assumes that such membership can be literally and directly tested. The Nationality Act requires that naturalization applicants demonstrate a knowledge of U.S. history and principles of government. It also requires that applicants demonstrate a basic facility in the English language.[13] But neither requirement can capture something distinctively American, even in an approximate fashion. The impossibility of testing membership in the national community, perhaps more than any other element of citizenship law, demonstrates the fading of America.

Considered through the lens of cultural identity, both the English language and civics requirements cast increasingly insubstantial parameters to the admission decision. First of all, many are exempted from the requirement. The act excuses applicants over fifty-five years of age who have been resident for at least fifteen years, or over fifty and resident for at least twenty years.[14] Waivers for those who claim mental and developmental disabilities are liberally dispensed.[15] For those to whom the requirement applies, it is administered to test for rudimentary skills only. Applicants are asked to read or write sentences drawn from samples relating to history and civics or to "everyday life," such as "Martha Washington was the first First Lady," and "They buy many things at the store." As Gerald Neuman observes, the language requirement does not "require such a high level of fluency that applicants would have to abandon their former languages and conduct their personal interactions in English in order to acquire sufficient facility."[16] In other words, the test itself does not demand linguistic assimilation. In this respect the English language requirement cannot sustain any putative linguistic definition of the American community.

Query, in any case, whether English language capability really does present a baseline element of American identity. One can hardly question the fact that English has been and continues to be the dominant language of the United States. It is another thing to claim that English language facility is a necessary predicate to being an American. As a historical matter, other languages (most notably German and Spanish) have at times provided the lingua franca in particular geographic concentrations. The nation has never had an official language (and, indeed, Hawaii and Puerto Rico each have non-English languages sharing such a designation). As a contemporary matter, of course, Spanish is becoming the first and in some cases only tongue of an increasing number of Americans.[17]

Not that language could have ever provided a free-standing definition of the community. For tens of millions outside the United States, English is also a native tongue; English is an official language in more than sixty countries and is "routinely in evidence, publicly accessible in varying degrees, and part of the nation's recent or present identity" in more than seventy-five.[18] For an increasing number of people, especially among the professional classes, English is a necessary second language. Estimates of those with some facility in English run as high as a quarter of humanity.[19] It has become the common language, in practice, of the European Union, to the point where a German-identified corporation such as Siemens uses it for all in-house meetings and memoranda.[20] To speak English does not suffice to establish American identity or membership in the national community.

Nor does facility in English qualify as a necessary, if insufficient, condition to membership (which in fact is how it figures in the naturalization regime, as combined with other requirements). It might be rationalized as an extension of the residency requirement, on the theory that incidental identity absorption through presence can only occur with knowledge of English. But even that argument withers in the face of an explosion in non-English-language media outlets. The major satellite television provider offers 50 international and foreign-language channels, Time Warner cable has 37; New York City alone has more than 140 foreign-language newspapers, and access to thousands more is now just a click away.[21] An inability to understand English no longer poses a barrier to understanding American culture. Much of what passes for American culture is also featured in non–English-language media. Of course, one would expect a different slant on that culture from a non–English-language channel, insofar as that outlet is likely to cater to a particular community with particular interests. But the difference on this score between an English- and Spanish-language outlet might not be so different as between a supermarket tabloid and the *New Yorker*. And many primary vehicles of today's popular culture—*People* magazine, for instance—now print Spanish-language editions. The upshot is that membership, defined as familiarity with American culture, no longer requires a knowledge of English.

ROTE CITIZENSHIP

Insofar as English language facility is both insufficient and unnecessary to establishing American identity, the civics test sits as a backstop of sorts, preventing (in theory) the admission of those who, notwithstanding a period of residence and a knowledge of English, have not in fact assimilated to the community. But the civics requirement is wanting at several levels. First, it is not clear that membership in the American community is as a practical matter amenable to measurement. Naturalization examiners typically ask ten or fifteen questions selected from a hundred sample questions distributed by the immigration service. History-based questions include why the Pilgrims came to America, which president is called the "father of our country," who said "give me liberty or give me death," and which state was the forty-ninth to join the Union; questions about the structure of the federal government ask, for example, the number of constitutional amendments and who serves as the applicant's congressional representatives.[22] Some questions relate to the naturalization process itself, including

"What form...is used to apply for naturalized citizenship?" (answer: N-400, which the test taker will have filed); and "Name one benefit of being a citizen" (among possible answers: to obtain federal government jobs). One sample question asks the applicant to "name one purpose of the United Nations" (the official answer: "For countries to discuss and try to resolve world problems or to provide economic aid to many countries").

The test is a joke. Leaving aside the fact that it measures only rote memorization (in this respect the civics exam resembles nothing so much as the test for a learner's permit for driving), it is not clear that such knowledge is a predicate to membership. One can be an American without a familiarity with even the basic elements of American history or government, much less the names of representatives and senators. That is as much as proved by the fact that many citizens by birth (more than half, by one estimate)[23] would fail. The test now represents a waste of valuable processing resources (as the immigration service caught up on a massive naturalization backlog in the late 1990s, it created another one in processing green-card applications).

Addressing this objection is not just a matter of rewriting the test, something that the INS and now its successor have contemplated for many years.[24] (A revised version is being administered on a pilot basis, but the new test is not much different from the old. Patrick Henry is out; Ben Franklin is in. There are now 140 sample questions rather than 100, but the basic approach will remain the same.) Leave to one side powerful arguments against the use of tests of any kind as a barrier to citizenship. The test is firmly in the tradition of literacy qualifications for the franchise, and some people do fail or are deterred from applying for naturalization in the first place.[25] Moreover, the deterrence factor may be especially high (particularly for those without formal education) in the face of the widespread belief among applicants that failing the test will result in deportation. (It doesn't. Failing the test results only in the denial of naturalization, not the revocation of permanent residence status.) But even accepting a justifiable basis for requiring some knowledge set as a threshold to membership, and assuming some meaningful way in which to execute a testing requirement, in the American case the question of content remains formidable. If there is any message of the culture wars, it is that the meaning of American identity is contested; to the extent that this meaning is unclear, it becomes difficult to pinpoint what sort of knowledge proves membership. Indeed, there may be no common body of factual knowledge that defines the American identity. Various subconstituencies maintain their own historical lore, and an understanding of specific governmental structures is simply beyond the interest of many.

To the extent that there is a common knowledge, it is most likely found in the stuff (almost by definition) of popular culture. Some have suggested that the civics exam include questions, for instance, relating to Levi's jeans and the like.[26] That modification might create a greater congruence between the knowledge expected of would-be members and the knowledge of existing members themselves. High school seniors would know in much higher proportion the identity of pop and television stars than of their congressional representatives. Relative to the current content of the civics exam, one could argue that popular culture better defines the American identity, in which a corresponding knowledge requirement would be justified to measure community affiliation.

The problem is that "American" popular culture no longer distinctively defines the American community. American popular culture has become a globalized popular culture. American movies, television shows, music, and books dominate foreign markets. The top fifty all-time movies for non–U.S. box office receipts includes not a single non–U.S. film. Fox News is now part of the Djakarta cable package; MTV can be seen in 164 territories via 41 channels in 18 languages. McDonald's has become a familiar sight in all the developed world; Mickey Mouse is surely known to a majority of the world's children; even the world's poorest now wear clothes that would be familiar in any American city, university T-shirts and Nike sweats.[27]

AMERICAN/ABROAD

Of course, not all globalized culture is American in origin; that only means that not all American culture is American in origin, and will only make an immigrant's familiarity more likely. It is also true that exported American culture is sometimes indigenized. McDonald's is a well-documented example, adapted to local tastes (no hamburgers in India, for example) and blending in to the point where it is no longer always identified as being American at all. (As the CEO of McDonald's observed, "in Japan, the average Japanese child thinks McDonald's was invented in Japan and exported to the United States."[28]) But that can be said of McDonald's in America as well (lobster rolls in Maine, fajitas in Texas), and any laundering of national origin does not eliminate the common theme and symbols of such establishments. A person who has been introduced to McDonald's in Singapore will feel at home in a McDonald's in Des Moines. Likewise, the rising occurrence of non–U.S. ownership (at both corporate and share-holder levels) does nothing to undermine the proposition. As Bertels-mann CEO Thomas Middelhoff noted in defending the company's share of the U.S. market, "I'm an American with a German passport."[29] Even if global culture has not yet fully infiltrated all parts of the world—the states of fundamentalist Islam presenting the most important exception—the penetration rate is now high enough to support the generalization that such symbols of American life are not only recognized but lived with the world over.

At one level, the global pervasion of American artifacts makes unneces-sary both the language requirement and the civics test. If familiarity with American idioms is what that test is after, it is redundant; most immigrants will already be well versed in them before arrival in the United States. The civics test may once have been meaningful. It first emerged as a matter of custom in the early twentieth century, when judges, then still exclusively responsible for administering naturalization oaths, would on an ad hoc basis examine applicants on their understanding of the American system. It was adopted as a statutory requirement, administered by the INS, in 1952. In that context, the test may have been more readily justified. If familiarity with culture is the badge of membership, immigrants in the era before globalization would not necessarily have been exposed to things American before their arrival, and perhaps not even after, to the extent that they remained in insulated immigrant communities. They arrived truly alien to the American landscape. Today the very concept of "alien-age" grows more obsolete—the use of the word, if even superficially inter-rogated, seems anachronistic.[30]

But the observation goes beyond the narrow policy question of whether the test stands as an appropriate or meaningful threshold to naturaliza-tion. Once again, this element of citizenship law points to the arbitrari-ness of the formal citizenship designation. The naturalization regime in this respect can be taken to define the national community in terms of a common knowledge base. At one time in history, that knowledge base was distinctive; it set Americans apart from persons of other nationality. Today, that knowledge base is shared by much of the rest of the world. The community's boundaries transcend territorial ones; the human geography of America envelopes, in degrees at least, much of the rest of the world. At the same time, some within the territorial boundary may be more insulated (in diasporic communities or other separated groups) from the culture than those not territorially present.

On this basis, one can also question the continuing relevance of the durational residency requirement. At the same time that some immigrants will be able to resist cultural incorporation while present in the United States, others will have, in effect, been incorporated before they arrive. Many of today's immigrants to the United States—clearly more than in the great waves of the early twentieth century—know what they are getting into. They have seen the movies and television shows, read the news, and heard about American life from those who preceded them. For most, the arrival and early years in America can present nothing like the dramatic change that faced immigrants of earlier eras. For these would-be Americans, five years of residence is superfluous.

Indeed, one can, if only as a thought experiment, play with the possibility of naturalization without residence of any length. How is someone who lives and understands all the cultural components of the American identity not American, regardless of where the person is located? What of the Indian living in India, the Pole living in Poland, the Peruvian living in Peru, all of whom are willing to express their faith in America, its system of government, and everything else it stands for? The challenge is not so easily repulsed as one might expect. The answer cannot be that the person wasn't born or hasn't lived in the United States; for we have seen (in the context of birth citizenship on the basis of parentage) that this does not bar others from membership, others who themselves are not required to demonstrate any particular knowledge of American culture. As we will see, neither does holding citizenship in another country preclude citizenship in the United States. If the person were to declare her support for the United States, why should she not be allowed to sign up? Indeed, why wouldn't other Americans want to embrace her?

DEFENDING A DEMOCRATIC ISLAND

The conclusion applies with greater force if one limits the conception of America to a political one. This persists as a backstop definition of what

America is: above all, a "civic" nation. That has always, especially among liberal theorists, been the way around cultural diversity; for all of our differences, Americans are united by a common belief in constitutional values and the democratic process. The notion of a civic nation also shores up the community in the face of immigration. Even if newcomers don't in fact share the community's past, they become members through their assumption of its constitutional faith and fate, by being, in the old long-discredited term, "Americanized." As the 1997 Jordan Commission report on naturalization suggested, immigrants should be "cultivat[ed]" in a "shared commitment to the American values of liberty, democracy and equal opportunity."[31] In this sense, America looks more like a religion, allowing for conversion of belief in the place of any need of lineage.

In the past, America's constitutional orientation presented a distinctive characteristic of the American community, distinguishing it from the peoples of other nations. It was then necessary to ensure the political education of newcomers as a condition to membership in the polity, for the success of the system was premised on republican virtue and responsible political participation. Today, that education is unnecessary; most immigrants come to the United States well versed in the ways of democracy. What used to set America apart most clearly no longer does so; the question once again is left hanging, what remains?

The political conception of citizenship permeates naturalization requirements and their historical origins. All naturalization applicants since the Founding have been required to take an oath to support not the United States per se or its government but the Constitution itself. The other original naturalization requirement—of durational residence— was also intended to ensure that immigrants were politically acclimated to democracy before being granted a political voice. As one congressman asserted in the 1790 debate over the first naturalization law, the residency requirement "would give a man an opportunity of esteeming the Government from knowing its intrinsic value," failing which "an alien [would] be entitled to join in the election of your officers at the first moment he puts his foot on shore in America, when it is impossible, from the nature of things, that he can be qualified to exercise such a talent." James Madison similarly cautioned, "What could the newcomer know of the Government the moment he landed? Little or nothing: how then could he ascertain who was a proper person to legislate or judge of the laws?"[32]

Likewise for more recently imposed requirements. The language requirement was intended to further responsible political participation. As the sponsor of the original 1906 provision noted, the language requirement was intended to ensure that the new citizen "could familiarize himself with our laws and take part in the discussions and listen to the discussion of questions affecting the welfare of the nation." The legislative report accompanying a 1950 amendment concluded that "[a]s a practical matter, it is difficult...to understand how a person who has no knowledge of English can intelligently exercise the franchise, especially in states which use the initiative and referendum. It is also difficult to understand how a person who does not understand, or read, or write English can keep advised and informed on the political and social problems of the community in which he lives." The civics requirement is also readily situated in this narrative. It originated as a customary practice, in which judges tested applicants of their knowledge of American government by way of ensuring that the oath-taking was meaningful. As administered today, much of the test focuses on the content and structure of the Constitution and government. Even the historical elements of the test can be explained not so much as pursuing cultural incorporation as ensuring educated political participation, on the theory that without knowledge of (for example) such central historical personages as George Washington, Abraham Lincoln, and Dr. Martin Luther King Jr., such responsible participation is impossible.

Taken on their own terms and in historical context, these requirements made sense. At least in a world where American politics unfolded primarily in the medium of the English language, one might expect English to have been a necessary condition to informed political participation. The civics test could also have been justified by way of ensuring that new members understood the rules they were agreeing to play by.

All of these rationales found ultimate support in the distinctiveness of the American system, and the fact that it had in most cases to be learned. At the time of the first naturalization measure, of course, American democracy presented an anomaly in the global political landscape, and a fragile one at that. One could have entertained genuine fears that immigrants—most of whom, after all, hailed from nondemocracies—would not necessarily adhere to the then-innovative principles of constitutional democracy. If admitted in large numbers, such nondemocrats could have undermined the very foundations of the constitutional system. A profession of belief in the Constitution was thus a necessary and significant threshold to membership in the American community. It was a world not only in which democracy faced competition from other political systems but in which the democrat was in fact the outlier, the heretic, the challenger of established hierarchies. It also was a world in which oaths were taken seriously, as part of personal honor of chivalric and almost religious dimension, so that swearing faith to the Constitution would have presented a meaningful qualification and protection against the threat of being subsumed by still-dominant non-democratic faiths. Hence, the oath was the only condition beyond presence; the new America did not demand much for membership, but that much it understandably insisted on.

Even in more recent times, the United States has stood tall among the relatively small crowd of genuine democracies. That explains the historical origins of the requirement that naturalization applicants understand principles of American government and the language requirement (at least to the extent that the latter was conceived as a means to the end of responsible political participation). Both emerged as the nation faced waves of immigrants whose distance from America, in political terms, was even more pronounced than those who preceded them. Where the English, German, or Scandanavian newcomer might have been expected to have had some exposure to democratic concepts, the immigrant from Southern or (especially) Eastern Europe might have had no such prior introduction. Many immigrants in the early twentieth century came from countries in which the individual counted for little, in terms of either rights or political participation. These were immigrants for whom democracy was as foreign as the moon. Those from the shtetl or the Sicilian hilltop were not likely to arrive with an understanding of constitutional values. They were considered more vulnerable to political exploitation and less likely to exercise political rights in a responsible, independent fashion, a fear to some extent supported by the historical record. Their own-language media might not itself have any grounding in democratic culture, and the instruments of government (including the ballot) were accessible almost exclusively in English. American democracy may not have been vulnerable to defeat so much as to distortion by the wide participation of political naifs. The imposition of a knowledge and language requirement on top of the oath may well have been justified in that context.

During the cold war era, constitutional democracy once again faced serious ideological competition in the form of communism, and much of the world continued to suffer other forms of authoritarian rule. Here the oath's significance may have been resurrected, at least in some eyes, as an important symbolic transfer of allegiance in a mortal world struggle. And even if immigrants from nondemocracies were not themselves subversive of democracy, many continued to come from countries in which democracy had yet to establish any foothold. Thus immigrants until recent years could be presumed not only unfamiliar with the American system of constitutional governance, but bathed in other, inconsistent political regimes. Again, in theory if not necessarily in practice, that fact grounded the civics requirement. If indeed the United States has been distinguished as a "civic" nation, then understanding the terms of government should have been the least that America could have expected of its new members.

UNEXCEPTIONAL CONSTITUTIONAL IDENTITY

But as with the social and cultural elements of what has been asserted to define the national character, constitutional governance is no longer distinctively American. This may represent the great historical contribution of the United States—that it served first as democracy's incubator and then its propagator. Leaving aside for a moment the question of whether democracy has supplanted all other models of governance, most people the world over are familiar with its rudiments, at least. That could be more safely said of those who seek to come to the United States, regardless of their homeland's regime. Indeed, those who come from repressive states are of course often motivated by their belief in democracy, whether as permanent immigrants or exiles.

In many cases, of course, the familiarity is much more than rudimentary. The international media covers U.S. politics in detail sometimes surpassing that of the U.S. media. The U.S. media is itself now widely available in other countries, including CNN and other broadcast networks, international editions of such papers as the *Wall Street Journal* and the *New York Times*, and the untrammeled access afforded by the Internet to the same product as is published in the United States. In the face of global media coverage, many newcomers are fully conversant in the details of American politics before even setting foot in the country, to the point that some have been identified as DOA—Democrats (as in Democratic Party) on Arrival.[33]

Whatever the level of familiarity, in contrast to earlier times most naturalization applicants understand the meaning of democracy. The oath requirement is now superfluous. Of course, the oath is a matter of agreeing to the rules of the game and supporting the enterprise one is seeking to join; existing members are justified in denying admission to someone who would work to undermine the community itself, even if that person is also denied rights as a result. (As Gerald Neuman notes, an applicant "who state[s] his utter hatred for the United States and its people...could surely be denied naturalization on the grounds that the government anticipates no benefit to society from his membership."[34]) But in this respect the oath no longer poses any obstacle to citizenship, for almost everyone supports the Constitution in some conception. It is perhaps telling that the requirement has now been waived (with legislation enacted in 2000) for those applicants who suffer a mental disability rendering them unable to understand the oath—the only group for whom the oath has presented a barrier to naturalization.

The language requirement, meanwhile, has long outlived its original purpose to ensure responsible political participation, which may explain why it is now administered in so pro forma a fashion. A proliferation of non-English-language media, print, broadcast, and Internet, now makes possible fully informed political participation without English language facility. The Voting Rights Act itself requires that ballots be printed in foreign languages in districts with significant non-English-speaking populations.[35] A recent blue-ribbon commission taking on the issue of voting practices in the wake of the 2000 election debacle recommended that new technologies be used to increase the availability of foreign-language ballots, a recommendation accepted by George W. Bush.[36] Presidential campaigns in both 2000 and 2004 were hard fought on Spanish-language turf, in advertising, speeches, and media coverage. As if to pose a more direct challenge to the citizenship requirement, naturalization ceremonies have themselves been conducted in Spanish (though the oath itself appears never to have been undertaken in a language other than English).

As for the civics test, it, too, is unnecessary as a condition for naturalization. All agree that its current incarnation presents a meaningless exercise in rote memorization. No longer does the existing community need fear the risk of political distortion by untutored aliens; naturalization applicants can safely be assumed to have an adequate understanding of democratic procedures and constitutional values. Insofar as the residency requirement was intended to protect against the same danger, it also becomes attenuated. In 1795, to take one lawmaker's comments, it may have been "a rash theory, that the subjects of all Governments, Despotic, Monarchical, and Aristocratical, are, as soon as they set foot on American ground, qualified to participate in administering the sovereignty of our country." Today such concerns seem almost quaint, in line with the Founders' obsession, now flagrantly anachronistic, that all naturalizing citizens renounce titles of foreign nobility. Eliminating the durational residency requirement may stretch political reality (reinforced by the fact that almost all other countries maintain such requirements), but one can today question its premises.

So much for the universal familiarity with democratic governance and its significance for particular naturalization requirements. To the extent that democracy is truly globalized—that is, to the extent that it becomes the only accepted form of government—there is a broader significance for the institution of citizenship and the meaning of American identity. It is America's achievement that all governments are measured against the yardstick of democracy, and that it has become virtually a given in the global political discourse. That is not to say that democracy prevails everywhere. One still finds a few old-fashioned autocrats, and of course Islam and some East Asian regimes continue to represent a challenge, at some level, to Western-originated democracy. But at no time have the prospects for dictatorship looked so grim—it is not a good time to be a political strongman—and even those regimes that do not claim legitimacy as democracies are challenged both internally and externally for failing to accept the yardstick. On the one hand, we may be entering into an era of clashing civilizations, in Samuel Huntington's vision, in which no system of government dominates. On the other, with the end of the cold war it is possible to situate the world on a trajectory at the end of which democracy alone emerges as a legitimate system of government.

If so, it will mark both America's triumph and its decline. To the extent that America has been defined by its adherence to a distinctive governance system, it loses that identity insofar as the system becomes universal. If individual Americans used to be identified by their faith in that system, they also lose that identity insofar as others claim similar faith. *Once everyone is an American, no one is an American.* Identity and community boundaries are ultimately about difference. Once the difference disappears, the identity disappears with it. If indeed we have been a civic nation, we are on the way to being a nation no more.

FINDING THE INTERNATIONAL FUTURE
IN THE NATIONAL PAST

The history of America's domestic citizenship structure—in the relationship of national citizenship and citizenship in the individual constituent states—supplies an illuminating comparative perspective on the future of American citizenship and identity in the global context. This history demonstrates both the practicality of eliminating naturalization requirements as well as the correlation of citizenship and identity. On both counts, the thinness of the states as communities may foretell the path of nations.

As a formal matter, state citizenship has never been an important quantity in the American constitutional scheme. Even in the antebellum period, when it might have been possible as a constitutional matter, state citizenship appears never to have been differentiated from national citizenship on the one hand or residence on the other; that is, no state extended state citizenship to persons not holding national citizenship, nor denied it to national citizens residing within their jurisdictions. Adoption of the Fourteenth Amendment, by providing that "all persons born or naturalized in the United States...are citizens of the United States and of the State wherein they reside," eliminated any possibility of denial. As with the birthright element of the Citizenship Clause, the lack of discretion afforded the states is explained by the racial context and the intention to prevent the denial of state citizenship on the basis of race.

Nonetheless states were able until the 1960s to discriminate against new state citizens/residents. For purposes of drawing the naturalization parallel, the imposition of a durational residency requirement for the franchise is most interesting. Typically, these measures required a new resident of the state to have resided there for one year before becoming eligible to vote. The states argued that such requirements were important for protecting the integrity of state political processes. Newcomers, the argument ran, would not have an adequate understanding of state issues and politics, knowledge that would come only with some period of presence.

That justification precisely tracks the basis for durational residency requirements for national citizenship (as well, secondarily, for the English and civics tests). Yet in its 1972 decision in *Dunn v. Blumstein*, the U.S. Supreme Court rejected the constitutionality of such restrictions on the franchise of new citizens.[37] The result is that after a period sufficient to establish bona fide residency (no more than thirty days) the new resident/

citizen of a state is eligible to vote in that state's elections. The mandate was implemented without difficulty, notwithstanding the high rates of in-migration confronted by some states. Of course, new residents may be unfamiliar with state and local political structures or personalities. The former may vary as widely as the latter; at the local level especially, there is no institutional uniformity across jurisdictions. As a result, some newcomers may cast their ballots irresponsibly, in ignorance. But others will be able immediately to bring themselves up to speed; whatever the political heterogeneity among the states, their political systems all work from the same constitutional baseline. As the Court observed in the *Dunn* case, "recent migrants who take the time to register and vote shortly after moving are likely to be those…who make it a point to be informed and knowledgeable about the issues."

A similar observation can be made at the international level. Schooled in democratic procedures, most immigrants will have the capacity to participate responsibly almost from arrival. Indeed, to reverse assumptions, who is to say that the newcomer from a small town in Texas is better prepared to participate in New York City politics than the newcomer from London or Paris? Even the immigrant from Delhi or Moscow or Santo Domingo might have one up on the Texan, insofar as foreigners quickly fold into the "domestic" politics of their immigrant communities, where the Texan finds himself on his own. There would have been a time, not so long ago, when these comparisons would have decisively tipped for the fellow American, where today it might not be so clear.

In any case, the domestic interstate experience shows the efficacy of a regime in which citizenship is equated with residence, and the institution of state citizenship suggests the possibility of eliminating naturalization requirements altogether. The United States may as a nonformal matter already have moved in that direction, determining many rights on the basis of residence rather than citizenship status (leading, in Linda Bosniak's felicitous phrase, to the "citizenship of aliens").[38] The result may be a citizenship regime of *jus migrationis* not seen since the late Roman Empire, under which settlement automatically brought citizenship with it.

The domestic citizenship structure also demonstrates how thin citizenship regimes correspond to thin identity constructs. It is not coincidental that the low threshold to state citizenship is paired with a generally low level of affective attachment to the states as communities. The absence of any qualification beyond residence both reflects and contributes to the relative weakness of communal bonds as defined by state lines. It contributes to this weakness by making the formal definition of community overinclusive. Take a state such as Texas, which more than most states sustains a distinct state-based identity. Anyone who moves to Texas can claim state citizenship, which inevitably tends to dilute the identity, especially in the face of substantial in-migration.

At the same time, the lack of conditions to citizenship, other than residence, reflects the insubstantiality of state ties. For indeed the states now only exceptionally comprise the primary locus of an individual's identity. Texas is highly unusual in this respect, for there are many who indeed might identify themselves primarily as such. (Not coincidentally, Texas is the only state to have once enjoyed independence as a nation.) But someone from Maryland, or Missouri, or Arizona? There are some territorial identities other than those defined by states that are significant, even resurgent; both cities and regions are coming increasingly to define individual identities and interests. The resident of New York City identifies himself as such before he would identify himself as a citizen of New York state; a person in Montana or Wyoming would accept "Westerner" before the label of the particular state.

The thesis can be tested with a counterfactual in which the states were permitted to impose requirements for citizenship beyond residence. Assume that as a condition for citizenship in the state of Maryland, a new resident were required to pass a test about Maryland history (about the Calverts, the state bird, Francis Scott Key, etc.) and pay a fee of $100. Assume also that no benefits were to come with citizenship status beyond a certificate of naturalization, suitable for framing. The upshot, I think, would be a large proportion of newcomers not bothering to apply. On one hand, that might marginally reinforce the state identity among those who did (or those who came to the status by birth, assuming a regime of jus soli for state citizenship to accompany a naturalization regime). To the extent it was something that one had to affirmatively seek, as opposed to passively receive, one would expect only those who entertained some affinity and commitment to the state to bother with the hassle and expense. In this scheme, Marylanders might be more inclined to wear the identity on their sleeves. On the other hand, the identity itself would emerge as fairly inconsequential, something in the way of the Knights of Columbus or other civic associations.

Of course, one might add incentives to acquiring citizenship in the form of such benefits as the right to vote in state elections, eligibility for welfare, and the like. The normative basis for conditioning the enjoyment of such benefits would, to begin with, seem weak. One could, for instance, hardly make a case that familiarity with Francis Scott Key determined one's capacity to engage in self-government at the state level and enjoy returns on tax dollars paid into state coffers. More significant for present purposes, adding such incentives would do little to enhance a sense of identity with the state. An individual who goes through the exercise of memorizing test answers with only the instrumental motivation of receiving public benefits is unlikely to cement any community attachment in the process. One can't build a community through tests alone. And even with the incentives (assuming they did not implicate widely utilized benefits, such as public schooling), one would find many interstate migrants failing to apply for membership at the state level in the face of any threshold to membership.

THE PRICE OF CITIZENSHIP

So, too, with national citizenship. The relatively low existing threshold for naturalization both reflects and contributes to a diminishing sense of national identity. If the community admits to membership those who really do not share significant commonality with the existing community (as is the case under the current naturalization regime), than the community is undermined. But one cannot restore the community simply by raising the membership threshold. Beyond a point, individuals will refuse to sign up, even if membership is otherwise for the asking.

Consider the fee required of naturalization applicants, which in 1996 was raised from $75 to $250, and more recently to $675. The jump was justified as covering the administrative costs of processing naturalization applications and provoked little opposition. The fee is problematic insofar as it conditions the status and any associated rights on a monetary payment. In the context of status change in other legal contexts, most notably divorce proceedings, the Supreme Court has found nonwaivable fees unconstitutional.[39] Nothing could be perhaps more alien to American political culture than to make the right to vote contingent on a payment, and yet that, in effect, is the result of the naturalization regime. Even though it provides for a fee waiver where the applicant can demonstrate an inability to pay—only obtainable by opening another cumbersome bureaucratic avenue in a process already burdened by administrative inefficiency—imposing a monetary threshold for full membership in the polity seems distasteful, if nothing else. (The fee applies to all individual applicants, so that families can see the cost easily surpass $2,500, hardly a trivial amount for many new immigrants, even if they don't qualify for the waiver.) The naturalization oath ceremony—the grist of Fourth of July stories celebrating the great immigrant roots of the nation—would hardly seem so solemn if they kicked off with the collection of substantial money orders from families of marginal means. Unlike other naturalization requirements (the oath ceremony included) there can be no argument that payment of the fee somehow enhances the new member's sense of community.

Whether the fee is justifiable, however, its imposition may not ultimately serve the interests of the existing community. If the price is too high—literally—American citizenship will find fewer takers. As fewer benefits attach to the status, it may prove perfectly rational to forgo the bureaucratic headache and expense of naturalization and remain a permanent resident alien. Even for the alien for whom the money is proverbial pocket change, one might see the rationality of forbearance. How much is citizenship worth? For the average law-abiding able-bodied alien, who doesn't have to sweat the risk of deportation and is unlikely to require those forms of public assistance limited to citizens, the advantage of citizenship boils down to the right to vote and in some cases estate tax benefits.[40] As we see among citizens today, the right to vote is not exploited by many where free, much less were it to come with a price tag, and the estate tax benefit affects only a small number of wealthy couples.

Indeed, although naturalization applications spiked dramatically in the early and mid-1990s, and again after the September 11 attacks, they have since shown signs of receding. The first spike could be attributed to the sudden, aberrational reintroduction of a citizen-based benefits differential and the generally heightened sense of insecurity among aliens during a period of vocal anti-immigration sentiment. (There are other, more pedestrian explanations, including a deadline under which all resident aliens had to replace their old green cards with new, counterfeit-proof ones. That required all aliens to deal with the immigration bureaucracy; the possibility is that many took the opportunity to upgrade, so to speak. A more recent increase found applicants trying to beat the hefty application fee increases.) But the restoration of many benefits barred to aliens in 1996, and the evident move from an anti-immigrant environment to a more embracing one diminished the urgency many felt to naturalize, at least before 9/11. Unsurprisingly, the attacks themselves spurred significant numbers to acquire citizenship. In some cases naturalization was prompted by what might alternatively be described as patriotism or sympathy. In others, anti-immigrant measures (or the threat of such measures) prompted naturalization as insurance against deportation or other activity targeted against noncitizens. As of the middle of 2003, however, applications were returning to pre-9/11 levels, well below those witnessed in the mid-1990s.[41] More significant than the absolute number of applications, the proportion of foreign-born residents who naturalize has been steadily decreasing, from 63.6 percent in 1970 to 37.4 percent in 2000. Even controlling for length of residence, the naturalization rate has declined precipitously. Among those foreigners in the United States for ten to fourteen years, for instance, the proportion naturalized has fallen from 57.5 percent to 29.4 percent.[42]

Naturalization in the past has seen periods of persistently depressed rates. That may have been attributable to the relatively more formidable barriers that naturalization once presented, in periods when some were ineligible to naturalize because of race and others came without English or any conception of the American way, however defined. Today, the failure to naturalize may be more a matter of apathy—rational apathy. If it means less to be an American, there is less reason to become one.

3

Not Only American

PLURAL CITIZENSHIP POSES a central challenge to citizenship as an organizing principle of world order and individual identity. Dual citizenship was once thought an offense against nature, a stain on a person's character, an immoral status akin to bigamy. One might be a dual citizen by virtue of the interplay of different citizenship regimes, but one could not openly maintain allegiance to more than one nation. This jealous defense of exclusive national ties had significant implications for the nature of the citizenship tie and the community it defined. Singular affiliations inherently have greater meaning than nonexclusive relationships, especially where the type of affiliation is common practice. The contexts of marriage and religion present ready examples; because (for the most part) those affiliations are exclusive, the resulting bond—the "community," if you will— looms larger on the individual's horizon. So, too, was it with nationality. The fact that individuals could have one nationality and one nationality only rendered national identification a more important quantity. It starkly drew the lines between the "us" and the "them," a sort of legal circling of the wagons that inevitably reinforced the meaning of citizenship.

Perhaps more dramatically than any other area of citizenship law, that is all changed. Nations have come mostly to accept plural citizenship. Indeed, some states have embraced the status, by encouraging those who emigrate and naturalize elsewhere to maintain their homeland nationality. States have also moved to allow the many children born with multiple nationality, through mixed-national parentage or birth in a country other than that of parental nationality, to retain the status into maturity. A growing number seek to regain the nationalities of their immigrant grandparents while remaining Americans. Dual citizenship has become a commonplace.

Just as a regime of mono-nationality reinforced thick national identity, the rise of plural citizenship both implies and facilitates its erosion. Acceptance of plural nationality suggests a less intensive competition among states, the accompanying decline in invocations of "loyalty" and "allegiance" further demonstrating that individuals need no longer throw in their lot with one and only one nation. Multiple, same-category attachments will on average be less meaningful than exclusive ones. Acceptance of multiple attachments also lowers the threshold for membership. It becomes cheaper, in effect, for the would-be member to acquire one tie where she doesn't have to give up another. The end result, once again, is an increasing disconnect between the legal definition of the citizenry and strong community on the ground. Plural citizenship blurs the boundaries of human geography. The less distinct the lines that separate national communities and the more overlap one detects among them, the less likely that nationality will singularly define an individual's place on the global landscape.

As with other transformations in the architecture of citizenship, acceptance of dual citizenship is neither lamentable nor reversible. By allowing individuals to formalize the multiple national attachments of globalized existence, it furthers liberal goals of autonomy and identity, a sort of international version of the First Amendment protection for free association. State interests in accepting the status are too great to turn the clock back; states are no longer in a position to extract exclusivity. Plural citizenship is a fact of the new world and a reflection of citizenship's smaller place within it.

THE HISTORICAL IMPERATIVE OF BOUNDED CITIZENSHIPS

It is not as if multiple national connections present a new phenomenon. Earlier migration brought to the United States millions whose lives had been molded in their homelands and who maintained persistent sentimental attachments to their countries of origin even after resettlement. Hence the rise of vaunted American pluralism, of the hyphenated Americans whose affective identities were found in communities defined by ethnicities, ones typically coinciding to other nationalities. These communities were of more than merely sentimental significance. It was a tenet of pluralism that ethnicity defined political interests as well, so that immigrant Americans and their immediate descendants were thought to vote the left side of the hyphen. The story of America is clearly not one of national homogenization.

But through the waves of immigrants who defined themselves along other-worldly lines, there was little tolerance for the voluntary maintenance of formal citizenship ties to other states. Citizenship in the old world was a binary proposition. You were in or you were out. In the hyphenation paradigm, "American" enjoyed decisive primacy. One's country of origin may have oriented various interests, but only within the American system. Political energy and commitment were channeled through U.S. institutions; one came to the table as a person of German or Italian or East European origin, but the table itself was American. That was acceptable. It was not acceptable to also sit at another table, defined by another citizenship.

The disfavor provoked by dual nationality became embedded to the point that it was reflexive. One did not need to explain what exactly was unacceptable about the status; it simply was. The disfavor took on heavy elements of moral opprobrium. Dual nationality was not merely unacceptable. It was an abomination. As the prominent American diplomat George Bancroft wrote to Lord Palmerston in 1849, states should "as soon tolerate a man with two wives as a man with two countries, as soon bear with polygamy as that state of double allegiance which common sense so repudiates that it has not even coined a word to express it." Senator Henry Cabot Lodge announced that he could "not assent for a moment to the proposition that such a thing as dual citizenship is possible." Theodore Roosevelt called the "theory" of dual nationality "a self-evident absurdity."[1]

Why this intense, deep-seated resistance to dual nationality? The question was draped in conceptions of loyalty and allegiance; as Attorney General Jeremiah Sullivan Black observed in 1859, "no government would allow one of its subjects to divide his allegiance between it and another sovereign; for they all know that no man can serve two masters."[2] The status conjured up images of shadowy saboteurs and menacing fifth columns. In fact, the roots of historical disfavor were far more prosaic, though hardly less imperative. A world of hostile nation-states could not tolerate the threat that dual nationals posed to international stability. Just as states battled over pieces of territory, they struggled for domain over individuals.

Traditional international law allowed a sovereign to treat its own subjects as it pleased, but significantly constrained its treatment of the subjects of other sovereigns; when a state mistreated a foreigner, the foreigner's state could intercede on her behalf. Italy, for example, could do whatever it wanted to an Italian national, but if it abused an American citizen, the United States could take it to task. The two precepts came into conflict in the case of dual nationals. One state asserted its right to govern its own subjects without interference, where the other claimed its right to protect the very same individuals. In the historical setting, the individual dual national represented a potential spark in the global tinderbox. The supposed immorality of the status was not so much the problem as the international dangers that could flow from it. So great were those dangers that they infected the very vocabulary of citizenship. If the status was against the supposedly natural order of things, then no one could lay rightful claim to it.

The societal stigma associated with dual nationality backstopped a legal regime that (in the American context at least) faced difficult challenges in policing the status. A blanket rule against dual nationality was impractical. From *Calvin's Case* through the end of the nineteenth century, most European states conceived of nationality as ordained by nature, a matter of "perpetual allegiance" that could never be cast off by the individual. Those states refused to recognize the transfer of nationality; it was a system of "once a subject, always a subject." The United States had little choice but to accept dual nationality arising from the naturalization of individuals from such states, assuming the young republic was to expand the ranks of Americans through immigration. Many naturalized Americans also remained nationals of their countries of origin. The result was millions of immigrants who were dual nationals, at least as a formal matter.

This population of dual nationals posed a major destabilizing element in U.S. relations with other states. It was a significant cause of the War of 1812, as British naval forces sought to conscript naturalized British Americans serving on American vessels. The United States found itself in numerous serious mid- and late-nineteenth-century disputes when naturalized citizens returned to their homelands for temporary visits, only to find themselves subject to conscription or other obligations of their original nationality. In those cases, the United States expended significant diplomatic capital in trying to insulate American citizens from the imposition of their would-be former homelands. United States officials considered such individuals to be American and only American, refusing to recognize the continuing claims of birth countries. A condition to naturalization ever since the Naturalization Act of 1795, a naturalization applicant was required to "absolutely and entirely renounce and abjure all allegiance and fidelity to every foreign prince, potentate, state or sovereignty whatever, and particularly by name, the prince, potentate, state or sovereignty, whereof he was before a citizen or subject."[3] This renunciation oath was taken seriously. "The moment a foreigner becomes naturalized his allegiance to his native country is severed forever," wrote Secretary of State Lewis Cass in an 1859 circular. "He experiences a new political birth."

POLICING DUAL NATIONALITY

Such pronouncements notwithstanding, when naturalized citizens returned permanently to their homelands, it often made little sense to put important bilateral relations on the line for them. No less than President Ulysses S. Grant decried the phenomenon, in his 1874 annual message to Congress, of "person[s] claiming the benefits of citizenship, while living in a foreign country, contributing in no manner to the performance of the duties of a citizen of the United States, and without intention at any time to return and undertake those duties, to use the claims to citizenship of the United States simply as a shield from the performance of the obligations of a citizen elsewhere."[4] Hence the development of the first administrative defense against the threat posed by dual nationality. When a naturalized citizen returned to his homeland permanently, the U.S. government refused protection against his homeland sovereign. In those cases, in effect, nationality reverted and American citizenship was forfeited. The practice was codified in 1907, providing for the loss of U.S. nationality acquired by naturalization after two years' residence in a country of birth.[5]

Abhorrence of dual nationality also explains, at least in part, citizenship practices discriminating against women. Until 1934, U.S. citizenship descended only to the children of American citizen fathers born abroad, not those born to American citizen mothers and noncitizen fathers. This reduced the probability that a child of mixed parentage would be born with dual citizenship. Mixed-nationality marriages were themselves the target of citizenship law. Also pursuant to the 1907 law, American women lost their citizenship automatically upon marriage to an alien.[6] The premise worked from dominant notions of patriarchy and the unified identity of the family; the idea that wives could stand on the other side of national borders from their husbands offended the very concept of marriage. But the rule also worked to diminish the incidence of dual nationality. Under the laws of most other states, foreign women were automatically naturalized on marriage, so an American woman marrying, say, a British subject would acquire British citizenship through the marital union. The expatriation measure prevented dual citizenship through the termination of original citizenship. The rule was partially repealed by Congress in 1922 in the face of vigorous pressure from the suffragette movement, which had only just won the right to vote, lingering until 1931 in those cases in which an American woman married an alien himself ineligible to naturalize.[7]

Perhaps most significant on the legal front was the eventual abandonment of perpetual allegiance on the part of European states. In a series of treaties negotiated in the 1860s (the so-called Bancroft treaties, after diplomat George Bancroft, who undertook their negotiation), more than two dozen mostly German and Scandinavian states recognized naturalization in the United States as extinguishing original nationality, except in the case of return. Other countries also came to recognize a right to expatriation. In the wake of the uproar provoked by the trial of several naturalized Irish Americans as British subjects in connection with an Irish uprising (one which, in the description of Secretary of State Seward, produced protests "throughout the whole country, from Portland to San Francisco, and from St. Paul to Pensacola"), in 1870 Great Britain recognized the capacity to transfer nationality.[8] By the early twentieth century, a majority practice emerged under which naturalization in another state resulted in the automatic termination of original citizenship. The abandonment of perpetual allegiance and the effectiveness of renunciation dramatically reduced the numbers of immigrant dual nationals.

Dual nationality resulting from the interplay of jus soli and jus sanguinis rules of birth citizenship (as opposed to that resulting from naturalization) was both more intractable and less of a threat to world order. The nationality laws of many European states extended nationality to the descendants of emigrants, even after the emigrants naturalized and in some cases beyond the second generation. At the same time, as we have seen, the United States (the case of blacks aside) followed a strict rule of jus soli, under which all persons born in the territory of the United States acquired American citizenship, regardless of parental immigration status. Thus, the early twentieth-century child of an Italian immigrant was born with both Italian and U.S. nationality. The upshot, again, was a huge population of resident dual nationals, in the sense of each of two countries claiming the individual as its own.

The law could hardly outlaw dual nationality in this context. The administrative task of determining who acquired the status at birth would have itself been momentous. Nor was it necessary to root out birthright dual nationality. For many, the status was inchoate. For those born and thereafter continuously resident in the United States, dual nationality had no concrete repercussions; these dual nationals did not threaten the interstate order. Many birthright dual nationals no doubt lived out their lives unaware of their status as such. But birth dual nationality nonetheless posed a potential threat of the sort posed by dual nationals by naturalization. Even in nineteenth- and early twentieth-century immigration, some families went home (by some estimates, for example, more than half of all immigrants from the southern provinces of Italy).[9] Those who returned brought with them children born in and thus citizens of the United States. Children born to U.S. citizens abroad (including naturalized citizens returning to their homelands), would also have dual nationality at birth by operation of jus sanguinis descent under U.S. law. Birth dual nationals could provoke diplomatic difficulties, insofar as they subsequently sought the protection of the United States against their country of eventual residence and alternate nationality. It may be something of an overstatement to characterize birthright dual nationals as ticking time bombs, but their status, even if inchoate, was antithetical to international stability.

So citizenship law supplied backstops to address the potential dangers of birth dual nationality. The first took the form of a so-called election requirement, under which many states tolerated the status at birth, but thereafter required the dual national to opt in or opt out at the age of majority. In some countries, the requirement was formal and statutory. In the United States, an implied election requirement was imposed as a matter of administrative practice, under which habitual place of residence and other factors were considered in deciding whether to extend protection to individuals with dual nationality. When a dual national came running to an American embassy for protection from his other country of nationality, for example, the United States would not assist those who, on the basis of place of habitual residence and other factors, were considered to have cast their lot with their other country of nationality. Through the nineteenth century, the election requirement presented a significant tool in reducing the incidence of dual nationality in cases where the American tie was the subordinate one.[10]

But to the extent election was never codified under U.S. law, applied only as a matter of sometimes ad hoc State Department practice, it was always a crude tool for policing dual nationality. Precision came with the statutory adoption of a strict expatriation regime, under which almost all cases of active dual citizenship resulted in the loss of U.S. citizenship. The first expatriation measure, enacted by Congress in 1907, terminated U.S. citizenship when an American citizen naturalized in another country or took an oath of allegiance to a foreign state. The latter provision invariably resulted in the loss of U.S. citizenship where an individual served in the military or other governmental positions in other countries. The Nationality Act of 1940 made such service explicit grounds for loss of citizenship where the individual held nationality in that other state.[11] The 1940 law also mandated denationalization for the mere act of voting in a foreign political election. In 1952, Congress provided for expatriation of birthright dual nationals who lived continuously for three years in their country of alternate nationality, unless they took an oath of continuing allegiance to the United States before the end of that period.[12] These measures could also be deployed against naturalized citizens who maintained or revived active links to their homeland states.

The legal regime entrenched an almost complete and categoric prohibition on active dual nationality. One could participate in the polity of another state only at risk of losing one's U.S. citizenship. American courts upheld the constitutionality of the expatriation regime. In the 1958 decision in *Perez v. Brownell,* the U.S. Supreme Court affirmed the termination of citizenship of a native-born but mostly absent American who as a Mexican citizen had voted in a Mexican presidential election.[13] Justice Frankfurter's opinion for the Court concluded that political participation in foreign lands might evidence "elements of an allegiance to another country in some measure, at least, inconsistent with American citizenship." Even a strong dissent from Chief Justice Warren, decrying Perez's expatriation and framing citizenship as a central facet of human existence, acknowledged that naturalization in another state should result in the loss of U.S. citizenship. Dual nationality may not itself have been illegal, but more than passive membership in another state would result in forfeiture of American membership. Although a complete prohibition was impracticable, the law of citizenship clearly laid down a norm against dual nationality.

This echoed loudly in international law. Eliminating dual nationality would have required states to cede sovereign discretion and coordinate their nationality regimes, something they were unwilling to do. But dual nationality was condemned in various international instruments. A 1930 Hague convention on nationality sought to muster the very "efforts of humanity" to abolish all cases of "double nationality."[14] In 1954, the semi-official International Law Commission recommended multilateral measures based on the principle that "[a]ll persons are entitled to possess one nationality, but one nationality only."[15] A major 1961 study of state practice relating to the status deemed dual nationality "an undesirable phenomenon detrimental...to the friendly relations between nations."[16]

This was not simply a matter of technical national allocation, the perfection of some random global filing system. The law relating to dual nationality was both reflective and reinforcing of a strongly defined national community. One could be a German American or an Italian American or an Irish American, but one could not be German and American, Italian and American, or Irish and American. The law both evidenced and policed the priority of attachment. The national commitment was exclusive, all the more meaningful to the extent that it required the sacrifice of competing attachments. Hence the vocabulary of national associations, of "loyalty" and "allegiance," which have taken citizenship to a different, more intensive level than other forms of membership.

MY LAND IS YOUR LAND

In a quiet but dramatic development, dual citizenship is emerging as a core incident of globalization. If America can be reduced to a punctuation mark, the hyphen is being replaced by the ampersand. It is no longer unusual or problematic to hold more than one citizenship. As with the previous regime, the law (domestic and foreign) is reflecting and accelerating the shift, and illuminates the new meaning of citizenship. On the one hand, acceptance of plural citizenship may facilitate state-based identities insofar as it allows individuals to actuate genuine attachments to more than one polity. On the other, each multiple attachment will loom less large, on average. In some cases, acceptance of plural citizenship will allow for membership of convenience, in which citizenship status is detached from community integration. From an American perspective, the meaning of citizenship is inevitably reduced by dual nationality, and yet there is no practicable or just mechanism for reversing its acceptance.

The population of plural nationals has witnessed dramatic growth in the past decade. (It is now more appropriate to speak of plural rather than merely dual nationals, with the emergence of a significant number of individuals with more than two nationalities.) The growth is predicated on enhanced mobility, a defining feature of globalization. Individuals move more than they once did, for both permanent and temporary resettlement. Children are more likely to be born in a country other than the one in which their parents have nationality. They are also more likely to be the product of "mixed" marriages, in the sense of marriages between individuals of different nationality.

Those predicates are a necessary but insufficient condition to the growth in plural citizenship. After all, the turn of the last century was also marked by massive migrations. Those migrations did not give rise to an increased incidence in dual nationality, at least not of the active sort. Today's mixing of peoples could, in theory, be confronted in the same way, with the old rules requiring termination of citizenship on naturalization or other evidence of operative ties to another state. Multiple nationality is not an essential feature of immigration.

But the law hardly even pretends to bar plural citizenship in the face of these migrations. On the contrary, each of the old mechanisms for suppressing dual nationality has been abandoned under U.S. law and that of many other countries. First, election requirements are largely a thing of the past. Combined with general trends toward jus soli (historically a feature of American citizenship law, of course) and jus sanguinis rules allowing for both patrilineal and matrilineal transmission of citizenship (now nearly universal), the elimination of election means that the growing number of those born with multiple nationality are able to maintain the status into maturity.[17] A child born in the United States to a British mother and a Mexican father, for instance, will have three nationalities at birth and for life. No longer under U.S. law (nor that of most other countries) will activities in other polities result in the termination of original citizenship. In its 1968 decision in *Afroyim v. Rusk*, reversing the *Perez* ruling of only a decade before, the Supreme Court struck down as unconstitutional expatriation on the grounds of voting in a foreign election, in the absence of evidence that the individual intended to terminate his U.S. citizenship.[18] That decision, restoring the citizenship of an American who had voted in an Israeli election, did not expressly approve dual citizenship. But with *Afroyim* as a starting point, the government gradually came to assume that various activities undertaken as a citizen of another country did not imply an intent to abandon U.S. citizenship.[19] Today, there is no activity (including office-holding and military service) that will by itself result in expatriation. One can serve, even at high levels, in the government and armed forces of a foreign state without risk of losing one's U.S. citizenship. Examples include American citizens who have served as the foreign minister of Armenia, chief of the Estonian army, and prime minister of Yugoslavia.[20]

Ditto for naturalization in another state. Until the early 1990s, it was still presumed that the acquisition of another nationality evidenced an intent to terminate U.S. citizenship. That presumption has been abandoned.[21] To the extent one is eligible, one can in effect collect citizenships and the benefits that may come with them. As citizenship eligibility standards are relaxed in other countries, more Americans are signing up for additional nationalities, for sentimental and instrumental reasons. Most notable in this regard is Ireland. A single Irish grandparent is all it takes to secure Irish nationality. Many Americans qualify, and many are taking advantage of the option, both to formalize the Irish identity and exploit the practical benefits of EU citizenship that come with the status.

But perhaps the greatest source of plural nationals, at least in the U.S. context, is those whose status has been enabled by changes in the laws of their homelands. Roughly from the end of the nineteenth century to the end of the cold war, the renunciation oath sworn to by all applicants for U.S. naturalization was a self-executing proposition. Even though never enforced by American authorities, the oath was in most cases made effective by operation of the law of the country of origin, which would terminate a person's original citizenship on naturalization in the United States. That dynamic significantly reduced the number of naturalized citizens retaining their original nationality. But other countries have also liberalized their approach to plural citizenship, and a large majority now permits the retention of nationality upon naturalization in another state. In other words, when a person naturalizes in the United States, odds now are that the person will retain her original citizenship at the same time that she acquires U.S. citizenship.[22]

Countries now making retention the default position include such important "sending" states as Mexico, the Philippines, the Dominican Republic, most other Caribbean states, Ireland, India, Italy, and Poland. In fact, of the top twenty source countries of immigrants to the United States, nineteen now accept dual citizenship (accounting for 90 percent of total immigration),[23] and lone holdout South Korea is facing increasing pressure from its emigrant community to fall in with the rest of the pack. The trend is clearly toward accepting the dual citizenship of "residents abroad," as they are known in many countries. The bottom line, in the U.S. context: a majority of newly minted citizens maintain their original citizenship as a matter of course.

Moreover, with the abandonment of expatriation measures intended to preclude active dual citizenship, these naturalized citizens (as well as those enjoying the status by birth) will be able to participate fully in their homeland affairs, to the extent permitted by that country. Many allow nonresident citizens to vote in political elections, in some cases providing polling places at consulates in the country of residence but increasingly allowing postal or even online balloting. Mexico, the Dominican Republic, Belgium, and the Philippines are among those that have recently liberalized electoral participation for external voters. Newly enfranchised overseas Italian voters tipped the balance in the electoral demise of Silvio Berlusconi.[24] Those who return to their countries of origin will be able to take their U.S. citizenship back home with them, without risk of losing it.

NO PAIN, SOME GAIN

The growing acceptance of plural citizenship, whatever the source, can be attributed in large part to the rise of human rights under international law. The formerly intense distaste for the status, remember, was rooted in the conflict generated by dual nationals between states, where one state sought to protect a national against another country also claiming the individual as its own. That was a world in which all rights were national rights, as Hannah Arendt famously observed.[25] Under international law, individuals had no rights except as protected by states. Today, of course, individual rights are human rights, inherent in personhood, not nationality.

Against the backdrop of human rights, dual nationals pose no more of a threat to world order than do mono-nationals. In the old regime, a dual

Italian and American national might (as many did) provoke controversy between Italy and the United States, as the latter sought to intervene on the individual's behalf against the former's mistreatment. The interests of the individual were recognized only as an incident of his nationality. Human rights recognizes these interests regardless of nationality. If Italy treats a person inconsistent with human rights norms, it has violated international law, and all states have standing to complain of that violation, even if the individual is merely an Italian. Plural citizenship thus no longer presents a special threat to world public order. The "fifth column" take on dual nationals, meanwhile, has never had any basis in reality; the historical record appears not to contain a single significant instance of espionage by a dual national (indeed, those engaged in spying and sabotage would be the last to advertise the competing loyalty).

So much for any imperative to suppress the incidence of plural citizenship. But both states and individuals now see benefits from the status. From the individual's perspective, where multiple nationality was once associated with multiple obligations, the additional memberships generally (if marginally) present additional rights. Plural citizenship can also be situated in a liberalism framework in which autonomy values (including autonomy in defining one's identity) present the prevailing normative benchmark. If I consider my Irish ancestry to be important to my identity, it is a good thing I can formalize the tie to Ireland, in the same way that formalizing membership in such associations as the Republican Party, the Catholic Church, and Amnesty International would presumptively advance my autonomy and sense of self. In that sense, the historical obstacles to maintaining dual citizenship amounted to a constraint on associative expression—I could only express my Irishness in the approved manner, perhaps as a Hibernian but not with a passport.

From the perspective of sending states, meanwhile, dual citizenship has also come to promise affirmative benefits. Emigrant communities are often a critical source of foreign exchange, through remittances to families remaining in the homeland and other forms of economic support. Allowing—even encouraging—the retention of homeland citizenship presents a mechanism for cementing such ties. The Philippines, Mexico, Turkey, and Taiwan are examples of states with large, prosperous diasporas that have recently seen the light through this lens. One might tag the phenomenon as the "new perpetual allegiance," in which homeland states offer continuing membership in expectation of indirect returns.

In the long run, maintenance of dual citizenship status may become the stuff of international human rights rather than something to be accepted or rejected by states as a matter of sovereign prerogative. Suggestive of this possibility is the 1997 European Convention on Nationality. In contrast to its 1963 predecessor (styled as a "Convention on Reduction of Cases of Multiple Nationality") and other international agreements on nationality, the 1997 accord abandons the premise that dual nationality is inherently problematic.[26] Moreover, the 1997 agreement obligates parties to permit multiple nationality where it results from mixed-national parentage. Although the convention is regional in scope, it may mark a watershed in global perceptions of the status, which in turn could point to some acceptance of the status as a matter of right rather than grace. That would lock in recent changes in state practice as well as put pressure on lagging states to conform with the liberalized approach.

In any case, particular features of the law of U.S. citizenship make reversal of the trend improbable here. The citizenship of native-born persons who acquire other nationalities is protected under constitutional rulings from the Supreme Court. (Recently proposed legislation would criminalize the active maintenance of dual citizenship, rather than terminate U.S. citizenship as a result, but that end-run around the *Afroyim* decision stands no chance of enactment.[27]) It would be impracticable to start enforcing, for the first time in U.S. history, the renunciation oath against naturalizing citizens. Homeland states could simply insist on the continuing citizenship of their emigrants, in which case the United States would either have to accept plural citizenship or exclude entire national categories of individuals from naturalizing. Even if the United States could enforce the oath (by requiring proof of the termination of original citizenship), naturalized citizens could subsequently reacquire their original citizenship. In short, as other countries come to accept plural citizenship, U.S. law will not be able to plug the breaches in the dam.

Not that anyone is really demanding that they be plugged. A few commentators aside,[28] there has been little agitation in the United States to reverse the growth of plural nationals. Mexican constitutional reforms allowing for the retention of nationality after naturalization elsewhere attracted some media interest in 1998, but mostly in the way of feature stories. The development laid the groundwork for a huge, concentrated population of dual nationals. Yet that prospect attracted virtually no interest on the part of policy makers. The lack of a response may be explained in large part by the growing number of dual nationals across the board, including in such powerful constituencies as Irish, Italian, and Jewish Americans, which also explains why future constraints on the status are politically as well as legally improbable.

At a conference dinner around the time of the change in Mexico's law, I asked a conservative Republican staffer on the House Immigration subcommittee about the possibility of legislation to address the question. He told me there was nothing in the works, noting that he had nephews and nieces who were Irish and American, and "they're good people, too." That seemed pretty much to close the case for him. The rest of American political culture should soon adapt to these new realities. No longer is dual citizenship considered freakish or immoral; one would find few in the mainstream who would persist with the analogy to polygamy. Many Americans, perhaps a majority, are now acquainted with one or more dual nationals, and many would be able to point to extended family members who (especially by birth or marriage) hold the status. It is a quiet revolution, mostly below the radar screen, but a revolution it may be. From a world that demanded singular nationality we are moving to one that accepts, even celebrates, the holding of many.

DUAL CITIZENSHIP IN THE SERVICE OF (SHORT-TERM) STATE INTERESTS

More than any other development, the rise of plural citizenship may foreshadow the diminished significance of citizenship itself. It does not mark the end of citizenship; indeed, at one level, it affirms the continuing relevance of national identities. Just as singular nationality reinforced the intensity of an individual's particular national identity, however, acceptance of plural affiliations will dilute that intensity, blurring the boundaries of the human geography of citizenship. For an immigrant-receiving, ethnically heterogeneous country such as the United States, this consequence will be more pronounced. American citizenship will often be subordinated to ethnicity-based alternate nationalities, and acceptance of plural citizenship will facilitate the social, political, and economic ties of large immigrant communities, perhaps even beyond the first generation. Plural citizenship compounds the disintegrative features of birth citizenship and naturalization rules, and further detaches citizenship from any meaningful locus of community.

One cannot, it is true, find the end of the nation-state in the growth of plural citizenship. After all, citizenship is about membership in states, plural citizenship as much as singular citizenship; in that respect, plural citizenship may evidence the continuing relevance of states in the world order.[29] Plural citizenship facilitates the identification of individuals with state-based communities by allowing them to formalize the multiple national attachments they may have as a matter of fact. In the world that frowned on dual nationality, an individual who would have liked to be associated with each of two states was forced to choose between them, diminishing the attachment to the state not chosen. Today, both attachments can be sustained and cultivated through uncompromised full membership.

As described, plural nationality can serve state interests in sending countries by way of cementing important ties between homeland and emigrant populations. But plural citizenship can be in the interests of receiving states as well. A system of singular nationality places a high price on naturalization, insofar as terminating original nationality is perceived as costly by the would-be naturalization applicant. For some that cost will be too steep, and notwithstanding their eligibility to naturalize, they will refuse to opt in. The failure of a large proportion of immigrants to naturalize poses a challenge to receiving states. Such a denizen population will not (almost by definition) be politically assimilable, which may in turn also retard social and cultural integration into the community. At some point, the territorial presence of political nonmembers will undermine the liberal premises of the modern democratic state, even if the nonmembership is a matter of choice. Accepting dual citizenship addresses this challenge. By eliminating the cost of renouncing original citizenship, it facilitates naturalization and political incorporation. In this view, plural citizenship is a tool of assimilation.[30]

That may make for good naturalization policy, but plural nationality in the long run will further erode the American national community. America was once in a position to offer naturalization on a take-it-or-leave-it basis. Today, that the United States might have to lower the barriers to naturalization to entice applications betrays the diminishing bargaining power of the American state vis-à-vis potential members. The United States may no longer dictate the terms of admission, or do so only at the peril of deterring a significant population of permanent residents from becoming full members of the polity and corroding the representative democratic process as a result. On this score, it is interesting that liberal theorists have moved beyond advocating that naturalization be at the option of the immigrant (in other words, that naturalization be reduced to a matter of signing up) to calling for the automatic naturalization of long-term residents.[31] That is improbable as a real-world option and problematic even from a liberal perspective, insofar as it constrains the autonomy of individuals to define their own identities. But the shift shows that immigrants can no longer be assumed to prefer citizenship in their country of resettlement, even if they are eligible for it. In this frame, the increasing difficulty of "the sale" indicates the diminished quantity that citizenship represents.

A NATION OF SECOND-CHOICERS

The growing incidence of plural citizenship does more than evidence the decline of citizenship, it also contributes to that decline and the decoupling of citizenship status from actual parameters of community. First, there is the "second choice" problem. In a world that demanded singular citizenship, individuals could be assumed to opt for a particular citizenship because it was their first choice. On average, that choice would reflect a balance of the sentimental ties and material benefits of one citizenship relative to another. These factors would often point in the same direction and reflect an actual priority of community membership. Thus, the naturalization decision would reflect a reprioritization of identity; the acquisition of American citizenship—accompanied by the loss of original citizenship—would (again, on average) reflect a change in the order of community ties. The old ties would not necessarily have been abandoned (in the American tradition, of course, they more often were not), but naturalization would evidence their subordination to the new affiliation. The phenomenon worked in reverse, as well. An American resettling abroad who naturalized in his new country of residence could not retain his U.S. citizenship. The naturalization would likely reflect the primacy of community ties to the other country and the subordination of ties to the United States. The result was a community in which citizenship status defined a core, because it coincided with the group for whom American identity was the first choice among national identities.

This construct is destroyed by the acceptance of plural citizenship, for there is no longer any implicit ranking in the citizenship choice. One can acquire citizenship in states to which one has a subordinate or even nominal ties without sacrificing one's primary attachment. This means that some citizens will sustain a substantial tie to another polity, in terms of their identity and commitments. That possibility may not be identity-dilutive, at least to the extent that identity and commitment are not zero-sum quantities. One can still be meaningfully attached to the American community at the same time that one holds more significant attachments to other nations. But plural citizenship also facilitates the citizenship of convenience. There are certain advantages to maintaining or acquiring citizenship, at the same time that obligations specific to citizenship (as we shall see in the next chapter) have been reduced to virtually nothing. It is a world in which one can collect citizenships at very little cost and without any meaningful attachment to those states in which citizenship is maintained. In the near-parody version, citizenship is held for the purpose of securing access to faster passport inspection lines at airports and other ports of entry. In a world of second-, third-, even fourth-choice citizenships, the lesser ones may reflect no actual community ties.

With the United States playing global polestar, the second-choice phenomenon will be more prevalent than elsewhere. As an immigrant-receiving country, there is greater probability that U.S. citizenship will either be subordinated to original citizenship (which, as Peter Schuck suggests, may be akin to first love, never completely eclipsed by later attachments)[32] or acquired for the convenience and security it affords residents. One fascinating study of an extended Dominican family in New York City by sociologists Greta Gilbertson and Audrey Singer, for example, found several naturalizing as a predicate not to assimilation but to departure and return to their homeland; with American citizenship in hand, they could live in the Dominican Republic without any risk of getting cut off from relatives and better medical care in the United States.[33] The American end of multiple citizenship facilitates transnationality, with the passport as a sort of global free pass rather than a signifier of allegiance to the American nation. And to the extent that attributes of American-ness, political and cultural, have insinuated the globe—"everyone is an American"—it will lose its distinctiveness as an identity, in which case another citizenship will particularistically define the person. To the extent that plural citizenship is normalized, America may become a community of second choicers, with a corresponding loss of filial intensity.

Plural citizenship also becomes the accelerant that fuels the community-diminishing effects of birth citizenship and naturalization rules. The strong norm of singular nationality limited the extent to which other membership criteria could undermine community definition. The rule of jus soli may well have extended citizenship at birth to some individuals who would not thereafter actually assimilate into the community; relaxed naturalization requirements (up until the early twentieth century, involving little more than a period of five years' residence) may have afforded citizenship to some who remained in insulated immigrant communities or who returned thereafter permanently to their homelands. But the birth citizen who ended up living her life in another national community would have forfeited her U.S. citizenship as a result of active membership in that other polity. The immigrant whose primary commitments were to his homeland would have been unlikely to exploit otherwise relaxed naturalization requirements if terminating the homeland tie remained a precondition; those who returned to their homelands lost their naturalized U.S. citizenship under the expatriation law. In short, to the extent that other citizenship rules allowed a blurring of community boundaries or a dilution of identity, the rules against dual citizenship reimposed definition and maintained intensity. Take those rules away, and the imprecision of these other conditions is fully actualized. There is no policing the happenstance birth citizen or the diasporan, both of whose affective and other attachments may lie elsewhere.

BLURRING THE BORDERS OF IDENTITY

The notion of imprecision points to plural citizenship's assault on citizenship as a primary locus of identity. If one paints the question as one of human geography, the norm against plural citizenship enforced community boundaries. As with territorial delimitation, under the old rule an individual was on one side of the line or the other; there was no straddling or overlap between communities. Territorial borders created spatial disjunctures—in the days before globalization, a border was consequential, in terms of social, cultural, and (of course) political development; a border even on a level field would amount to a barrier as important as a mountain. So, too, did the boundaries of citizenship. By minimizing overlap in state-based communities, the norm against dual nationality made those communities more distinct. That approach eliminated scalar possibilities, instead creating clear binary arrangements which reinforced the sense of other in cross-community perceptions. A world in which the "us" and the "them" are rigidly separated is one in which both will loom larger. (Think sport teams and religions, and other institutions that demand exclusive loyalties.) In this respect, citizenship rules suppressing the incidence of dual nationality contributed to community identification. The rules were themselves consequential in a world that would otherwise lend itself to multiple, equivalent associations in the wake of immigration and lingering homeland ties.

Acceptance of plural citizenship erodes this distinctiveness among national communities. As a matter of human geography, it becomes impossible to say where one community leaves off and another begins. A graphic representation of citizenship status would now be much more complex than a territorial map, characterized by overlapping spaces (especially tangled as triple nationality becomes more common) rather than separated ones. It is as if territory were to come under various joint regimes, in which more than one government exercised jurisdiction over the same piece of territory. (Indeed, insofar as territorial boundaries once represented, under the doctrine of sovereignty, zones of exclusive jurisdiction, those lines are also being blurred as various forms of trans- and supranational power emerge. Although our atlases may look basically the same, with the neat carving up of territory, the geographers of globalization are developing other maps to capture the new geography of power.) The arrangement is no longer binary; one can be both and many.

In short, plural citizenship saps national identity of its distinctiveness. If one can be American and also be Dominican or German or Filipino, it becomes more difficult to say what it means to be an American. That already presented enough of a challenge in the old world of singular nationality, but at least then it was more plausible to isolate the characteristics attaching to membership in the American polity to the exclusion of formal membership in other polities. What of assertions of a uniquely American creed when many citizens are not uniquely American? Plural citizenship emerges as another tool in the global infiltration of American ideals, in this case through the participation of American citizens as citizens in other political systems. But that infiltration undoes the identity as it loses differentiation. One can play on the old saying, "we have met the enemy and they is us," in unpacking the significance of plural citizenship. It is difficult to rally the "us" against a "them" when the two overlap. Attachment to state is no longer amenable to loyalty tests. The need to choose between states no longer presents itself, as states themselves seem less competitive, not only for purposes of defense (a mostly obsolete function, at least against other states), but also for general community self-definition. The core is no longer distilled.

Again, this is offered as a matter of description, not lamentation. Nor, as with other citizenship practices that reflect a diminished national identity, is there anything really to be done about it. Into the next generation, as more children of mixed parentage and children of immigrants are able to sustain claims to alternate citizenship, plural citizenship may emerge a defining feature of a new era in which membership in states is demoted to the level of membership in other forms of association. As citizenship loses the sacral elements of exclusivity, it becomes just another form of belonging.

4

Take It or Leave It American

WHAT DIFFERENCE DOES citizenship make? Previous chapters have implicitly challenged the premise of a public vocabulary in which the citizenry is taken to comprise a meaningfully bounded community. When a national public official appeals to his fellow Americans, he is no longer talking to a coherent audience. This chapter takes on another mainstay of the political discourse, "the rights and obligations of citizenship." As used in public and social policy debates, the unstated premise here is that citizenship is consequential in the relationship of the individual to the state; in short, that citizenship makes a difference.

But in fact, citizenship makes very little difference. What the state extracts from you and what it owes you are minimally contingent on citizenship status. Citizens are privileged in only a few dwindling contexts. Leaving aside the context of immigration law, resident aliens have essentially equivalent rights. Even in the political arena, in which aliens are largely excluded from voting for or holding public office, citizenship is not a barrier to political influence. The restoration of most public benefits denied resident aliens under the 1996 welfare reform act highlights a near equality for purposes of state assistance. In the immigration context, long the one in which aliens suffered dramatic rights deprivations, the landscape has been changing to extend protection. The lack of a significant differential explains why many long-term immigrants fail to naturalize. For those who don't otherwise identify with the American community, it may not be worth compromising their identity. For others, it simply isn't worth the bureaucratic hassle.

The lack of differential is even more dramatic on the question of obligations. The "obligations of citizenship" is a favorite buzz phrase of mainstream public intellectuals, usually to the end of reviving civic virtue. But in effect there are no obligations of citizenship. With the relatively minor exception of jury duty, citizenship imposes no additional societal burdens not also shouldered by noncitizen residents. The most notable duties extracted by government—taxes and military service—fall with essential equivalence on citizens and aliens alike. Taxes are based largely on residence. Conscription is a thing of the past in the United States—even in the wake of the September 11 attacks, very few have spoken of reinstating the draft—and thus imposes no duty on anyone. Americans, as such, are required to do nothing for their country that they would not be required to do as mere residents.

That has not always been the case. On the rights side, although aliens have always enjoyed some constitutional protections on an equal basis, they were historically disadvantaged with respect to important privileges, including the right to own property and engage in some kinds of business. As for obligations, the highest duty demanded by the state—to be asked to give one's life in its service—was once demanded only of the citizen or the citizen-in-the-making. These narratives are less amenable to periodization than others in the law of citizenship; in a country of immigrants thirsty for the strength that immigrants represented, history reflected the pressures of drawing into service those who were on the way to but had not yet perfected their membership status. But one can trace a trajectory in which citizenship status has grown less consequential in terms of situating an individual within society.

That trajectory further evidences and reinforces the decline of American citizenship as an institution. The strength of collective associations can be measured by their power to extend benefits to and extract obligations from their members. The more intense the community, the more likely it will extend itself to protect and provide for the individual member (in a way different from its protection and provision for nonmembers), and the more likely it will be able to enlist the service of individual members to that end. Along that measuring stick, the institution of the American state has diminished. But the lack of a citizenship differential also undermines the capacity to extend and extract. Insofar as the community does not make special provision for its members, members will feel less special in belonging. To the extent that the community makes minimal demands on its members, less of a bond will emerge among them.

We saw how the conditions of membership—respecting citizenship at birth and through naturalization, and respecting plural nationality—not only reflected an increasingly undelimited national community but also contributed to its further erosion. The same dynamic appears with respect to the incidents of citizenship. As with the citizenship rules, dwindling rights and obligations cannot be reinflated through simple policy-making exercises. Of course, citizenship contingencies can be legislated, as occurred in 1996. But they are unlikely to stick where citizenship boundaries bear a diminishing correlation to community lines. In the end, the determination of rights and obligations moves to other institutions that do correlate with associational attachment—institutions other than the state.

MEMBERSHIP HAD ITS PRIVILEGES

Citizenship is central to some modern narratives of individual well-being. Chief Justice Earl Warren once declared, "citizenship is man's basic right for it is nothing less than the right to have rights."[1] The popular conception, shared by some public intellectuals, holds that there are certain significant rights peculiar to the citizenry. Although there are some (most notably, Yale law professor Alexander Bickel) who have minimized the institution of citizenship in the American political landscape,[2] it is vaunted in the dominant republican tradition under which individual actualization can occur only through formal rights of political participation. The conventional wisdom has ascribed to American citizenship a special power to benefit its holders, a shield against transgressions abroad and a marker of full membership at home.

But even a cursory survey of U.S. law reveals few important rights that hinge on citizenship status. With regard to the protection of many important rights, the courts are blind to citizenship status. In the realm of civil rights—that is, rights of the person to protections against arbitrary official action, to free expression, and the like—resident aliens enjoy equivalent rights to the citizenry. Indeed, such rights are enjoyed by all who are territorially present, regardless of their immigration status. Thus, the undocumented alien who faces criminal prosecution is entitled to all constitutional due process protections afforded accused citizens.[3]

These due process rights have been extended to noncitizens since their judicial creation. They were not applied out of judicial solicitude for aliens, however. Rather, they were a function of the strict territorial application of the Constitution. The Constitution governed the treatment of all persons within the United States and none outside its territorial boundaries. The Constitution wasn't portable; citizens and aliens alike left their rights to due process at the water's edge.[4]

A similar story can be told of the application of the equal protection clause. The Supreme Court long ago extended its coverage to aliens. Even in the late-nineteenth-century context of intense West Coast antipathy to Asian immigrants, the Court found aliens—including the "obnoxious Chinese"—to enjoy equal protection against discriminatory state legislation.[5] But in this context as well, neither citizenship status nor solicitude for aliens has been the dispositive factor. Rather, state discrimination has been quashed by way of protecting the exclusive federal power over immigration. One could not have the states interfering with federal decisions regarding the admission of aliens.[6] Equal protection became the vehicle for ensuring institutional prerogatives. Of course, with respect to rights to both due process and equal protection, whatever the cause, the result was to equalize the position of aliens before the courts.

That is not by any means to say that aliens historically enjoyed equal legal status. Aliens were subject to various discriminatory regimes sanctioned by the courts and the common law. Thus, for instance, some states in the nineteenth century barred aliens from owning real property, consistent with long-standing common-law traditions. Others that permitted such land ownership restricted its transfer by inheritance (in other words, a noncitizen could not pass real estate to his noncitizen children). The federal government, moreover, restricted homesteading to citizens or immigrants who had applied for naturalization.[7] In an economic context that remained largely agrarian, these disabilities were significant.

Other economic disabilities were pervasive. Many states made aliens ineligible for the licenses required to operate certain kinds of businesses, especially those involving natural resources (hunting and fishing licenses, for both commercial and recreational purposes) and such regulated establishments as pawnbrokers and liquor stores. Every state in the Union barred aliens from the practice of law, and many jurisdictions excluded noncitizens from such other professions as medicine, accounting, and nursing. Between 1871 and 1976, for example, New York enacted thirty-eight laws requiring citizenship for occupations ranging from architects, private investigators, physicians, dentists, and pharmacists to embalmers, plumbing inspectors, and blind adult vendors of newspapers.[8] In some states, aliens were barred from serving as corporate directors. These measures had the cumulative effect of setting down a clear line between members and nonmembers (especially to the extent that they reinforced racial criteria for naturalization), and presented powerful incentives for eligible immigrants to naturalize. The courts upheld these discriminatory measures as rationally advancing legitimate state objectives.[9]

These disabilities are now largely a thing of the past. In cases of discrimination on the part of state governments, the courts now afford legal aliens elevated protection ("heightened scrutiny," in constitutional diction) similar to that extended those who face racial or gender discrimination.[10] Restrictions relating to land ownership, inheritance, professional licenses, and the like have failed to pass that raised bar. Only with respect to a limited number of positions involving core "governmental functions," such as police officers and public school teachers, are states now constitutionally permitted to deem citizenship a job qualification.[11] Permitted but not required—many states, for instance, make noncitizens eligible to teach. Blanket civil service ineligibilities have been struck down. By 1999, such states as Florida, California, and Texas had abandoned all citizenship-based criteria for employment or licensing. Noncitizens thus no longer face significant categorical obstacles to economic or professional advancement. Nor may state governments discriminate against aliens with respect to the incidents of the welfare state, at least not in the absence of a federal imprimatur.[12]

LOCATIONAL SECURITY

The courts have, it is true, afforded the federal government wide discretion in its treatment of aliens. Under current constitutional doctrine it remains clear that the courts will not stand in the way of federal discrimination against noncitizens.[13] In the realm of immigration control, citizenship status is indeed consequential. Aliens can be deported from the United States (or never allowed to enter in the first place). One might be a decades-long resident and face expulsion for even a relatively minor crime. Especially since the elimination of discretion in many deportation cases with the 1996 immigration law, the media has been awash with stories in which the consequences of removal have been harsh indeed.[14] Citizens are free to come and go as they please; whatever other punishments can be imposed on citizens (including, of course, death), banishment is not among them, for that is a fate, as Justice William Brennan observed, "universally decried by civilized people."[15] Citizenship thus affords a certain security of location. The Immigration and Nationality Act also privileges citizens with respect to securing the entry of some family members; where citizens can petition for the admission of parents, siblings, and married adult children, permanent resident aliens cannot. Spouses and children of noncitizen residents are subject to annual quotas that in recent years have resulted in long waits for admission where visas for equivalent relatives of citizens are not capped.[16]

But even this citizenship differential is less meaningful than would appear. Most permanent resident aliens are just as locationally secure as their citizen neighbors. Congress has never provided for the deportation of aliens on the basis of nationality or status alone. Even in wartime, although so-called enemy aliens have been in some cases subject to internment (as was most notoriously the case with Japanese—and Japanese American citizens—during World War II), there has never been a mass deportation of aliens for reasons unrelated to individual conduct. The average law-abiding permanent resident can rest easy about his entitlement to remain in the United States.

To be sure, procedural constitutional protections have, at least in the past, been diluted in the immigration context, so that there has been a more serious danger of wrongful deportation. (To make the analogy to criminal law, the risk of an "innocent" alien being deported has been greater than the risk of an innocent criminal defendant being convicted.) But this risk is small. Congress has extended extensive procedural protections to aliens in deportation procedures, even if the Supreme Court would not always require them as a matter of constitutional law. For instance, a permanent resident alien is entitled to mount a defense to deportation charges in a trial-type proceeding, in which the government must demonstrate by "clear and convincing evidence" that the alien is deportable.[17] What risks remain from gaps in procedural protection (for instance, indigent aliens are not entitled to an attorney in removal proceedings) are minimized by the inefficiencies of immigration law enforcement. Millions of aliens who are deportable are never apprehended, in light of which the numbers of aliens wrongfully deported must be quite small (in something of the same way that the number of persons wrong-fully accused of jaywalking will be minuscule).

Beyond the prospect of deportation, the immigration-related disabilities of permanent residence status are minimal. Although there are technical restrictions on a resident alien's right to come and go—stay away too long and, at least in theory, the green card holder may be deemed to have abandoned his residency status—in practice any presence requirement is underenforced, at least where the alien maintains a U.S. address, is absent for no longer than a year at a stretch, and pays her taxes.[18] As for differential treatment for purposes of immigration benefits, it only applies to those seeking the admission of family members, and even then not significantly. The waiting list for visas for siblings of citizens (a category for which only 65,000 admissions are allocated annually) now stands at more than ten years; on the other side, Congress has recently moved to speed the entry of the children and spouses of noncitizen residents who have faced quota-driven delays. It is now even the case that permanent residents use the same lines as citizens at such U.S. airports as New York's JFK and Washington's Dulles; a U.S. passport doesn't get you back in any more quickly than does a green card.

Of course, noncitizens without permanent residence status face more significant deprivations in the immigration context. For those present in the United States, locational status is not legally secure, either because their legal nonimmigrant status is temporary, barring the adjustment of which they will have to depart, or because they are out of status altogether, and thus face the prospect of removal. But even here, the disabilities of noncitizen, nonpermanent resident status may not be as dramatic as one might expect. As a legal matter, the drawbacks of conditional or illegal presence are obvious. As a practical matter, however, they may be if not insignificant, then at least manageable. Many who enter the United States as nonimmigrants subsequently acquire equities (a U.S. citizen spouse, for example) rendering them eligible for permanent residence status. More than 60 percent of those issued green cards in 2006 were already in the United States. In the meantime, so long as they comply with the terms of their nonimmigrant admission, their presence is secure.

As for undocumented aliens—those who entered the country illegally or who overstay or otherwise violate the terms of a lawful nonimmigrant admission—the inefficiency of immigration enforcement, especially in the country's interior, makes the probability of apprehension so slight as to be almost inconsequential. Nationally, there are fewer than 2,000 investigations officers tasked with the identification of deportable aliens, approximately one agent for every 5,000 undocumented aliens present in the United States. Many of those agents are focused on cases involving criminal aliens or national security. Less than 7 percent of investigative work hours are directed at the interior apprehension of aliens who entered without inspection or who are otherwise out of status.[19] One can live in the United States as an "illegal" alien with little fear, on a day-to-day basis, of removal. Immigration law enforcement is so dramatically inefficient in the nation's interior that even the out-of-status alien faces minimal locational insecurity.

Obviously, the undocumented alien faces steeper risks at the border, where the government focuses the overwhelming majority of enforcement resources. It is much less easy for an illegal alien to come and go. But even on this score, it remains a matter of cost rather than of possibilities. The borders remain porous. Even with a tenfold increase in border enforcement resources over the past twenty years, the probability of apprehension for an illegal border crosser stands at an all-time low. The Border Patrol collars fewer than 5 percent of all illegal entrants, and most of those who are caught will (after being released back into Mexico) simply try—and succeed—on the next attempt.[20] Although it is not as simple as buying a plane ticket, undocumented aliens go home for holidays and other visits, confident that they will be able to return to the United States.[21] In this respect, even the nonterritorially present alien who is ineligible for an immigrant visa is not categorically disabled by the status. Aliens who want to get into the United States usually can, one way or another. Many will enter on a nonimmigrant basis, with full intention of overstaying a time-limited visa or violating a no-employment condition. Others will do it the harder way, through clandestine entry, involving greater but by no means insurmountable additional costs.

Thus, even with respect to immigration rights and locational security, the differentials among citizens, permanent resident aliens, and other aliens are better situated along a scale than in a binary system. Were one to draw a line, moreover, it would not fall along the citizen/noncitizen divide but would rather distinguish citizens and legal aliens, on the one hand, and those out of status or with no basis for securing it, on the other. Where one would expect it to count the most, the rights of citizenship don't add up to much.

NONCITIZENS AND THE SOCIAL SAFETY NET

Citizenship counts for even less with respect to federal benefits beyond the immigration context. As noted, state governments are today restrained from discriminating against aliens in most respects. Federal benefit schemes such as Social Security disability insurance, Medicare and Medicaid, food stamps, and Temporary Assistance for Needy Families (TANF, or "welfare," in the popular conception) have discriminated on the basis of citizenship status only at the margins. Alien eligibility has at times been conditioned on five years' permanent residence. Otherwise, however, federal benefits programs had placed permanent resident aliens on a par with citizens, up until the enactment of the major 1996 welfare reform bill.

The 1996 act rendered even permanent resident aliens ineligible for a variety of federal benefits. Aliens were barred from Medicare and Medicaid unless their state of residence opted for eligibility; with certain minor exceptions, they were counted out of the SSI and food stamp programs altogether.[22] In the wake of the 1996 act, there were widely voiced fears that citizenship was making a comeback as a tool of deprivation and exclusion.[23] Indeed, the exclusions were sobering and, at least in modern times, without precedent; coupled with intense anti-immigrant sentiments in the mid-1990s, the resident alien ineligibility was understandably perceived as another stage in the circling of the wagons.

It hasn't turned out that way. First of all, for the most part the states filled the gap where they could. Far from a predicted race to the bottom, in which no states would have opted for alien eligibility when given the choice under the federal measure, almost all extended benefits to large proportions of their noncitizen populations. Indeed, some states adopted alien-eligible programs to replace those federal benefits categorically denied by the 1996 measure (food stamps and SSI, most notably). The extension of state benefits was followed by the piecemeal restoration of most benefits at the federal level. Except for the first five years following admission and with the exception of SSI disability, permanent resident aliens are once again eligible for all major federal benefits programs.[24] Otherwise, in most cases permanent resident status implicates the deprivation of no concrete benefits.

Of course that may say nothing about the status of nonimmigrant and out-of-status aliens, who continue to face a variety of disabilities. In contrast to permanent resident aliens, they are ineligible for many forms of public benefits, falling outside the social safety nets at both the state and federal levels. Various avenues of economic advancement are effectively precluded. Many nonimmigrant aliens are barred from employment. An "illegal" alien can never hope to hold a public sector position, nor any in those professions in which employers rigorously enforce legal prohibitions on hiring aliens who do not enjoy work authorization. In many contexts, such aliens must in effect live underground, denied the foundational identity that comes with a Social Security number and a driver's license. Never mind the fact that the undocumented alien is hardly free to come and go. The lack of permanent residence status is plainly consequential.

But it is perhaps not as great a disability as one might expect. Those on nonimmigrant business visas are in many cases (under the H-1B program) eligible for a six-year stay, during which they are often able to convert to permanent residence status. They are not particularly disadvantaged as nonimmigrants; many are in well-paying professions where they are unlikely to require access to public benefits such as welfare. The corporate executive from a European state holding a multiple-entry visa will not feel any deprivation owing to his immigration status. Those who are not employment authorized (on visitor or student visas, for instance) often work anyway, with very little fear of effective enforcement against them.

Even illegal alien status need not represent a significant cost. For starters, the fact that an estimated 12 million individuals are in the United States in violation of the immigration laws demonstrates that for that large population the benefits of presence outweigh any disadvantages of undocumented status. Many undocumented aliens are able to secure work, which is usually the incentive for illegally entering or remaining in the United States. Much of this employment is at the lower end of the labor scale.

But it is possible, as many cases have shown, to prosper here even as an illegal alien. Nothing about their immigration status bars membership in the various spheres of civil society, including churches and ethnic community associations, some of which may extend the sort of safety net that they cannot secure from the state. Undocumented aliens are members of unions; indeed unions consider aliens in general as a major new source of growth, and are vigorously advocating for the labor-related rights of aliens, legal or not. Beyond unions, a growing number of "assistance centers" help undocumented aliens assert their substantially equivalent rights under labor, housing, consumer, and other legal regimes.[25] Illegal aliens are eligible—as a constitutional matter, per the Supreme Court in its 1974 decision in *Plyler v. Doe*—for public elementary and secondary education, and of course they benefit from the public infrastructure (including police and fire protection services). They are generally eligible for social services in kind—shelters, soup kitchens, and the like—as well as for federal aid for emergency medical care, which, not surprisingly, creates strong incentives among medical professionals to diagnose emergencies liberally.[26] Some states have made illegal alien residents eligible for in-state tuition rates in public institutions of higher education. Others have moved to make them eligible for driver's licenses, which in turn can pave the way to bank accounts, credit cards, mortgages and other accessories of everyday American middle-class life.[27] Indeed, many banks and other businesses are accepting Mexican and other foreign country identity cards for dealings with individuals.[28] Undocumented immigrants may be forced underground but not necessarily that far under the surface.

In any case, whatever the disabilities faced by nonimmigrant or undocumented aliens, that still draws the line somewhere other than at the boundary of citizenship. No doubt a green card is a valuable commodity, something that individuals pay thousands of dollars for, usually in the form of legal bills and government-imposed fees. If there were a global auction for immigrant visas, they would command a substantial price. But citizenship is another story. As a product, it has almost gone begging for customers. Part of the explanation is that it doesn't offer much as a package. In recent years, it has had some appeal as a defensive investment— against the possibility of deportation, however remote, and the deprivation of federal public benefits. That may have caused the spike in applications through the mid-1990s, although as described in chapter 2, even more prosaic explanations are available. But as anti-immigrant sentiments subside, and the basic equivalence returns, the long-term value added in citizenship is relatively insignificant. It doesn't give the resident alien much that he doesn't have already.

PARTICIPATING IN THE POLITY

The one area in which citizenship is assumed to make a clear difference is in the realm of politics. With few exceptions, aliens are barred from voting; from that, it is not hard to construct an account in which they lack a political voice. But this account fetishizes the ballot and fails to consider multiple other entry points that are open to noncitizens. Indeed, as the importance of individual votes diminishes and the weight of "special interests"—of which many noncitizens comprise a part—has increased, noncitizens are able to exert considerable political pressure notwithstanding their lack of formal membership in the polity. If anything, this influence has grown in recent decades, a trend almost certain to continue in the future.

As a general matter, aliens lack the franchise. A few oddball jurisdictions, most notably Takoma Park, Maryland, allow legal resident aliens to vote in local elections. In New York City, even undocumented aliens could vote in school board elections if they had children in the public schools (before the recent abolishment of the school board there). But the proportion of aliens thus able to cast votes is tiny.

This has effectively always been the case in the United States. Contemporary advocates are quick to assert a historical tradition of alien voting. From the mid-nineteenth century into the early twentieth, twenty-two states at one point or another allowed aliens to vote even in federal elections. There was a time when a substantial number of aliens could vote for president.[29] But alien suffrage was typically restricted to so-called declarant aliens, that is, aliens who had formally declared their intention to become citizens. Although an anachronism today, this was at one time an important step in the naturalization process. One could take out "first papers" after only three years' residence (before the five required for naturalization itself); it served as a notice of a purpose to transfer national allegiance, amounting (in Hiroshi Motomura's formulation) to a "form of precitizenship that conferred significant benefits on a lawful immigrant who could not yet naturalize."[30] Thus, alien suffrage was extended to citizens-in-the-making, individuals for whom the acquisition of formal membership was imminent. That qualification rationalized it, albeit imperfectly, to a world in which allegiances counted for so much. It was hardly by way of empowering aliens per se that the practice was engaged, in the spirit that some today support the concept of noncitizen voting.

That is not to say that there is any necessary logic to the current citizenship eligibility requirements for the franchise. Among European states, alien voting in local elections is now routine (indeed, among EU members states it is the law), and some countries, including New Zealand and Denmark, allow long-term alien residents to vote in national elections. Powerful normative arguments can be marshaled in its favor, especially at the local level. But one might first ask (as advocates do not, for obvious tactical reasons) whether extending the franchise is more than a marginal issue in the political inclusion of aliens. In fact, aliens already enjoy multiple channels of political influence, in the context of which voting emerges a relatively minor deprivation.

There is first of all the direct political influence that aliens can bring to bear with the most potent of political tools—money. Under federal law, permanent resident aliens can make campaign contributions in federal elections.[31] One need not go out on any policy limb in asserting that money is where the primary influence has been in modern-day politics. With money, one can run the expensive, media-focused campaigns that translate to victories at the polls; it is with the checkbook rather than the ballot that one's voice is amplified. This route is open to both resident aliens and citizens. The practice was tested during the Clinton administration, when it was discovered that some resident aliens had acted as conduits for nonresident aliens, and legislation was introduced that would have precluded campaign contributions by any noncitizens. Congress rejected that proposal, in the wake of which one can assume the legality of resident alien political fundraising into the future.[32]

Then there are the various indirect levers available to aliens in advancing their political interests. As already noted, aliens are eligible for membership in virtually the entire spectrum of civil society. This membership is obviously important in itself, as a matter of individual self-actualization (indeed, as I will describe in chapter 6, on that score it may pose a threat to the dominance of the state). But membership in civil society organizations is also an important tool of political influence. Thus, the alien who is a member of a union or a church or is an employee of a large corporation is afforded political voice with respect to that element of his identity. Noncitizens can belong to and work for political parties; there are reports of them hitting the ground running as political volunteers on arrival.[33] An alien who is black or Asian or Hispanic is likely to have his interests advanced by powerful racial advocacy groups, at least for purposes of affirmative action and related issues. Perhaps most significantly, aliens will often find powerful and more completely aligned advocates in the form of ethnic lobbies. Thus, to take two of the most prominent examples, Jewish and Irish aliens in the United States could hardly be said to be disenfranchised in any meaningful sense. The observation may not be as self-evident with some other groups, but almost all ethnic immigrants have some form of community organization. They also have relatives here who are citizens and can vote. So even if one does continue to place faith in the primacy of the ballot—not easy to do, in the face of ever-decreasing turnout rates among voters—there is a form of virtual representation at work here.

Finally, aliens enjoy powerful advocates in the form of their homeland governments. Under traditional international law, foreign governments had the right to exercise "diplomatic protection" on behalf of their citizens against mistreatment at the hands of another state. This practice is broadening, so that foreign governments are interceding in the United States not just to shield their nationals from perceived injustices (although they continue to do this vigorously, especially in the death penalty context) but also to advance social interests. Mexico has been particularly aggressive on this score. With more than fifty consulates in the United States, Mexican government officials are working to advance the interests of Mexican nationals across the board, from school benefits to health care to labor rights, in the courts, state capitals, and Washington.[34]

All this adds up to considerable political leverage for noncitizens, the lack of the franchise notwithstanding. The proposition holds for both legal and illegal aliens; although plainly permanent resident aliens are better positioned to protect their interests, undocumented aliens enjoy the proxy efforts of civil society groups (including unions), ethnic communities, and home governments. The proof is in the political bottom line. If noncitizens were in fact politically defenseless, one would expect them to be routed on every front. Yet aliens have held their own and more. As described, outside the immigration context resident alienage is effectively equivalent to citizenship. With respect to immigration, Congress has adopted a litany of substantive benefits and procedural protections that would never have been forced on it by the courts. (Indeed, there are many instances in which an immigrant has lost in court only to win on the Hill.) Undocumented aliens, although obviously suffering legal if not actual disabilities, have scored significant legislative gains in the form of various amnesties over the past two decades.

The significant legislative setbacks of 1996 don't offer much of a counterargument, although they do show that noncitizens may be more vulnerable to short-term reversals. Largely driven by intense anti-immigrant sentiment in California, three 1996 laws—the welfare and immigration reform acts, and a criminal procedure measure aimed mostly at accelerating executions but also the removal of criminal aliens—made it an annus horribilis for immigrants. Resident aliens lost significant federal benefits eligibility, the result of an eleventh-hour move to save billions of welfare dollars. The rules governing deportation were tightened; decades-long resident aliens could now be removed for relatively minor offenses, with no possibility of discretionary relief and in some cases no allowance even for judicial review. The 1996 laws generated a slew of desperate tales of immigrant woe; at the time aliens did seem wholly disenfranchised.

But subsequent developments have told a different story. First was the significant coverage devoted to the harsh consequences of the "reforms," and a general recognition that they went too far. In the case of benefits eligibility, the damage has largely been undone. An unusual coalition of conservative Reagan administration veterans and immigrant advocates came together in 1997 to win passage of partial relief for nationals of various Central American and East European states, as well as Haiti and Cuba. There has been considerable momentum building for some softening of the 1996 provisions eliminating discretion with respect to the deportation of criminal aliens. A major amnesty came close to passage in 2007, with backing from the Bush White House. In the absence of some other resolution of the issue, amnesty (however vigorously politicians of all stripes sprint from the label) will no doubt be back on the legislative table before long.

SEPTEMBER 11 AND THE RIGHTS OF ALIENS

The move toward significant immigration liberalization itself suffered a setback in the wake of the September 11 terrorist attacks. But in fact that episode provides further evidence of the contemporary resiliency of alien rights and political interests. In the wake of so concussive and unprecedented an assault, carried out by alien visitors, one might have expected significant anti-alien immigration measures. Such measures were both proposed and feared, and yet the ultimate legislative response to September 11 was calibrated and considered. That noncitizen interests could weather the episode essentially unscathed demonstrates the deep entrenchment of the equivalency between citizens and others territorially present.[35]

In the immediate wake of the attacks, it appeared that the episode would result in significant curtailments of alien rights. More than a thousand aliens were rounded up (no phrase better describes it) on minor immigration or criminal violations, denied access to family or counsel, and threatened with secret removal proceedings. Initial legislative proposals from the administration would have authorized the attorney general to remove any alien certified as a terrorist, permanent resident aliens included, with no review of either the certification or the removal. A presidential order authorized the establishment of military tribunals for use against non-citizens for charges relating to the attacks, with only the most rudimentary procedural protections. The notorious Palmer Raids following World War I and the internment of Japanese aliens (and Japanese Americans) during World War II seemed fairly invoked as cautionary historical parallels. Civil libertarians and immigrant advocates raised the specter of massive rights deprivations.

Left to its own devices, the Bush administration might have pressed ahead with extreme measures (although even the John Ashcroft Justice Department was careful to warn against taking retribution against Arab Americans). In the end, however, Congress emerged an effective agent of restraint on most fronts. In particular, it rejected administration demands for expansive, unreviewable authority to remove suspected terrorists. The major September 11–related legislation, the USA PATRIOT Act, afforded the attorney general the power to detain suspected terrorist aliens for seven days only; if immigration or criminal charges are not pressed within that period, the alien must thereafter be released. More than half of the text of USA PATRIOT concerns the extension of immigration benefits to survivors of those killed in the attacks, whose eligibility for immigrant status would have otherwise died with the victims. Congress has used committee hearings to highlight questionable executive branch practices undertaken on existing authority, such as the round-up detentions. The aliens detained in the weeks after September 11 (all on preexisting enforcement powers) have since been released or deported on other grounds, and it is not clear how far the Justice Department will be permitted to proceed with secret proceedings, after early rebuffs from the courts.

Nor has citizenship mattered much in the treatment of those involved or said to be involved in terrorist activities. The decision to prosecute the twentieth hijacker, Zacarias Moussaoui, in federal district court under normal criminal procedures made clear that the administration would not use military tribunals against aliens apprehended in the United States. Likewise, shoe bomber Richard Reid was prosecuted under ordinary criminal procedures. Indeed, two of the three individuals designated as "enemy combatants," through which the government attempted to deprive them of all due process rights, were U.S. citizens. Yaser Hamdi was subsequently released, in the wake of the U.S. Supreme Court decision finding the terms of his confinement unconstitutional, and Jose Padilla has since been plugged back into the ordinary criminal process after spending more than three years in a brig with no access to the outside world.[36] There is one permanent resident alien, Ali Saleh Kahlah al-Marri, who remains subject to the designation. Al-Marri has prevailed before the lower courts in challenging his detention. One might wonder if his continuing plight results from the lack of publicity afforded his case relative to the others. In any case, the administration clearly didn't consider citizenship a shield against extra-constitutional enforcement action on U.S. soil.

The post-9/11 result, then, is a far cry from the Palmer Raids or Japanese internment. Those episodes remain useful as historical benchmarks, against which the response against aliens post–September 11 looks tame. The new terrorist threat further demonstrates just how little citizenship means today; if the events of 9/11 didn't widen the diminishing gap between the status of citizens and noncitizens, then nothing will. Although some formal distinctions persist, in practical terms the rights differential has been reduced almost to zero.

NO EXTRA RIGHTS, NO EXTRA OBLIGATIONS

More often invoked than the supposed rights are the supposed obligations of citizenship. The phrase is ingrained in our political vocabulary, a refrain with which to bracket exhortations to a revived sense of national duty and spirit. As with the term "citizen" itself, like background music or a dead metaphor, the trotting out of its associated obligations rarely provokes examination. And yet the obligations that come with the status of citizenship are minimal. Residence, not citizenship, is now the determining factor in dictating what the individual owes the American state.

That goes for the two traditional burdens of citizenship. Above all others is the duty to bear arms and to face the mortal hazards of the battlefield. The willingness to die for one's country is as good an indicator of national fervor as any, the solemnized "ultimate sacrifice"; it has been closely identified, since ancient Greece, with the concept of citizenship itself. For able-bodied males, at least, it has been the primary burden of membership;

indeed, this differential burden, in terms of gender, was often used to justify the differential rights of citizenship that otherwise disadvantaged female citizens.

As a historical matter, citizenship status played a key formal role in defining the class of men subject to mandatory service. In the American context, it could never be so simple as drawing a straight line between citizens and aliens, for the population of aliens has always been too large not to exploit for military service purposes. Aliens have always been eligible to serve in the U.S. armed forces, in a tradition dating to Lafayette and other foreigners who served in the Revolutionary War. Declarant aliens—that is, those who had declared their intention to naturalize—were subject to conscription during the Civil War and World War I. Other aliens, however, could request exemption from the draft. Securing the exemption itself had a citizenship consequence: any alien relieved from military service on this ground was made permanently ineligible for naturalization. Along with desertion from the armed forces, this remains the sole ground for permanent debarment in all of the Nationality Act.[37]

Congress repealed the exemption possibility for aliens in 1951.[38] Since then, except as provided by treaty, permanent resident aliens and citizens have been treated as equivalents for military service requirements. They are no longer given the option of relinquishing naturalization eligibility in return for an exemption. (Even undocumented aliens are, at least as a technical matter, subject to conscription. Only nonimmigrant aliens are excused.) During the Korean and Vietnam conflicts, resident aliens were subject to the draft.[39] Today, they are subject to Selective Service registration requirements. Of course, military conscription now appears increasingly improbable; even in the wake of September 11, calls for a revived draft have fallen flat. Outside the citizenship context, that may say a lot about the future of the nation-state, for which military service has been a defining feature. The willingness to die for one's national community is what put it above other communities. But the formal abandonment of a citizenship criterion for conscription untethers a major traditional burden of citizenship from the status. One may still undertake, in the naturalization oath itself, to bear arms for the nation, but as a matter of law one has already done that with receipt of a green card.[40] Noncitizens, meanwhile, comprise an estimated 2–3 percent of the Iraq-era volunteer army.

The same basically holds true for the other major putatively distinctive obligation of citizenship, namely, the payment of taxes. But taxes are perhaps even less anchored in citizenship terms than military service obligations. Territorially present aliens—whatever their formal status—have long been obligated to pay income taxes. The same holds true today. Aliens who are present in the United States for more than 180 days must file tax returns as would any citizen, nonimmigrants and illegal immigrants included. This can't prove much of a surprise; if aliens were exempted from income tax, it is hard to imagine very many of them undertaking naturalization (yet another way of demonstrating the commensurable value of citizenship). Noncitizens are entitled to foreign tax credits for various tax payments made to the many nations with whom the United States has bilateral tax treaties, but then again, so are citizens.

That leaves jury duty as the sole differential obligation working from a citizenship criterion. Today, both federal and state courts uniformly exclude noncitizens from jury pools. With some state-level exceptions for declarant aliens, that has always been the case. Query whether it makes any sense. If one assumes in the contemporary world some basic level of acculturation to the rule of law (as described in chapter 2), immigrants are surely competent in most cases to comprehend the function of a jury, at least relative to the average, civically undereducated citizen. Jury service no longer implicates loyalty to state, as it may once have; noncitizen jury service would not likely undermine the justice system. Indeed, if one takes seriously the proposition that criminal defendants are entitled to a jury of their peers, the practice looks more like a deprivation of a right rather than an exemption from a duty. Think of a crime committed within an insulated immigrant community including a high proportion of noncitizens; in that case, the defendant is in effect subjected to the justice of outsiders. Noncitizen exclusion from jury service looks anachronistic.

Even assuming its perpetuation, the jury duty differential doesn't give much heft to "the obligations of citizenship." Resident aliens occasionally cite jury duty as a deterrent to naturalization. That might show the obligation to be substantial. On the other hand, it might just further demonstrate the low perceived value of citizenship. If noncitizens are unwilling to "pay" for the status with a day or two's inconvenience every three or four years, then they probably don't see much advantage to citizenship. In any case, those who invoke the obligations of citizenship would find their arguments deflated if the question reduces to a measurement of the burden posed by jury duty. This is not the stuff of civic revival.

This discussion of the difference that citizenship doesn't make has focused largely on rights and obligations within the territorial United States. From this follows a liberal nationalist challenge, in which citizenship's equality norm is reborn through territorial rather than status definitions. This challenge posits Bosniak's "citizenship of aliens,"[41] effectively redrawing the boundaries of citizenship to include not just formal citizens but others also territorially present. The redrawing is accomplished not through the extension of citizenship status itself (as some liberal theorists have proposed) but through the extension of rights attaching to the status. Thus, Bosniak argues, insofar as the Citizenship Clause of the Fourteenth Amendment anchors rights for citizens it can also anchor them for aliens, the use of "citizen" notwithstanding.

This is an attractive argument, as both a normative and descriptive matter. It cuts to the primary exclusionary tendencies of any citizenship regime that demands more than territorial location and the legal subordination of "those in our midst." The approach actualizes the attachments of aliens, recognizing the possibility of their de facto membership. It also largely coincides with the current state of the law, as already described, in which territorially present aliens (or at least those with permanent residence) are in fact extended many of the rights associated with citizenship. Perhaps the whole institution of American citizenship can be made to stand if we simply redefine it to include those who, while technically noncitizens, act and are acted on as if they enjoyed the status.

Ultimately, however, the "citizenship of aliens" falls on its territorial premise. Just as with the birth citizenship rule of jus soli, under which all persons born in the United States have been extended citizenship for life, the theory cannot process the fluidity of national boundaries incident to globalization. On the one hand, there is the question of who exactly is sufficiently "present" to qualify for the expanded category of noncitizen "citizen." Restricting the redefinition to add only permanent residents leaves a glaring question mark with respect to nonimmigrants and undocumented aliens, a large number of whom have accumulated the sorts of attachments that would otherwise qualify for recognition. On the other hand, one can't equate simple presence with citizenship. The two-week tourist, the undocumented alien who has been here a year, the H-1B who has been here for two—in none of these cases would presence alone seem to warrant the privileges of full membership. Indeed, in some cases that might be said of permanent residents, who may maintain the status notwithstanding long periods of absence and otherwise insubstantial connections to the community. The ease of transnational movement undermines territory's utility as a benchmark. Territorial presence is now a scalar quantity, not a binary one.

Nor can a theory asserting the extension of rights to those present justify the implicit denial of rights to those not present. For starters, as with jus soli, the territorial citizenship concept doesn't take account of border zones, real and virtual. The resident of Juarez, who may have family, a job, and property in El Paso, doesn't make the cut notwithstanding the clear stake in the "American" community. Even without the direct individual ties to U.S. territory, the Juarez resident will be directly affected by various elements of local, state, and federal decision making in the United States. It is not clear as a normative matter why she should be any less deserving of the rights of U.S. citizenship than the undocumented alien resident of El Paso—indeed, one might argue that the law-abiding Juarez dweller should be more deserving of consideration. The same sort of argument applies, albeit less dramatically, to the virtual border spaces of diasporic communities. There again, the putative presence binary no longer persists on the ground. Some diaspora members are in the United States as citizens, some as permanent residents, some as nonimmigrants (sometimes long-term), some as undocumented aliens. Many of those who have status spend long periods of time in their homelands, where they maintain businesses and other forms of property, and have family, both close and extended. Those non-U.S. residents, family and others, have an interest in various aspects of U.S. governance. That interest is not accounted for under the formal citizenship regime; it's not accounted for by the "citizenship of aliens" either.

Of course, many rights are territorial in their application (or at least they have been traditionally conceived as such), which perhaps explains the surface appeal of the territorial citizenship concept. A right to fire or police protection, or emergency medical service, depends on being there. Other government benefits, such as means-tested public assistance, have been as a historical matter implemented on a territorial basis. Administration of the law has as well been constrained by territorial rules of jurisdiction, as has judicial process. International law itself blessed the mostly territorial determination of rights as a core element of the doctrine of sovereignty.

RIGHTS BEYOND BORDERS

Some rights, even as a historical matter, have been determined not on the basis of location but rather on citizenship status, regardless of location. Today an increasing number of rights and obligations arise apart from either citizenship status or presence. That further gives the lie to citizenship as an organizing principle, whether as a matter of formal status or as a notional matter of territorial location. One is left with the possibility of modulated relationships to national authorities, undergirded by universal human rights norms. The possibility of modulation is inconsistent with citizenship's equality imperative; the consequentiality of universal norms inconsistent with its premise of a bounded community.

At one time, perhaps the most important benefit of U.S. citizenship took the form of so-called diplomatic protection, under which citizens were entitled to use the U.S. government as a shield against mistreatment by foreign governments. Outside the territorial United States, this right presented an extremely valuable commodity. The institution of diplomatic protection, as established under international law, predicated the dictum that all rights are national rights. As described in the last chapter, sovereigns could do as they pleased with their own nationals and stateless individuals, but were highly circumscribed in their treatment of the nationals of other states. In the nineteenth and early twentieth centuries, a U.S. passport amounted to an insurance policy, a mechanism for invoking the community's protection in the international context. (As the passport legend still intones today, "The Secretary of State of the United States of America hereby requests all whom it may concern to permit the citizen/national of the United States named herein to pass without delay or hindrance and in case of need to give all lawful aid and protection.") With a short-lived, limited exception for a small number of declarant resident aliens, these rights were available to citizens alone.[42]

The citizenship criterion remains in place today for passport eligibility. It is also true that the U.S. government will go to bat more vigorously for its own citizens than for others, all other things being equal. But the value of diplomatic protection has steeply declined in the face of the international human rights revolution. Seventy-five years ago, diplomatic protection was an individual's only hope of keeping nasty sovereigns at bay. Today, personhood, rather than citizenship status, presents a substantial restraint against mistreatment by governmental authorities. The fact aside that U.S. authorities are showing an increasing willingness to intercede on behalf permanent resident aliens in high-profile cases (most notably involving China[43]) at the same time that consular efforts in run-of-the-mill cases have been cut to the budget bone,[44] one might concede that a U.S. passport still provides some comfort to its holder abroad. But it is a bonus value—a sort of business class, if that—rather than a basic one.

Citizens abroad have also enjoyed formal protection against mistreatment by the U.S. government, rights not extended to aliens. Citizens are entitled to constitutional protections against U.S. government action regardless of their location where nonresident noncitizens are entitled to few. The Supreme Court has held, for example, that nonresident noncitizens do not enjoy a Fourth Amendment right against unreasonable searches and seizures undertaken abroad by American law enforcement authorities. A search of a noncitizen's house in a foreign country by U.S. drug enforcement agents can be undertaken without a warrant, and the detention of a noncitizen can be undertaken without any sort of probable cause. In theory, outside the United States, FBI agents can bang down any foreigner's door they want to, and detain and interrogate a noncitizen without any particularized evidence that the individual has engaged in unlawful conduct.

But it's not clear how defensible this result is as either a doctrinal or normative matter, and, more important, it's not clear how much practical difference it will make into the future. The Supreme Court's decision on the question, in the 1990 ruling in *United States v. Verdugo-Urquidez*, stressed the Fourth Amendment's use of "the People" to justify denying its protections to nonresident noncitizens.[45] Carried to its not-so-distant extreme, however, that textual analysis either leaves all noncitizens (regardless of location) stripped of Fourth Amendment rights, or else contemplates "the People" as including some group of them. The former proposition was too extreme even for the Rehnquist Court. The latter opens up "the People" in a way that doesn't lend itself to easy delimitation.

It is difficult, moreover, to argue that those who are being held to the substance of U.S. law shouldn't be extended the benefit of its procedural regularities. In this sense, one can indeed define "the People" as any individual, regardless of citizenship status or location, over whom the United States is extending its jurisdiction. As Justice Brennan observed in his dissent in *Verdugo-Urquidez*, "our Government, by investigating him and attempting to hold him accountable under United States criminal laws, has treated him as a member of the community for purposes of enforcing our laws. He has become, quite literally, one of the governed." Thus defined, the People would have as a historical matter largely coincided with territorial boundaries, as law was largely administered on a territorial basis. Today, it becomes a potentially universal quantity—hardly something one would conceive as a "community" in any traditional sense—as the United States asserts extraterritorial jurisdiction in a growing number of contexts.

In any event, even if the Supreme Court sticks to the line set in *Verdugo-Urquidez*, it may not mean much on the ground. United States law enforcement will only exploit the nonapplicability of rights where they can be confident that they are in fact dealing only with nonresident noncitizens. As a practical matter, however, that must be a dwindling number of cases. As crime becomes increasingly transnationalized, and as U.S. citizenship becomes dispersed in the various ways I have described, the odds of facing an unexpected American increases. Where law enforcement has evidence that would support the issuance of a warrant in the United States, it now makes sense for them to deploy that evidence beforehand, by way of insurance against subsequent constitutional challenge.

And of course the United States is not the only country with rules against unreasonable searches and seizures, rules that U.S. authorities have to play by when participating in enforcement operations in those countries. Indeed, protection against arbitrary investigative activity is emerging as an entitlement under international law; article 17 of the International Covenant on Civil and Political Rights (ratified by more than 150 countries, including the United States) includes such a prohibition. These trends mean that nonresident noncitizens who may not enjoy Fourth Amendment coverage may get the same protection from other bodies of law, ones that effectively constrain U.S. enforcement activities on foreign soil. In other words, the fact that foreigners outside the United States may for some purposes find themselves outside the Constitution may not mean all that much.

The same may hold true for the post-9/11 rights differential in the context of extraterritorial enforcement against terrorism. Parallel to the designation of citizens apprehended on U.S. soil as enemy combatants, President Bush authorized the killing of U.S. citizens located abroad who are suspected of al-Qaeda membership where impractical to take an individual into custody. Citizenship thus affords no protection or due process to those individuals; in November 2004, a U.S. citizen was killed when a Predator drone took out a car in the Yemen desert (although the CIA was targeting a non–U.S. citizen al-Qaeda member in the vehicle). The military and intelligence officials have apparently desisted from holding U.S. citizens in so-called black sites, at which suspected terrorists were secretly detained and interrogated. But those facilities have been shut down in the face of withering criticism by international actors.

The same holds true with respect to Guantanamo, where no American citizens are held, and the military commissions that have been authorized for prosecuting post-9/11 terrorist suspects. The United States is under sustained pressure to close up shop there, at the same time that the U.S. Supreme Court ruled in 2004 that detainees there should enjoy access to federal court under the federal habeas corpus statute.[46] After being nullified by the Supreme Court in the *Hamdan* case and then revived in the last days of the Republican majority in Congress, military commissions have taken years to get up and running and even now are being deployed in only a handful of cases. In short, although noncitizens have been disadvantaged as adversaries in post-9/11 developments, the deprivation of noncitizen rights has been vigorously contested in a way that would have been unimaginable in, say, World War II. Guantanamo will be a tarnished precedent for future enforcement parameters. On the contrary, 9/11 notwithstanding, the extraterritorial treatment of citizens and noncitizens is likely to converge, for good or ill.

Questions of public benefits remain more keyed to territorial presence. An undocumented alien child in the United States, for example, has a right to public schooling; the Juarez child (much less one resident in Manila) does not. But of course the U.S. citizen resident in Manila will not be entitled to U.S. public schooling, either, nor indeed to SSI, food stamps, or TANF. There is a logic to benefits schemes that may sustain the residence distinction. Residents of a particular jurisdiction will, on average, pay more into the system in the form of taxes. Where benefits are on an individualized pay-in basis, as with Social Security, they are not always contingent on continued residence. Many noncitizens receive Social Security retirement income outside the United States, in most cases after returning to their homelands. So the benefits system cannot be wholly defined in terms either of citizenship or residence.

Finally, even political rights can be plotted in scalar terms. Citizens resident abroad, including those holding multiple nationality, are guaranteed the right to vote in federal elections.[47] This was foregrounded by the 2000 presidential election, in which at one point it looked as if nonresident citizens (last resident in Florida) might tip the balance.[48] As highlighted here, permanent resident aliens can't vote but they can give money; although they must maintain legal residence in the United States by way of holding on to their green cards, they can do so at the same time that they maintain significant links to other countries, including citizenship and property ownership. Otherwise, nonresident noncitizens can neither vote nor give money. But that doesn't necessarily translate into the absence of political heft. Foreign citizens can retain lobbying firms to make their case to legislative and other officials. Through organizational membership, both corporate and NGO, they can indirectly affect U.S. decision making.

And it's not clear why they shouldn't be given some formal role in "domestic" policy making to the extent that they are impacted by resulting decisions. Although admittedly impractical, Frances Stead Sellers suggests an interesting theoretical case for opening up U.S. presidential contests to a global electorate. After all, almost everyone is affected by the outcome, insofar as almost everyone is affected in some way by U.S. policy making. Basic democratic theory holds that the governed should have some voice in choosing their governors. Perhaps the growing informal channels of influence for noncitizens reflects advancing global democratic norms; as the influence of the United States grows, so to does the influence of international elements on U.S. processes.

This is not to prove that all persons wherever located already have or should be extended the same rights and status vis-à-vis the United States. But the description of those rights that even nonresident aliens may come to hold gives the lie to the neat lines of a citizenship paradigm. The conventional wisdom already holds that citizenship doesn't make much of a difference within the territorial United States. That it may be a diminishing quantity beyond its borders reinforces the suggestions of its declining salience as an institutional affiliation.

EXPLAINING THE VANISHING DIFFERENTIAL

This has been mostly by way of description, setting out the ways in which "the rights and obligations of citizenship" has become an empty proposition. This trajectory can be explained as a consequence of the ways the citizenry has been defined, and the ways the boundaries of citizenship are increasingly detached from the boundaries of any underlying human community. This chapter's consideration of the incidents of citizenship is in effect a corollary of the previous ones, which set out criteria for acquiring the underlying status. As the definitions of citizenship become artificial, they will become less consequential. This explanation denies the possibility of reversal, at least not through any effort of the lawmakers.

If citizenship does not meaningfully coincide with actual community, it is unlikely to be determinative of rights and duties. To demonstrate, one might posit the constituting of a "community" on some random basis, say the group of individuals whose surnames begin with the letter S. In theory, there is no reason why a group defined in those terms couldn't serve as the basis for various redistributive undertakings (which, after all, perhaps best defines what is at the bottom of "rights and obligations"). Those more prosperous in the group could be required to make payments that would be given to less fortunate members, and payments from the group could be used for such other purposes as schools for member children. Able-bodied members could be assigned to provide security to the elderly. Members could be enlisted to help decide disputes among other members. To frame the system, one would need articulate a set of rules governing the various requirements and entitlements that would come with various types of membership in the group, as well as for rules relating to questions of membership. What of the person who changes his name, or acquires an S surname through marriage?

Rather obviously, such a group would never come into being, at least not as anything more than a parlor game. The group's definition would be completely artificial, one's placement in the phone book having no bearing on one's identity. Members of a group so constituted would be unwilling to share with other members of the group, at least not by cause of membership. Even though the group had a "law" attempting to benefit its members, it could never build a reality to match.

That is not to say that rules relating to the entitlements and burdens of members and membership are inconsequential. As I will discuss in chapter 6, they can figure importantly to an individual's well-being, even in the context of nonstate entities and civil society. They can be entrenching and facilitative of community bonds; they regularize a community, allowing for its growth. But rules cannot be generative of community, nor, at a certain point, can rules sustain community.

In the context of the state, rights and obligations can cement an identity. If law on the basis of membership both extends entitlements to you and demands service from you in return, it can enhance the feeling of specialness that comes with membership and distinguishes members from nonmembers. But that facilitation can only build on prior commonalities, and once those commonalities are lost, the law cannot perpetuate them. If citizenship reflects a relatively distinct community, then the status can support a differential. Insofar as the distinctiveness degrades, however, the community will be able to offer fewer benefits to members and extract fewer obligations. Citizenship cannot be resuscitated by its legal revaluation. As the incidents of citizenship fade, the identity itself further dwindles.

5

American Defined

BEHIND ALL CITIZENSHIP talk lurks a premise that the state is the natural unit of community. In most cases, this premise is unthinking. When a speaker addresses a proposition to citizens, there is an unstated assumption that the appropriate audience is the group of members in the state, and that the audience is in fact composed of such individuals. On both counts these assumptions are increasingly untenable. "Citizens" almost always intends an audience that includes noncitizens; to the extent that it does, some community other than the state is implicated. The observation applies to all rhetorical appeals invoking the term, political and otherwise. The "citizenry" becomes an obscure proposition, and the polity's foundations are put into play.

That moves us beyond the vigorous public debate of recent years on the nature of the American nation. Three basic intellectual schools are represented in this debate. First, there is a small and largely discredited circle of new nativists who would return the United States to its allegedly northern European cultural and ethnic roots. Second are the nationalists, who hold out the nation as humankind's best institutional hope and who almost of necessity assert the existence of a distinctive and all-encompassing American identity. This group subdivides into conservative and liberal variants. Conservative nationalists preach a hard-edged assimilationism, typically pressing cultural as well as political attributes of American nationality; they accept the class of Americans as a privileged and exclusive group. Liberal nationalists, by contrast, articulate a thinner, civic notion of American identity, and consider citizenship a pillar of inclusiveness and equality. Both versions of nationalism have been defined at least in part in opposition to a third competing paradigm, that of multiculturalism. Although multiculturalism emphasizes group difference at the expense of national unities, it too is premised on the persistence of a strong state, if only as an agent of redistribution.

In this array, the new nativism merits only brief attention as a clearly losing entry, descriptively and normatively. Conservative nationalism, though accepting of newcomers, is left fighting the metaphorical last war, anchored in and unable to extricate itself from early twentieth-century conceptions of citizenship and belonging. Liberal nationalism and multiculturalism, by contrast, present powerful visions of the purpose and future of the American nation. But both are challenged by my opening predicate—that before one can consider what it means to be an American, one must consider who is an American. Liberal nationalism and multiculturalism are ultimately premised on an America whose community boundaries remain distinct against the global backdrop. As those boundaries are blurred and breached in the various ways described in earlier chapters, the logic of liberal nationalism unravels, and multiculturalism also becomes unsustainable, at least in the framework of a national polity.

That leaves the state bereft of intellectual girders, and further highlights its demotion in the scheme of human organization. But then what supplants the state in that scheme? What becomes of citizenship after the state? This and the following chapter eschew the notion of a global citizen, a favored strawman of the liberal nationalists; no time soon are we going to witness a global super-state as a universalizer and unifier of humankind. Rather, we will likely see an increasingly diffusion of identity to various nonstate, and in many cases, nonterritorial forms of association. Membership in the state is no longer the only game in town.

THE LOST HOPE OF AN ETHNIC AMERICA

The new nativists sing the praises of an ethnic America. These are the inheritors of the Know-Nothings. "The American nation has always had a specific ethnic core," writes Peter Brimelow in *Alien Nation*. "And that core has been white."[1] The new nativists have little use for the rest of the world, on this front or any other. Represented on the political stage by

Patrick Buchanan, their platform hardly concedes the value of admitting any outsiders as immigrants, much less as citizens, for foreigners are taken to represent (for the most part) the dilution of this putative historical purity. In the realm of immigration policy making, new nativism calls for highly restrictionist measures; indeed, the new nativists find in this wave of immigrants a major threat to the nation as they define it.

With good reason: recent immigration has irrevocably destroyed this vision of the United States. The new nativists may find much historical support for their definition of the American people. Racial restrictions were imposed on both immigrant admissions and naturalization applications well into the twentieth century. Citizenship was also internally stratified, so that large portions of the polity (blacks and women, most notably) were legally subordinated, their citizenship status notwithstanding. As Rogers Smith has exhaustively documented, American citizenship as a historical matter has been a vehicle of exclusion.[2]

The position also fits with the logic of citizenship, although its proponents are unlikely to frame it as such. Like an exclusive club, the greater the barriers to entry the more valuable the membership. Insofar as citizens in a particular polity do share ethnic, religious, and linguistic roots, the more significant the status is likely to be. That is why European national communities, at least until recently, have supported redistributionist policies that would never fly in the United States—in some cases (Scandanavian states presenting the best examples) because citizens in a particular country could almost literally trace family relationships among themselves. Although redistribution was not its object, the bond of American citizenship through the mid-nineteenth century was probably stronger than in any of our modern lives (in large part, as Smith demonstrates, because of its exclusionary, ascriptive premises). On average, citizenship implied significant commonalities. In the historical tradition of republican citizenship, independent (read: propertied) individuals, all white, all male, would gather in the reasoned exercise of governance, working from shared ideals but also mostly shared backgrounds. As citizenship disperses along various dimensions, so that citizenship implies little in the way of distinctive bonds, the status itself inevitably dissipates. That is perhaps the primary theme of this book.

It is also a primary theme that the past intensities of American citizenship cannot be recaptured. The new nativism is untenable, as both a practical and a normative matter. According to the 2000 census, almost

25 percent of the those resident in the United States define themselves as something other than white, and more than 15 percent speak something other than English as their first language, numbers that are surely growing in the face of further immigration. New nativism has few takers among either policy makers or intellectuals. Pat Buchanan flamed out as a national politician; the publication of Brimelow's *Alien Nation* raised the critics' hackles in the press and academe. New nativism just wouldn't work in today's world, short of installing a limited circle of artificially privileged insiders. One can't actually stop the flow of immigrants; new nativism would permanently subordinate these newcomers. The new nativist agenda would lead to something not so different from ancient Athens, in which a small group of individuals comprised the blood aristocracy of citizens, the rest relegated to legally lesser status. In the end, the new nativism is finding its place somewhere other than the state. Thus, the antistatism of white militias is grounded in the impossibility of advancing their agenda through national institutions; it is only through a kind of separatism that their conception of America can be vindicated. In that vein, the new nativists are becoming contemptuous of the very institution of national citizenship, seeing it as embodying a different America than the one they seek.[3]

THE NOSTALGIA OF THE CONSERVATIVE NATIONALISTS

Conservative nationalists vaunt citizenship as a sacred quantity. As the columnist Georgie Anne Geyer writes in lamenting its decline, citizenship "is the unique and ennobling story of the postfeudal, modern relationship of the individual human being to the state, of the state to the individual, and of the human being to his fellow man."[4] Unlike the new nativists, conservative nationalists accept newcomers as long as those newcomers accept the old assimilationist premise of American immigration. Conservative nationalists do not shy from relentlessly asserting allegiance to an "American way of life," and take the "Americanization" movement of the early twentieth century as the model of incorporation. "Without assimilation," writes John Miller, "the *pluribus* threatens to drown out the *unum*, imperiling the very concept of American nationhood."[5] The English language figures prominently as cultural glue; on the domestic side, conservative nationalists launch fierce attacks on bilingualism, especially in education. Samuel Huntington highlights America's "Anglo-Protestant culture and its religiosity" as defining a distinctive national identity.[6] Conservative nationalists take as self-evident not only the continuing primacy of the nation-state as the primary institution of governance but also the United States as enjoying primacy among them. They would, however, allow that the American ideal can be successfully adopted by immigrants regardless of race or previous nationality.

Conceding the potential virtue of immigration itself (though they, too, may have a generally restrictionist orientation), conservative nationalists have come increasingly to highlight the gatekeeping function of citizenship policy. They condemn dual citizenship and are open to limitations on territorial birthright citizenship. They have made a whipping post of the naturalization process and its failure alternatively to instill or to detect American values among new citizens.

But conservative nationalism fails even superficially to present a coherent ideology in the contemporary context, and it seems unlikely to advance on the ground. There are too many pressures at work here beyond the capacities of national policy makers. Take dual citizenship. Conservative nationalists hew to old world comparisons of the status to polygamy and the impossibility of "serving two masters." They suggest that dual citizenship results in irreconcilable psychological conflicts, produced by a "narcissistic conceit" in "unlimited identities," and that its toleration will further fuel antiassimilation trends.[7] But they don't back up those tired incantations with explications of how exactly dual citizenship poses concrete harms in today's world—as indeed they can't. Although some conservative nationalists evoke the specter of a sort of electoral fifth column, especially in the context of Mexican and American dual citizenship, they offer no persuasive distinction to the grand tradition of American ethnic politics, in which immigrant communities have applied political pressure in the American system to benefit their homelands. Beyond vague suggestions that the renunciation oath actually be enforced, conservative nationalists don't have a recipe for how the United States can police dual citizenship. On this score, conservative nationalism looks naive and nostalgic.

Likewise with respect to another favorite lament of conservative nationalism—the rote nature of the civics test administered to most naturalization applicants. In the gatekeeping perspective, the civics test plays the part of "a powerful instrument of unity, an engine of assimilation that turns newcomers into U.S. citizens who understand our political traditions and are proud to be Americans."[8] As described in chapter 2, the test as now administered is fairly described as a farce, a sample 10 or 15 questions taken from a widely available list of 100. Conservative nationalists are quick to center this in their picture of a "dumbed-down" citizenship. But devising an alternative, as to both content and administration, is beyond conservative nationalists (or for that matter their liberal counterparts, who also put some stock in the exercise). Conservative nationalists would place a greater emphasis on what they perceive to be the traditional canon of American history and politics, and call for a tougher test that would (they hope) measure more accurately the applicant's understanding of this tradition.

But there is little chance of these recommendations becoming a reality, either. As a political matter, the content agenda crashes head into the multiculturalist perspectives, and this is one context in which the multiculturalists are unlikely to back off. And perhaps with good reason. Native-born Americans would in large numbers fail the sort of exam proposed by the conservative nationalists, yet one could hardly argue that they thus lose claim to citizenship. Surveys show that a majority of high school seniors would fail the current naturalization civics test; one recent poll found that more than 70 percent of graduating seniors at such elite institutions as Harvard, Princeton, and Brown did not know the purpose of the Emancipation Proclamation—a sample question on the naturalization exam.[9]

On the process question, it is all very well to argue that the test should be more searching and less of an exercise in rote memorization. But the more searching the test, the more resources that would have to be devoted to its administration. The INS and its successor agency have had immense difficulties keeping current with increased naturalization applications. At one point in the mid-1990s, the backlog was running as long as three years in some districts, and the agency has caught up only by cannibalizing resources from the processing of other immigration benefits (the backlogs have now been transplanted, in effect, to the consideration of applications for green cards among nonimmigrants already present in the United States). To make a fifteen-minute naturalization interview into something more extensive, written or oral, would add another burden to a system always on the verge of breakdown. The recently released revision of the test keeps the same basic format and only tinkers with the substance. So much for reviving the civics test.

As a general matter, conservative nationalists preach a thick assimilationism, one that welcomes newcomers but only insofar as they conform to putative American traditions. But conformity is so little a part of American society today, at least in any distinctively American way. Of course, there is the common knowledge set of popular culture, but that knowledge set is now shared with most of the world. Conservative nationalists are unlikely to call for test questions about the likes of Snoop Dogg—who enjoyed 99 percent name recognition in that same survey of elite graduates; even if they did, there would be nothing about such questions that would evidence a segregable American identity, because on a worldwide basis everyone (except perhaps some highbrow American citizen readers of this book) knows those answers. An undertaking to impose American-ness on immigrants emerges a hopeless enterprise. It is thus improbable that American citizenship will be resuscitated on conservative nationalist terms; there will be no turning back of the clock.

LIBERAL NATIONALISM AND ITS FALLACIES

Liberal nationalism presents the most formidable theoretical foundation for American citizenship into the future. The liberal nationalists retreat to a more defensible perimeter, with a thin and inclusive articulation of American nationality centered in political values. In line with pluralist conceptions of American politics, liberal nationalism vaunts membership in the vehicles of civil society, including those relating to ethnicity, but holds the national identity above all of them. In the tradition of liberal political theory, liberal nationalism sees the state as central to the vindication of individual rights and of equality, which renders citizenship an essential institution. Indeed, all of liberalism, and not just some subthesis relating specifically to the admission of new members, depends on the defense of "democratic citizenship." If citizenship falls as an institution, liberalism falls with it.

And falling it is, on this theoretical testing ground as elsewhere. At its deepest foundation, liberal nationalism cannot reconcile its tenet of inclusiveness with the inherent exclusiveness of citizenship regimes. This failing becomes more pronounced as the civic conception of America itself becomes increasingly less distinctive, as democratic constitutional values take hold at the global level. The inclusiveness imperative can't be saved by a territorial corollary, for all the reasons that the territorial premise fails as a mainstay of citizenship determinations. Nor can the pluralist strand of liberal nationalism process the new transnationalism of civil society. The nation no longer stands as an umbrella for other forms of association; once those boundaries are breached, this theory of America loses its normative edge to global forms of governance, a migration of authority the features of which are coming into focus.

Liberal nationalists look, in effect, to take the best qualities of the nation-state as a form of human association and put them to work in the advancement of liberal ideals. Political scientist Rogers Smith asserts, for example, that the nation presents "the best hope available to [Americans] for leading free and meaningful lives."[10] (Liberal nationalists, as Bonnie Honig so nicely frames it, "read democratic theory according to the genre conventions of a popular or modern romance, as a happy-ending love story."[11]) This requires first an understanding and abandonment of historical exclusions and then the adoption of inclusive, egalitarian aspirations. Insofar as the nation is defined in ethnic, racial, or other ascriptive terms, inclusiveness is (and has been) obstructed. In the American context, however, inclusiveness may be enabled with a civic definition of the national community and its detachment from ethnic or cultural signifiers.

This sets the liberal and conservative nationalists apart—where the conservatives would assert thick cultural parameters to American nationality, liberals would pose few, if any. As Michael Walzer puts it, "If the manyness of America is cultural, its oneness is political."[12] Kenneth Karst similarly holds that "an American demonstrates that she belongs to America primarily by acting out the civic culture's ideals,"[13] and Michael Ignatieff finds a civic nation "united in patriotic attachment to a shared set of political practices and values."[14] (Political theorist Jürgen Habermas has adopted a similar strategy in the context of the European Union, articulating a "constitutional patriotism" on which to base EU citizenship and untether it from the various national/ethnic components of the federation.[15]) If indeed citizenship is secured by professing belief in the constitutional system, it is an inclusive institution, available to all wishing to subscribe.

THE OPT-OUT CHALLENGE

The first difficulty is that liberalism assumes that everyone present wants to subscribe; the second is how it defends the exclusion of those elsewhere who would like to. In other words, it assumes nearly complete coincidence between citizenship status and territorial jurisdiction, and it rationalizes barriers to physical entry even to those who would otherwise opt in to the liberal vision of the nation. On the first score, the greatest conceptual challenge is posed not so much by barriers to citizenship. Liberals have always decried obstacles to naturalization, at least as a general matter,[16] and indeed, those obstacles, at least in comparative perspective, have never been particularly formidable (leaving aside historical exclusions based on race and current ones involving immigration status, for only permanent resident aliens are eligible to naturalize). If one assumes that everyone present wants membership, then barriers are the natural focus; once the barriers are leveled, all become members, and the inclusiveness and equality values are perfected.

But not everyone wants in, even among permanent residents; that is, many permanent residents do not opt for citizenship even though they are eligible for it. That gives rise, in effect, to a significant population of second-class citizens by choice. These are individuals who, although they live here as do citizens, are not formally equal to them, and who have eschewed a political voice in the government that exercises jurisdiction over them. The phenomenon thus calls into question central liberal assumptions about equality and political rights, especially when the group becomes something more than an anomaly. In areas with concentrated immigrant populations, one can reasonably characterize some electoral districts as "rotten boroughs" in which a rump group of citizens (as the liberal might have it) is overrepresented relative to citizens in other districts and is able to exercise preferences without regard to the noncitizen community in its midst.[17] As Honig asks, "What will become of state citizenship when it is transformed from a supposedly universal category into a property of a self-chosen few?"[18]

The concept of territorial citizenship, as described in chapter 4, of drawing the "citizenship" circle to include certain classes of territorially present noncitizens, offers one possible liberal response. Resident aliens could be extended all the rights of citizenship, including for instance the right to vote. But this strategy fails for all the reasons that it fails to supply a workable mechanism for either explaining the insignificant rights differential between citizens and noncitizens or eliminating what remains of that differential. A territorial binary (in which you are either in or out) no longer reflects a reality in which a spectrum of presence and interests cuts across time and space. It does not offer a clear answer to such common cases as the long (or not so long) present undocumented alien; the permanent resident alien who splits her time between the United States and her homeland, where she maintains substantial connections; or the nonresident noncitizen who has various interests in the decision making of the U.S. government. Deploying territorial criteria will not make the liberal goal of a national community of equals any more easily accomplished.

Moreover, the denizen class highlights the place of individual volition in defining the national community, which further undermines the possible liberal nationalist retreat to territorial criteria. If nothing else, liberal nationalists premise their conception of the American nation on the individual's will to belong and to maintain the civic faith. We have posed the existence of a significant population that has—as a matter of choice—decided not to join. The problem is most obvious when one considers the territorially present Islamic fundamentalist who abhors American democracy and everything it stands for; it is difficult to draw the membership circle in any way that includes such an individual. This population of active antagonists may be small. But the difficulty also arises with the individual who may believe in democracy but would just rather not be identified as an American, or indeed the individual who never naturalizes out of simple laziness.

Much the same critique applies to Ruth Rubio-Marín's proposal that formal citizenship automatically be granted to individuals after a ten-year period of residence.[19] On the one hand, by extending formal membership, this proposal operationalizes the territorial premise; that is, it addresses the challenge by formally redrawing the citizen/noncitizen line rather than by allocating citizenship attributes to noncitizens (e.g., by affording voting rights to aliens). On the other, it draws in those who may have no allegiance to the civic nation. It would seem, moreover, to violate autonomy norms of liberalism, insofar as it imposes an identity on some who would otherwise affirmatively reject it. If nothing else, the Rubio-Marín proposal evidences an understanding that individual opt-outs pose an increasingly serious challenge to the liberal conception of a territorial community composed of equal members.

THE INEVITABILITY OF EXCLUSION

So liberal nationalism cannot account for the presence of a large population of volitional nonmembers. The flip side is that it has a hard time justifying the exclusion from membership of nonresidents who would like to opt in.

To the extent everyone wants to sign up, the resulting community will be less intensely felt among its members; it will be a less important form of identity insofar as it is less distinctive. If the American nation were indeed the "universal nation," as Hans Kohn rhetorically characterized it in 1957, based on "a universal right—the right to citizenship,"[20] it would not be much of a nation, in the same way that membership in the Holy Roman Empire didn't supply much of an identity in Renaissance Europe. Much of the world's population can now be said to subscribe to once-distinctive basic American concepts of constitutional government, individual rights, democracy, and the rule of law. If that's what it takes to be a part of the American nation, then we are talking a much larger group than the current citizenry, one that isn't bounded in any meaningful sense.

But the liberal nationalist would be hard pressed to offer any other condition to membership, insofar as citizenship starts once again to look like an instrument of exclusion. In earlier times (and of course the principle of inclusive citizenship is nothing new as an ideal, discursively dating to the founding of the republic), there were the limiting factors of ideology and presence. In the context of the last great wave of immigrants, democracy was still the minority practice, and many wouldn't subscribe even if given the opportunity. More important, there has been the implicit limitation of territorial location. When the likes of Woodrow Wilson espoused a civic conception of America, they had in mind the inclusion only of those present in the United States. In the era before immigration controls, that could be reconciled with aspirations to inclusiveness, saying, in effect, that if you could get here, and you commit to the constitutional project, we will embrace you.

That, of course, doesn't work any more; not just anyone can come through the door. So liberal nationalism has either to call for open borders or to defend immigration controls, which surely qualify as a kind of exclusion. Citizenship issues aside, liberals have always had difficulty situating immigration in their paradigm. John Rawls, the father of modern liberal theory, famously dodged the issue by assuming a society in which entry was only by birth.[21] Most liberal theorists (open-borders proponent Joseph Carens presenting the notable exception) accept the legitimacy of immigration control. Some justify it on a public order basis, asserting that to allow free entry would overwhelm the system, resulting in the downfall of liberal order; as Bruce Ackerman observes, "the *only* reason for restricting immigration is to protect the ongoing process of the liberal conversation itself."[22] That proposition is disputable on an empirical basis. It also seems morally problematic, insofar as it privileges certain individuals on the basis of birth alone, giving rise to the modern-day serfdom of those unable to secure entry permits to the countries of their choice. In light of their strong support of domestic interstate freedom of movement (the constitutional right to travel constituting an important innovation of the Warren Court), the unwillingness of liberals to embrace its international counterpart is suspect.

One can isolate the citizenship correlate of this difficulty by posing—if only as a thought experiment—liberal nationalist rejection of membership for those not territorially present. If I live in Juarez, or, for that matter, Calcutta, and am willing to subscribe to American civic nationalism, why shouldn't I be enrolled as a member on that basis alone?

FINDING "SOCIETY"

Walzer and other liberal theorists might first respond that such individuals are not a part of the national community because they do not share a "common life" together with existing members.[23] Another unconscious strategy here is to bound all discussion as applying only to a given "society." But that just begs the question of what a "common life" or a "society" consists of. Most simply assume the matter as prior, that is, as not requiring analysis. Others, such as Walzer, find them territorially contingent. "The link between people and land is a crucial feature of national identity," he insists. "[T]he focus of political life can never be established elsewhere."[24] Seyla Benhabib likewise highlights the "crucial link between democratic self-governance and territorial representation."[25]

This effectively adds a presence requirement to the requirement of democratic faith. That may have been an understandably unexamined predicate in the past, even the recent past. Today, one might demand a normative explanation. As discussed in the context of noncitizen rights, given the expanded exercise of U.S. jurisdiction beyond U.S. territory, there is a theoretical case, at least, for nonresident noncitizen participation in American political processes. Walzer observes that "[m]en and women are either subject to the state's authority, or they are not; and if they are subject, they must be given a say, and ultimately an equal say, in what the authority does."[26] Globalization and the erosion of the territorial premise undermines the first proposition in the various ways I have already described. The Juarez resident may be subject in everyday ways to U.S. authority, including the authority to restrict entry to a different sector of the same metropolitan area. If I traffic in narcotics or engage in violations of U.S. antitrust laws I am subject to U.S. authority even if I have never set foot in the United States; if I hold U.S. investments I must pay U.S. taxes. Obviously, the territorial resident will be subject to greater authority. But subjection to substantial authority, as is now true for many nonresidents, casts doubt on how to complete Walzer's equation. To turn another liberal nationalist proposition on its head, if "[g]oing to court to claim a right under the United States Constitution is an assertion of membership in the national community,"[27] then there are many noncitizens (potentially all) who qualify.

Nor are other boundary-driven delimitations of the "common life" self-evident today. Given the dispersion of mass communications, shared cultural understandings are transcending political boundaries; the era of free trade makes the probabilities of cross-border economic interaction almost as great (and sometimes greater) than internal ones. Some level of human interaction is inescapably physical and direct, but that is about neighborhoods, cities, and regions, not about nation-states.

So if the (usually unstated) territorial predicate no longer holds, and America really is just about an idea, then membership should not be locationally contingent. This is not so silly as it might seem at first hearing, although the challenge is obviously one to the theory rather than to any practice. As described in chapter 1, nonresident children of U.S. citizens may be extended citizenship at birth, citizenship they will be able to retain even if they never set foot in their parents' homeland. The theory there, from a liberal perspective, must be that such individuals will be parentally inculcated in American values. Given the expansion of global democracy, it would now seem possible to assimilate American civic ideals without such generational transmission. The example of the newly arrived Bangladeshi immigrant who self-identified as a Democrat again provides a stunning example—an individual who was fully versed not just in the basic principles of American politics but in the nitty gritty long before he was able to come to the United States, in a way that surpasses the political knowledge of most native-born citizens.[28]

The logic of liberal nationalism offers no basis for excluding even the nonresident from the polity. Nor does the next line of retreat—that

America is also defined by a common history, its members by their "shared recollections"—offer an answer. This trope has figured prominently in liberal nationalist articulations dating back to John Stuart Mill.[29] "Above all," writes Arthur M. Schlesinger Jr., "history can give a sense of national identity."[30] It also explains why liberal nationalists are unwilling to give up the civics and language requirements for naturalization, even though it makes them fidget; for these thresholds will exclude some individuals (those who fail the tests) who would otherwise qualify for membership. But this shared-history argument only works if one attaches it to the shared blood—that is, we have a common identity because our ancestors fought the same battles, suffered the same travails, shared the same triumphs. If one concedes the possibility that the history can be adopted—as all but the new nativists must, to allow for the possibility of newcomers—then the argument's perimeter is breached, for that knowledge is no longer exceptional and no longer requires presence. Nor, finally, could the liberal nationalist dismiss the proposition of nonresident citizenship by playing the dual citizenship card. That the resident of Santo Domingo is a citizen of the Dominican Republic is no longer inherently incompatible with a commitment to constitutional democracy, nor with a knowledge of U.S. history, politics, and culture.

Indeed, plural citizenship subtly but foundationally tests the liberal nationalist perspective. On one hand, the fact of alternate citizenship would not seem by itself to undermine the civic orientation of American nationality, at least not in a world in which states are no longer in the sort of zero-sum competition that once characterized the global system. The associational rights implicated by citizenship ties—the expressive element of citizenship, citizenship as identity—are ordinarily sacrosanct in the liberal worldview. That may explain why liberal nationalists are willing to accept plural nationality in a way that conservative nationalists are not.

On the other hand, plural citizenship challenges the liberal nationalist equality norm, insofar as it affords some individuals more rights than others. A dual Irish and American citizen, for instance, has rights in another polity not enjoyed by her mono-national American citizen neighbor. That concern is addressed, at least in part, by the suggestion of some liberal nationalists that dual citizens be allowed to vote only in their country of residence.[31] Perhaps more troubling to the liberal nationalist is the possibility that the dual citizen will not put membership in the American state above other memberships, and that its acceptance will undermine civic solidarities. Hence proposals that naturalizing citizens who retain their original citizenship pledge their primary loyalty to the United States.[32] As liberal nationalist Noah Pickus concludes, "prudence calls for a cautious approach toward plural citizenship."[33]

But these objections to plural citizenship and the proposed remedies lack theoretical coherence, never mind their impracticality. The equality objection draws a first response that life in unfair. I may belong to various clubs, organizations, religions, and companies for which my neighbor is ineligible; I may be advantaged by those memberships, but any system that protects rights of association will have to tolerate the resulting inequality. Dual citizenship, moreover, does not give rise to formal inequality within the confines of either state. My dual Irish and American neighbor doesn't get an extra vote in U.S. elections by virtue of her additional citizenship. That also argues against the proposed remedy of limiting the franchise to one polity or the other. Indeed, the real inequality created by such cases of multiple nationality will be with respect to professional opportunities and rights of movement. My Irish and American friend can compete for jobs in the European Union for which I would be ineligible, and reside there without restriction. But the only way to address that inequality is by prohibiting the maintenance of plural citizenship altogether.

THE END OF THE SELF-CONTAINED NATION

The question of primary commitment cuts more deeply into the liberal nationalist paradigm. There is nothing inherent about a civic vision of the nation that requires such commitment. But the liberal nationalist hesitation on plural citizenship puts into relief an organizing principle of liberal theory generally: that attachment to state stands above all other attachments. This is the "Chinese box" component of pluralism, its way of processing the many nonstate attachments, including ethnic attachments, that might otherwise challenge the primacy of the state. Thus, David Hollinger sees American nationality as "mediat[ing] . . . between the species and its ethno-racial varieties."[34] Walzer puts this at the center of his definition of citizenship: "A citizen, we might say, is a man whose largest or most inclusive group is the state."[35] The nation becomes the umbrella entity under which all other associations fall. At the cornerstone of pluralist theory, citizenship becomes the one common membership that holds these potentially conflicting other groupings together.

That order gets scrambled once one contemplates plural citizenship. For now one confronts memberships that will inherently spill over the confines of the state. Obviously, for instance, not all Irish citizens are also American citizens; so those American citizens who also hold Irish citizenship will belong to a group that doesn't fit under the umbrella of the state. The community of the Irish may have conflicting interests with the community of Americans; there is no mediating institution, at least not a national one, to hold the two communities together. Liberal nationalism attempts to resolve this with the primary loyalty requirement, so that when push comes to shove the attachment to the American nation plays the trump.

But once one accepts the fact of plural citizenship, there is no neutral principle by which to demand that primary loyalty be vested in one state of nationality over another. Why should I put my American nationality above my Irish nationality? To elevate the normative value of one nationality over another seems a tough proposition for liberalism to support, certainly where the nationalities at issue share a basic liberal orientation. (One might have an easier time justifying primary loyalty where the alternate nationality is, say, North Korean.) To take the standard Rawlsian perspective from behind the veil of ignorance (that is, the choice an individual would make if she were unaware of her own circumstances), there is no reason to expect that the interests of the American nation would be placed ahead of others. In this respect, liberal nationalism betrays an unattractive feature of all nationalism, namely, that its holders will still consider themselves (or be expected to consider themselves) more worthy than the holders of other nationality.

Of course, as a practical matter, the liberal state can tolerate the holding of multiple nationality because the conflicts of interest among nationalities are dwindling. Where once the interests of one state could translate into the destruction of another (still true, perhaps, in throwback contexts such as the Israeli-Palestinian conflict), there are few matters today on which a benefit to one national community translates into a detriment to another, and none where that detriment poses any sort of fundamental threat. That renders largely irrelevant questions of "loyalty"; indeed, that traditional vocabulary (of loyalty and allegiance) appears increasingly obsolete. As a practical matter, of course, it would be impossible to police any profession of primary loyalty to the United States over another state of nationality, in something of the same way as it would be impossible to enforce the existing oath of renunciation.

Similar observations now apply to nonstate attachments. They did, for the most part, neatly fit into the Chinese box paradigm before the advent of globalization. Membership in racial, ethnic, religious, labor, corporate, and other interest groups (as they have been labeled in pluralist framings) was mostly nationalist in orientation; although many of these groups had international connections (classically, in the form of occasional congresses), with few exceptions—the communists being a notable one, the Catholic Church another—their bread was almost entirely buttered within the national space. As identities, they were clearly subordinate to national identity. In that way, they all fit within the national box—in Walzer's terms, the state remained the individual's "largest or most inclusive group," notwithstanding the existence of nominal ties outside the nation. One could still conceptualize the nation as being the one identity that cut across all others.

But that no longer holds true today. Civil society has gone dramatically transnational. Many elements of civil society that are located in the United States and are nominally "American" will include many members who are not American. Even more obviously, most elements of "domestic" civil society have operationalized their international connections. For many, national organizations are chapters of international umbrella organizations with substantial or ultimate policy-making authority. All of today's prominent identity/interest group orientations—including environmentalists, human rights advocates, animal rights advocates, ethnic groups, indigenous peoples, religions, professions, women, gays, children, the disabled, the elderly, and consumers, to set out a noncomprehensive list—have important and in some cases dominant international institutional vehicles. Many corporations are no longer the multinationals of the 1960s—basically national (read: American) in identity, with global operations—but have evolved into genuinely transnational entities, with mixed nationality among shareholders, employees, and management, as well as multinational operations. As Robert Reich has noted, "the 'American' corporation is becoming disconnected from America."[36] Purely local organizations (which of course are themselves not national in definition) stop short of transnational orientation, though even local organizations are now bypassing the national state to establish significant international connections.

This reorientation (about which I'll say more shortly) poses a fundamental challenge to the pluralist axis of liberal nationalism. The pieces of the Chinese box no longer fit together. Many Americans now belong to organizations that are not exclusively or even primarily American in composition. Take an American who is also a member of Greenpeace, Amnesty International, and the Catholic Church, is an employee of Toyota, and is a woman. For good measure, one might throw in an additional nationality, so that the individual is also a citizen of, say, the Dominican Republic. That is not an exceptional profile, the substantial transnational elements included. Can we say of this person that her "largest and most inclusive group" remains America?

This takes us back around to the inclusiveness norm of liberal nationalism. Yes, the United States remains the most inclusive of these groups in the sense that it will include antienvironmentalists and those for whom human rights are not important, members of other religions, employees of other companies (as well as the unemployed), and men. But that is totally circular—these other groups are all more inclusive than the United States insofar as they are not limited to U.S. citizens. In other words, America is no longer the most inclusive group that many Americans belong to, or at least it is no more inclusive than many others groups of which we are members.

That takes the nation down from its pedestal. If the nation is no longer the most inclusive group, the one over all others, then it just becomes another form of association. That doesn't make it unimportant, for the association defined by the state is still clearly among the most important. But it cannot be essentialized. It is not prior—that is, it is not ordained by nature, something that can go unexplained or assumed. It is not inherently different from other forms of association. States come and go—and indeed, the state may come and go. As with all forms of association, particular states need to satisfy a function for their members. To the extent that they do, they will persist, and to the extent the function is critical, they will prosper. But if they satisfy only marginal needs, or none at all, they will wither. The liberal nationalists have a tough time playing at this level.

THE END OF MULTICULTURALISM AS WE KNOW IT

Liberal nationalists have been forced to confront this postnational challenge, and I will address their response here. But first, a short detour to consider the multiculturalist conception of citizenship, for if the Chinese box is shattered, it shatters the dominant strain of multiculturalism as well.

Multicultural conceptions of citizenship elevate diversity over unity, as implied in the rallying call of "the politics of difference." In contrast to pluralism's interest groups, in multiculturalism some forms of group membership qualify as identities, and some of these identities are said to entitle group members to differentiated treatment. That is, membership in some groups affords a legal status different from that held by nonmembers. At its core and in the American context, multiculturalism has been mostly about race—in particular, members in historically disadvantaged groups. Today it has been broadened to include others, perhaps most notably on the basis of sexual orientation. Equality and inclusiveness also feature prominently in multiculturalist articulations; positive action on the part of the state recognizing group identity is justified to correct entrenched historical discrimination against those groups.

Although it elevates group membership, multiculturalism has been very much oriented to the state and what Iris Marion Young characterized as the "heterogeneous public."[37] Multiculturalism focuses on what group membership will get you by virtue of your national membership, on what the nation owes the group. Multiculturalism focuses on special protective and redistribution regimes that benefit individuals through national policy on the basis of group membership. It depends on the existence of national community. As liberal nationalist David Miller puts it, "the politics of recognition makes sense only if we assume that these more encompassing identities already exist."[38] Multiculturalism works from the premise of mutual duties among citizens, positing that some special duties are forthcoming to subgroups that have been disadvantaged.

But the perspective offers no rationale for the national community, nor can it survive its dissipation. Unlike liberal nationalism, which attempts to extract an overarching unity among citizens in the state, multiculturalism offers only difference. In this respect, multiculturalism reifies the state, leaving its existence unexamined. It undermines the possibility of national community insofar as it locates primary identity somewhere other than the state and offers no substitute basis for its persistence, no commonality by which to bind its members. Liberal theorist Joseph Raz attempts to build a common culture out of multiculturalism itself, in which respect for value pluralism becomes the glue of society.[39] But that seems the basis for the thinnest of distinctive identities, and hardly one that sets the United States apart from other countries. The more typical response from nationalists, liberal and conservative alike, tars the multiculturalists as "separatists" and "Balkanizers." "The ethnic revolt against the melting pot," writes Schlesinger, "has reached the point... of a denial of the idea of a common culture and a single society. If large numbers of people really accept this, the republic would be in serious trouble."[40]

Perhaps. By at least implicitly denying the basis for national community, multiculturalism may help defeat its immediate aim of redistributionist national policies. Those who claim only difference are unlikely to evoke supportive sentiments in others. But whether or not multiculturalism contributes to the dissipation of national community, it will surely be a victim.

In citizenship terms, the challenge to multiculturalism can be illustrated with the use of the term "African American." On the one hand, the substitution of "African American" for "black" was another step in securing symbolic equality, bringing the group's identification into line with those of other ethnic groups (Italian American, Irish American, Asian American, etc.). On the other, it may not pose a coherent group at all. There are many individuals of African descent present in the United States who are not Americans, in the sense that they are not U.S. citizens. Can they be described as African *American*? So that we would speak of Afro-Brazilians, Afro-Dominicans, and Afro-Haitians? Or is perhaps their ethnicity—bounded not in citizenship terms but by common origins, traditions, and experience—the better representation of their identity? For purposes of the multiculturalist agenda, it would be hard for the African American community (defined by citizenship) to exclude individuals of African descent from their self-identified group (at least those territorially present in the United States), for the group has been defined in racial terms.

On the other hand, the multiculturalists would have good reason to wish away these noncitizen counterparts. If one assumes the bounded national community containing various groups—a multicultural version of the Chinese box—then one can assume a national community even if one doesn't have to rationalize it. If redistribution were just among citizens, one would at least have the commonality of status, and a course of intergroup interaction and opposition. Thus, if the United States were a totally closed system, with no in-migration, one might be able to justify racially based reparations for slavery on the grounds that all living white citizens were descended from slaveholders and all living black citizens were descended from slaves. Assuming the validity of intergenerational justice claims, reparations could be sustained. One might even be able to make that case if all immigrants naturalized, on the argument that those who accept membership must accept responsibility for the past misdeeds of fellow members (in the same way that new members of business partnerships may be held liable for misconduct antedating their participation). But it seems more than a stretch to suppose that the noncitizen resident from Ghana should be entitled to slavery reparations from the noncitizen resident from Poland. The same analysis holds for such core components of the multiculturalist agenda as affirmative action in employment.

The substantial spilling of group identities over citizenship lines thus threatens the logic of multiculturalism as we have primarily known it—that is, as a "domestic" force focused on the formulation of national policy. That is emphatically not to diminish the significance of group difference—indeed where such differences will be defeated at the national level, I believe they will triumph on a global scale. But multiculturalism can't be sustained on a national playing field, at least not in the long term. Together with other forces, multiculturalist policies further undermine a distinctively national identity. As that identity and associated solidarities erode, there will be increasingly less inclination to undertake the sort of sharing and mutual support that multiculturalism demands.

THE SEPARATISM OF SOVEREIGN STATES

Multiculturalist theory supplies a useful frame for thinking about representational dynamics at the global level. The segmentation of the world into nation-states has long been accepted as a natural state of affairs, one that does not require justification. But if one conceives of national communities as simply another kind of group, the vocabulary of multiculturalism applies, and the national segmentation can be explained as a form of multiculturalism. That allows the liberal nationalist critiques of multiculturalism to be turned back against liberal nationalism by way of demoting the state as a preferred form of community.

In setting the parameters of group delimitation and recognition, leading multiculturalism theorist Iris Marion Young explained that

> My "affinity group" in a given social situation comprises those people with whom I feel the most comfortable, who are more familiar. Affinity names

the manner of sharing assumptions, affective bonding, and networking that recognizably differentiates groups from one another, but not according to some common nature. The salience of a particular person's group affinities may shift according to the social situation or according to changes in her or his life.[41]

Young had in mind the kinds of groups that have sought a differentiated status within the nation-state, those based on race, ethnicity, language, sexual orientation, and the like. But her description would also fit the national community, conceived as an "affinity group." As a historical matter, certainly, members of national communities have shared certain assumptions, engaged in affective bonding, and networked among themselves. Multiculturalism is sometimes conceived as "identity politics." What have international relations been but that? At the international level, national affiliation has long stood as the primary form of identity.

International relations have also been the "politics of difference." Multiculturalism demands redistributive and other forms of justice from the state, but it also seeks group autonomy in social, cultural, and even political spheres. Multiculturalism borrows key concepts from global characterizations of group distinction. The term "self-determination," a familiar doctrine of international law protecting the claim to nationhood and sovereignty by certain communities, is also deployed by multiculturalists in the domestic context to advance group autonomy. The multiculturalists have at times borrowed the language of nationality, as in the sometime articulation of African and "queer" nations. The terminological connection is apt. At its zenith, the doctrine of sovereignty protected the group autonomy of the nation-state, affording groups qua nations complete independence with respect to matters of internal governance and insulating their practices from any external tests of legitimacy. Sovereignty emerged from the Thirty Years' War, an answer to the question of whether monarchs could freely choose the religious orientation of their realms; as pronounced in the Peace of Westphalia, "cuius regio, eius religio." It is deeply ingrained in our perception of the world that there are differences among nationalities. At least until recently, it has also been accepted that national differences should be reflected in the structure of the global system.

Drawing these parallels further undermines the coherence of liberal nationalism. If the state system has been a kind of multiculturalism, then the liberal nationalist critique of multiculturalism applies to the state system. Nationalists indict multiculturalism as "separatist." The same could be said of the international system and its recognition of national groups, insofar as it quite effectively separated nations from one another. Yet liberal nationalism is itself premised on the state system. By vaunting the value of national identity, it necessarily buys into a global system of distinct nations; in that sense, the liberal nationalist norm is as separatist in its foundations as multiculturalism is. Liberal nationalism works from group difference defined by nationality. Multiculturalism works from group difference defined along other metrics. But they share a focus on groups that offer identity to individuals. Nationalists might argue that multiculturalism constitutes an unworkable or unstable form of nationalism; this is implicit in the use of the term "Balkanization," itself out of the international context. But that goes to mechanisms of recognition, not to the legitimacy of the group definition.

All this is not to say that the separatism posed by the state system still reigns unchallenged; it is the central thesis of this book that the "group" defined by American nationality is breaking down, as reflected in its membership regime. The doctrine of sovereignty is now vigorously contested. To the extent that sovereignty still represents a meaningful quantity, it has been diluted by the various ways that international law has come to insinuate itself into the core of domestic governance, most notably in the form of an increasingly thick regime of human rights norms. So the autonomy of groups defined by nationality is now circumscribed.

More important, nor is it to say that differentiation at the global level is a bad thing, or in any event that it is avoidable. Among the fundamental attributes of human character is the need for community. Communities are in fact defined by difference. In the recent history of humankind, at the international level, community and difference have been located in the territorial nation-state. That has been a history on a grand scale, full of both tragedy and triumph. The nation-state has been the vehicle for both the loftiest and the lowest of human ambitions. As among all communities, relationships among national communities have been locked in competition, sometimes healthy and peaceful, sometimes, of course, in murderous conflict. Just because the state may be retreating as the primary locus of global identity does not mean that community differentiation will be a thing of the past. Community identity will persist along different and more complex metrics.

This reveals yet another failing in liberal nationalist orthodoxy. In addition to its other putative virtues, liberal nationalists have come to defend the state as preferable to any other form of community. In the process, they prop up a strawman against which nationalism looks strong indeed, posing global citizenship as the only alternative to membership in the state. Walzer ventures life beyond the state: "We might opt for a world without particular meanings and without political communities: where no one was a member or where everyone 'belonged' to a single global state...a world of radically deracinated men and women."[42] A variant conjures up the global marketplace as defining social relations. In either case, global state or marketplace, community is the victim. In the liberal nationalist view, without the nation individuals are left as strangers to each other.

Painting the world with those numbers results in an inescapably grim picture, at least from a liberal perspective. Two pillars of liberalism appear its victim: redistributive activity and individual rights. Strangers practice only the thin mutual aid of good Samaritans, with obligations to assist others only where their need is urgent or the cost and risks of assistance are low. Fellow citizens, by contrast, are part of an ethical community whose solidarity allows for the sustainable provision of collective goods where ethical universalism would not. Such goods include national defense. Dearer, perhaps, to the liberal nationalists (for of course nationalists of all description will vaunt the national defense), it also includes the panoply of modern welfare programs. The rights argument takes a similar tack. "One can say that recognition [of rights] entails the mutuality of a common language, common conventions, and common consciousness," observes Benjamin Barber. "Rights lead then to citizenship; they are entailed by citizenship, they are the essence of citizenship—its finest product."[43] Without citizenship, one is bereft of this vehicle for individual security. As Walzer puts it, "statelessness is a condition of infinite danger."[44]

Not so long ago, these dicta stood mostly true. In the calamity of World War II and its lead-up, citizenship status was often determinative of well-being. To the victims of the Holocaust, international law provided not even a paper shield, prompting Arendt's observation that all rights are national rights. The international system had long before established the state as the provider of security; nations are above all security communities, the provision of defense once being the primary good supplied by the state and the function that brought otherwise disparate elements of the community together. It was also within the confines of the state that redistributive benefits schemes have reached a historical apex, at least as a matter of scale. The liberal nationalist vision is thus historically grounded; there has been a time when it more or less accurately described the world as it was.

But that vision is also historically contingent. The elaborations of liberal nationalism are not timeless truths. Even on its own terms, alternatives to the state are not so obviously fragile. Rights under international law are now clearly consequential. Only the most irrecondite Realist (the school of international relations theory that holds states and states alone to be the relevant actors in the world system, and interactions among them to be anarchical) would dismiss international human rights as a null set. All rights are not simply national rights any more. Where the stateless person once was as a matter of international law a person enjoying no protection (such protection being afforded only by states), today she enjoys an increasingly refined set of rights, lack of national affiliation notwithstanding. The discourse of international relations now puts human rights at its center, and human rights norms affect state behavior, even without the establishment of a global superstate. The regime's enforcement is imperfect—as is relentlessly pointed out by international law skeptics[45]—but that is true of all legal regimes, including, for example, domestic prohibitions on such crimes as murder. In this case, the strawman might be acquiring some bones, as it were. Yasemin Soysal goes so far as to compose a postnational model in which "universal personhood replaces nationhood; and universal human rights replace national rights."[46] Though national regimes will remain important to the vindication of individual rights, it is possible to conceive domestic institutions as agents of the international system and domestic rights as complementary to international ones.

As for security, the question is, security against what? When the nation-state reigned supreme, security was against other nation-states. Today, the threat is from elsewhere. With some exceptions (for historical evolutions will never be lockstep), states do not make war with other states. From a U.S. perspective, it is becoming increasingly difficult to present a scenario in which another state poses a serious threat to the community's well-being, in the way that Germany did during World War II or the Soviet Union during the cold war. Rather, as September 11 made clear, security is now required against terrorism and other forms of crime. But that threat is one against which the nation-state has no particular comparative advantage. Because the threat is constituted on a transnational basis and is directed against local targets, it requires the participation of actors both above and below the state if it has any hope of effectiveness. Because law enforcement has also been undertaken by national institutions, states will (as a matter of path dependency, if nothing else) play an important part in these efforts. As a matter of theory, however, there is nothing essential about national agents in the provision of security going forward.

Finally, there is the provision of welfare and other redistributive schemes. It is true that there isn't much hope of such activity significantly advancing at the international level, conceived as a system of states. For instance, it is unlikely that state-to-state subsidies (a.k.a. "foreign aid") will ever amount to much; there is no prospect of direct global taxation on individuals to support redistributive programs, even looking to the long run. The retreat of the nation-state and the rise of some sort of universal citizenship would lay a blow to public welfare-type undertakings. Again, the specter here is of unconstrained survival-of-the-fittest market relationships, with the dispossessed falling helplessly to the wayside.

But this perspective suffers a gaping middle. Nationality "is not the only form of identity that has led to self-sacrifice and altruism," notes Keith Faulks. "To assume, therefore, that we are faced with either a choice of nationality or atomism . . . is a gross simplification."[47] One finds the middle in what comes under the now familiar moniker of "civil society." Civil society is nothing new, in theory or on the ground. The organs of civil society are at the center of liberalism, as pluralist interest groups. These nonstate forms of association have long been understood as a part of the American experience; Tocqueville, for example, found nothing more deserving of his attention and astonishing to his European sensibilities than the breadth of associational activity. But civil society has always been conceived as only an element in the overarching national community, never as its competitor. As described, however, this "Chinese box" premise of liberal nationalism has broken down, and these other membership organizations may no longer gird the state.

That possibility has gone missing from modernist debates on defining America. The centrality of those debates will subside with the continuing demotion of the state; debates about America will be only as important as their object. The anthropologist Arjun Appadurai brilliantly captures the state of play in these tournaments of theory, as they accommodate a sense that plurality is the American genius and that there is an Americanness that somehow contains and transcends plurality. This second, post–Civil War accommodation with difference is now on its last legs, and the political correctness–multiculturalism debate is its peculiar, parochial Waterloo. Parochial because it insistently refuses to recognize that the challenge of diasporic pluralism is now global and that American solutions cannot be seen in isolation. Peculiar because there has been no systematic recognition that the politics of multiculturalism is now part and parcel of the extraterritorial nationalism of populations who love America but are not necessarily attached to the United States. More bluntly, neither popular nor academic thought in this country has come to terms with the difference between being a land of immigrants and being one node in a postnational network of diasporas.[48]

The energy of the theorists, if they are to be engaged in new challenges of institutional architecture outside the state, should move beyond questions of national definition and national meaning. That is not to deny the continuing importance of the state and national community into the immediate future. But the most formidable challenge will not be to further define the national community, as if it were a stand-alone entity, but rather to situate the national community among other communities, and to map the relationship of citizenship to other forms of membership.

6

Beyond American

IF IN FACT the center of community is migrating to locations other than the state, then rights and responsibilities are going with it. What we think of as "public" issues may increasingly play out in nonstate settings. If so, it is in that direction, and away from the state, that theorists, decision makers, and the media should start to turn their sights, looking at other forms of association as meaningful in their own right, not just as objects of state regulation. Public intellectuals almost without exception take the nation as a given, as something that we should simply assume to be the critical institutional juncture of human interaction. Defined as government decision making, policy making has taken on fetishistic proportions, as if policy was the source of most evil and the potential engine of most correction, as if all of it can be played out on Sunday morning talk shows.

The obsession with policy making and the premise of a coherent citizenry are discursively self-reinforcing. If the most consequential decision making is undertaken in the national government, then the most consequential marker of membership will be citizenship. Likewise, if citizenship marks the primary boundary of identity, then the most consequential decision making will transpire in the state. But the reality may be otherwise. I hope to have shown that citizenship no longer stands categorically above other membership organizations. It should follow, then, that the national government will no longer be the dominant node of decision making.

Of course, the nation-state has for centuries enjoyed such dominance, and the nation-state has been the primary object of public discourse—indeed, it has defined that discourse. In addressing the challenges of non-state organizations, that experience may provide an analytical starting point. That is, one can at least attempt to translate notions of community, democracy, and justice to the nonstate setting. In Appadurai's terms, this book has attempted to identify one element in "the current crisis of the nation." The discussion now turns to using that identification "to provide part of the apparatus of recognition for postnational social forms."[1] That undertaking is monumental, for it spans the whole spectrum of issues implicated by governance. Nor will the effort work on all fronts, as there are distinctive elements to governance through the state.

As a part of that undertaking, it is not clear whether modern conceptions of citizenship can survive the transition to an order in which the state is not supreme. Taken as a form of membership, the citizenship experience supplies important analytical metrics for membership rules in these other forms of association. On the other hand, some of these metrics, especially as driven by a liberal perspective, may not translate in the unstable dimension of nonstate communities. The institution of citizenship may be too anchored in the state, in the liberal state, to survive the ascendancy of these competitor organizations.

NONSTATE SECURITY

To frame this discussion, one might consider how different institutions impact our individual lives and how the nation-state ranks among them. Using the vocabulary of the state, the question is to what extent nonstate institutions frame rights and responsibilities. To the extent that other institutions are more important in situating individuals, those institutions are likely to determine individual identity, and loyalties will inevitably follow.

By way of backdrop, there is again the diminished importance of the state as a provider of security. The security function amounts to the provision of a right, because protection of physical survival is most important among individual interests. In the Hobbesian era of hostile nation-states, the provision of that right by the state overshadowed all others, even if it did not always determine the conduct of our everyday lives. The state provided defense against outsiders who would otherwise do their worst.

In return, the state extracted the highest obligation, namely, the duty to sacrifice one's life to the end of the community's security. The historical primacy of the state can be largely explained by thinking of states as security communities.

As discussed in the last chapter, however, that security function is dissipating, even in the face of the possibly cataclysmic threats posed by terrorism. The state as a territorial entity enjoyed primacy because security was undertaken on a territorial basis; outsiders were territorial outsiders, and victories were measured by territorial conquest. The tactics and strategy of terrorist attacks are not drawn along territorial lines, and so the defense against terrorism will not be established in territorial terms. Of course, there will be defenses that revolve around the movement of individuals; there will be territorial checkpoints that will sometimes coincide with national boundaries. But it is obvious—even to a Republican administration that otherwise thumbs its nose at multilateralism—that an antiterrorism strategy cannot be driven by such boundaries. Once the territorial orientation of the defense is lost, the function served by the state as protector of the "right" to individual safety inevitably starts to fade, because security will also be delivered by entities other than the state.

On the obligations side, the state also looms less large with the demise of conscription. Henceforth, no Americans will be required to give their lives "in the line of duty" as members of the U.S. armed forces. Even in the wake of 9/11, calls to reinstate the draft fell flat, and if it didn't happen in that context, it never will. Some will lose their lives in the course of voluntary enlistments, as in the conflict in Iraq. But given its clear failure, that sort of engagement—the genesis of which might be explained in part by a yearning to fight an identifiable foe on a more traditional battleground—is unlikely to be repeated anytime soon. In the meantime, the losses in the new conflict against terrorism are more likely as not in local police forces than in national armies.

So even if the position of nonstate entities were to have remained static, their position relative to the state would be enhanced. But they have moved into the various breaches of the eroding institutional battlements of the nation-state. Even at the level of security, once a state monopoly and still an area of state dominance, at least as a vestigial matter (NORAD still monitors the northern border for approaching ballistic missiles, presumably), other entities now act as security providers. Local law enforcement is perhaps as important as national law enforcement and military action in defending against terrorist threat, guarding the proverbial front lines. Though their tactics may be coordinated at and funded (in part) from the national level, they are not part of a military chain of command. The commissioners of the New York, Los Angeles, and Chicago police departments are not mere agents of Washington. The locality's role in protecting the security right starts to rival the nation's.

Nongovernmental actors are also playing a role here. At the global level, "private security forces" provide protection to corporations and corporate employees in those places where the state cannot be counted on. (This is aside from the expanded use of private contractors in the service of U.S. armed forces, notably in Iraq.[2]) Gone are the days when a corporation could call in the warships at signs of local unrest; corporations with sizeable facilities in potentially unstable environments will have security to match. These forces are akin to governmental security entities. Human rights activists now monitor their practices as they would the practices of states, as a matter of international law; and they are charging corporations with accountability to international human rights law, in the courts and elsewhere.[3]

Corporations will also provide the equivalent of diplomatic protection to their employees in foreign countries (including for noncitizens in the United States). Eighty-three companies among the *Fortune* 100, for example, subscribe to International SOS, a private concern helping corporations "ensure the health and security of their travelers and employees around the world." (When the Israeli bombing of Lebanon in the summer of 2006 raised safety concerns, International SOS quickly evacuated students from subscriber universities Harvard, Yale, and Princeton, while other Americans had to wait for days for poorly managed U.S. government evacuations.) The choice between a U.S. passport and an employee identification card for a company like Shell or Freeport-McMoRan while located in another country might not be so obvious these days. If one were to have trouble with local authorities, the corporate membership might buy you more protection than the national membership.

THE EVERYDAY OF RIGHTS AND RESPONSIBILITIES

If the state's relative role in what we used to think of as geopolitics is diminishing, it is more dramatically so in the realm of everyday life. "Citizenship education"—evoking the putative common status of all inhabitants—was once at the core of the curriculum, instructing on everything from hygiene to etiquette (framed essentially as societal obligations), where today it sounds quaint. Those rules of living are now more likely to be drawn up by nonstate entities. Some of these nonstate entities have been around for a very long time, where others are new. But even with respect to well-established nonstate institutions, the era of state primacy obscured the ways in which they governed our everyday lives. That's a matter of perception. As a matter of reality, as the state recedes, the relative importance of these institutions—new and old—grows, so that they loom larger in the realm of governance activity.

Religions supply the most prominent example of nonstate association, one long antedating the state. In the heydey of the liberal state, there has been a tendency to forget how comprehensively religions regulate the lives of their adherents, often imposing intricate standards of conduct. Religious dietary laws, for example, are far more intrusive than most forms of state intervention. Religions may also impose substantial obligations on members. The Mormon Church expectation of two years' missionary service presents a striking example of a persistent community service obligation that stands even as the state's equivalent (universal military service) has fallen away. Religious norms further implicate a broad swath of conduct and status relationships. They may lay down the norms of family law in ways that effectively override those mandated by the state. Procedural rights are allocated among members along with substantive ones.[4]

These sorts of issues are so obvious in the corporate context that we take them as a given. The outer parameters of conduct may be set by states (although vastly enhanced capital mobility has limited state power to dictate narrow constraints), but within those outlines corporate entities have great discretion in delineating the rights and obligations of particular constituencies. Corporate charters and bylaws play a constitutional function in this context. Shareholder voting rights, for instance, are determined within the entity. Corporations have wide berth to set employee rights and obligations within the bounds of public law, such as it is enforced.

Other examples abound. Gated communities and other residential collectives play home to more individuals (at least 7 million households as of 2002), extracting fees for various common goods in much the same way as the state collects taxes, and governing various elements of residential life, from paint colors to lawn mowing requirements, noise levels, and limits on solicitations, in addition to the provision of immediate infrastructure and basic services otherwise thought of as "public."[5] Educational institutions increasingly set standards of conduct deviating from legal ones, for instance, on questions of speech. Hate speech may be constitutionally protected against government suppression, but a private institution can prohibit such expression among its members (a prohibition enforced through institutionally internal justice mechanisms).[6] Sporting federations have the power to expel or fine member athletes on the basis of internally generated rules—rules that have become increasingly intricate (in both their formulation and enforcement) with the exponentially magnified financial stakes of the industry. The International Olympic Committee, and not any state or group of states, regulates the use of various drugs by athletes and then enforces prohibitions, and the private, Geneva-based Court of Arbitration for Sport gets the last word on related disputes.[7] On the Internet, various private entities in effect regulate privacy standards, intellectual property rights, and the allocation of domain names; expulsion from a listserv or other online community for violation of conduct standards may be unjust and unreviewable.[8] Professional associations often have the independent power to bar an individual from an occupation, as in medicine, law, and the securities industry. All institutions, from the neighborhood treehouse to Amnesty International, set governance standards that set the relative rights of members in formulating and accomplishing institutional purpose.

Enforcement in these nonstate contexts is imperfect. As a general matter private institutions, unlike the state, cannot resort to force to advance compliance. But the difference may be more a matter of degree than kind. On the one hand, enforcement of public law is far from perfect, even as supported by the use of force. The federal Occupational Safety and Health Administration may set various workplace standards, but with only a thousand or so inspectors (the same number as in 1979) to enforce those standards nationwide at 6.5 million workplaces, there is a huge margin for noncompliance (and that leaves aside the many businesses that avoid the regime altogether by going offshore). Even where resources are more generously dedicated, violations will go unpunished; some murderers, after all, get away with it.

On the other hand, nonstate standards can effectively regulate conduct even though they lack force to back them up. Take the kosher dietary prescriptions. Observance of these practices by members of orthodox communities is unenforceable in any formal sense; the kosher food police do not undertake larder inspections. But informal enforcement mechanisms loom large; the orthodox temple member is unlikely to consume non-kosher food in a family setting, much less a community one. "[B]ecause disapproval comes from family, friends, colleagues, or comrades," observe Will Kymlicka and Wayne Norman, "it is in many ways a more powerful incentive to act responsibly than punishment by an impersonal state."[9] The community cannot deploy police powers against offenders, but that does not preclude the availability of effective sanctions. Noncompliance with community standards can result in the withdrawal of various community rights. If you don't pay your dues, you're not going to be able to use the club dining room.

The state might still be thought to set the boundaries of conduct. No doubt that in many respects the state and its laws frame the conduct and governing rules of private organizations. But this impact is not seamless. First of all, many "rights" are enforceable only against public entities; a private organization cannot violate First Amendment free speech rights, for example. That dichotomy allows private entities considerable freedom, even in the face of the state, to set their own standards. As noted, to the extent that the state does purport to regulate private activity, public enforcement is imperfect, and legal standards may be circumvented. That club may admit a small handful of minority members to stay out of trouble with antidiscrimination measures, but the move may be essentially token. A ban on age discrimination may find corporations limiting—always on other grounds, of course—its hiring of older workers.

The state may be marginal even in episodes involving outrageous or criminal conduct. Consider the recent sex abuse scandals in the Catholic Church. The magnitude of the wrongdoing was clearly compounded by internal church rules regarding the response to known past offenders, in particular their reassignment to parish duty. Law enforcement was ineffective before the scandal broke, and only a small handful of offenders will actually be brought to justice. Monetary settlements may be extended as much by a sense of internal institutional justice as by the threat of civil litigation. In other less sensational contexts, resort to "the law" is unlikely to have much traction in the great majority of cases.

There is also once again the "Chinese box" premise to the assertion of state supremacy. As described in the last chapter, nationalists conceive of all nonstate entities as fitting neatly under the umbrella of the state, so that membership in a private entity is a subset of national membership.

To the extent that assumption no longer holds true, it has consequences for the state enforcement argument. The leverage of the state and of the law will be limited against transnational organizations, even if formal powers ("jurisdiction," in legal terms) persists. United States courts have the formal power to review decisions of the private arbitration system developed for deciding Internet domain name disputes, but that power is exercised in only one out of every hundred disputes.[10] The International Olympic Committee, likewise, is subject to little state discipline. Transnational corporations can evade a panoply of state regulatory measures by expatriating elements of production; the state might in theory have full power to set terms of employment, but to the extent that they increase corporate costs, regulatory targets can simply exit. In a sense, these transnational nonstate entities have accreted some characteristics of sovereignty, to the extent that the construction is equated with decision-making autonomy. That autonomy translates into power beyond the reach of the state.

REDISTRIBUTION BEYOND THE STATE

Among the commonly conceived rights of citizenship (as first theorized by British sociologist T. H. Marshall) are social rights.[11] This component of citizenship is central to liberal nationalism and multiculturalism; products of the Great Society both, they cling to the nation as the primary agent of redistribution. But this function is also being eclipsed by other entities. There are multiple institutional locations of mutual aid and other forms of associational support beyond the nation. At the national level, most benefits programs are now in the way of social insurance; like private insurance, eligibility is contingent on contributions. One is not entitled to Social Security as a citizen, only as a employee who has paid in to the program for the required number of years. (As we have seen, one need not be a citizen to participate.) Those programs may in practice be more redistributionist than private insurance (and participation is mandatory, although again, not seamlessly enforceable), but the orienting principle is the same.

Purer "safety net" vehicles at the national level are in decline. Most notably, much of welfare as we know it—especially since the welfare reform act of 1996—is largely implemented at the subnational level. Though territorial in definition, and compulsory in the same sense as national schemes (that is, residents and other taxpayers have no choice—other than to relocate their taxable activity—than to participate), these are founded on something other than the national community. Liberal nationalists surely perceive the federalism revolution in the United States as a threat to their general agenda—the threat from below. The assumption is that smaller territorial units, if left to their own devices, will necessarily be less generous in the provision of public goods. But there is nothing inherently more stingy about mutual aid schemes in smaller territorial units. An example from immigration policy: many states are assisting undocumented aliens in a way that the federal government hasn't, with respect to such matters as driver's licenses, in-state tuition for higher education, and welfare benefits.[12] Indeed, these subnational constructs are more likely to be thick; the smaller the territorial community, the more likely the existence of communal solidarity.

Subnational governmental schemes of redistribution do not pose a significant conceptual challenge, because they work from territorial premises in the same way that national schemes do. (Likewise on the other side of the spectrum with the European Union, which, notwithstanding its supranational position, remains a territorial entity.) They may challenge nationalism, of course; where territory is the baseline of community determination, there is no reason why those baselines need to be drawn expansively. Secession has been the result in some quarters, where (because the state is drawn more closely to coincide with actual community) state identities have been reinforced. In the Baltic states, for example, citizenship status may be more salient than in larger, less cohesive entities. But even there, the status of citizenship does not conform with a homogenous identity; large minority populations (in that context, ethnic Russians) undermine solidarity that might otherwise be defined in citizenship terms. That complication also helps explain the failure of secessionist movements in Quebec, the Basqueland, Scotland, and elsewhere. At the same time, the threat to national identity from below is a real one. This may be especially true from way below, at the level of localities, where spatial community will be most keenly felt, although not on a scale capable of competing with the nation-state on its own terms.

More interesting are private and nonterritorial forms of association. First there is the family, within which the instincts for mutual aid are best programmed. In the tradition of mainstream contemporary America, such activity has not typically extended beyond the nuclear family. In other cultures—cultures now increasingly represented in U.S. territory—kin obligations are more broadly defined. This may seem a thin, molecular form of support, hardly a substitution for public welfare schemes. But migration and globalization have transformed this form of redistribution into a significant transnational phenomenon. Remittances by migrants to the United States to family members back home in Latin America now total some almost $45 billion annually, more than twice the level of U.S. government foreign assistance. For many sending states of the Western Hemisphere, remittances exceed all others sources of foreign exchange; that is, they surpass the value of any export product.[13]

One level removed from these transnational intrafamily connections are diasporic networks of various descriptions. In some cases these are based in towns or regions within sending states, which maintain direct ties to erstwhile members in the United States. Patterns of migration will often find neighbors in the place of origin ending up as neighbors in their country of migration. This gives rise to associations in the receiving country, the purpose of which is to support activity in the place of origin. These support organizations are known to undertake what Americans would usually conceive as "public" works projects consisting of road and other commonly used infrastructure. More than 500 such "home town associations" have been established among Mexican immigrants alone.[14] These activities are undertaken in the absence of governmental compulsion and serve to redistribute resources within transnational communities. Within immigrant communities, banking and other mutually supportive activity is undertaken on an informal basis.[15] Diasporic support activity also takes places at the macro-level. This activity may include a state component, such as where the government of a sending state seeks to tap into diasporic resources. Israel and India have issued bonds targeted at nonresident populations. (In the Indian example, such bonds can only be purchased by ethnic Indians; in the Israeli example, the efforts include direct fundraising as well.) Notwithstanding the state element, though, this support activity does not fit into liberal nationalist models, insofar as it is voluntary and not territorially based. In the liberal nationalist view, diasporas are not part of homeland polities. They don't count for anything in the paradigm of democratic citizenship.

There are other nonstate institutions in which one finds redistributive activity, few of which coincide with national borders or "the citizenry." Religions provide perhaps the best example. Tithing in the Mormon Church may be voluntary in the sense that the church can't throw an individual in jail if he or she refuses to pay, but the payment is not voluntary to anyone who wants to remain a member. Compliance among Mormon Church members compares favorably with taxpaying compliance among American citizens (members give nearly 8 percent of their income—that is, 80 percent of their obligations under the tithe—where the U.S. government estimates that Americans pay 83 percent of what they should be paying in income tax); the return for members in need may be better than those who might otherwise claim support from the state.[16] In some religious communities, support functions are comprehensive, to the point where, for instance, the Amish don't need to purchase health and other forms of insurance. In others, monetary support functions within religions may be more ad hoc, varying according to context.

Various redistributive activity occurs within corporations as well. Corporate employees may well describe themselves as part of a "family." Aside from informal support (chipping in when someone is in need), employment policies not ordinarily conceived as redistributionist have that effect. The availability of parental and disability leave (beyond that required by law) qualifies as a form of mutual aid, for example. On a transnational basis, corporations now undertake various assistance schemes in locations of production.[17] The whole corporate social responsibility paradigm is, in a sense, about the more just distribution of corporate resources. The movement has massively snowballed in recent years; even foot-dragger Exxon-Mobil now issues a "corporate citizenship" report, complete with sections on transparency, human rights, and "strategic community investment." Of course, corporations have profits as a raison d'être. They can't work as wholly charitable enterprises. But mutual support activities are not inconsistent with that mission.

Rights and responsibilities are also being determined as nonstate communities act on one another. Representing and mobilizing sympathetic constituencies, NGOs often have the power to secure changes in corporate behavior, for example. When Greenpeace or Amnesty International have something to say, transnational corporations now listen. The annual meeting of global business leaders and policy makers at Davos includes top NGO officials as well. NGOs have demonstrated the capacity to drive consumer marketplace choices with material bottom-line impacts. This interplay has started to mature into a more cooperative dynamic in which NGOs and corporations negotiate the terms of corporate behavior on such issues as labor rights, human rights, and environmental impacts, with effectively monitored codes of conduct to serve as performance benchmarks. As globalization pares competitive margins and capital becomes more mobile, beyond the reach of any single state to control, these nonstate regimes have emerged as increasingly prominent instruments of governance. Tropical timbers, diamonds, branded athletic gear, child labor, and workplace health and safety are among the products and issues now subject to such nonstate regimes.[18] Technical standards-setting entities, meanwhile, are branching out into more policy-oriented areas. The little-known International Organization for Standardization is now a major force on environmental management issues; more than a hundred thousand corporations worldwide subscribe to its ISO 14000 series, which sets out requirements for establishing corporate environmental polices, determining environmental impacts of corporate activities, and planning and implementing corporate environmental objectives.[19]

The point here is not to draw a detailed picture of the many ways in which private bodies effectively regulate our existence. Rather, this discussion aims to demonstrate that the state is not the only game in town. There is nothing categorically different about state regulations; the state is just another (albeit powerful) form of association. We can think of the state as a membership body. We can also think of other membership bodies as we think of the state. As identities migrate to nonstate forms of association, the latter proposition may be the more important of the two. We are used to framing justice in "public" terms, in the terms of state institutions and state action. But if there is nothing essentially different about the state, then injustice can be perpetrated in nonstate fora in essentially the same way it is in public ones. To the extent identity migrates to nonstate associations, powers will migrate with it, magnifying the dangers of injustice. That argues for turning our sights on those entities in the way they have been trained for so long on state institutions.

THINKING GOVERNMENTALLY

On questions of governance, one can in effect import the entire canon of political theory in which the citizenship concept has been so prominent. The basic challenge of holding agents accountable plays out in private contexts as well as public. The notion of political democracy and the place of the individual citizen within it can inform other forms of association. The precepts of majority rule and one person, one vote, for example, can be applied in other entities. Labor unions and some other nongovernmental organizations, Amnesty International and the Sierra Club among them, have adopted this sort of democratic procedure, so that the organization directorates are selected on a one-member, one-vote basis.

Conceptions of public justice may also inform private discipline. Many associations provide some procedural protection, more or less elaborate, in taking action against members for noncompliance with organization rules. Educational institutions, for instance, almost always have procedures by which a student can defend against charges of cheating or plagiarism, or for faculty to respond to harassment complaints or other violations of school policy. The Inquisition was a historical form of nonstate procedure (for determining heresy), sometimes undertaken without the cooperation of secular governments. The Catholic Church still provides for trial in cases involving marriage, excommunication, and dismissal from the clergy; in a kind of religious version of the *Miranda* rule, priests are forbidden from revealing information secured during confession in such disciplinary proceedings.

More often than not, however, direct transference of democratic theory and citizenship principles proves difficult across the public/private divide. The equality norm of liberal democratic theory does not always lend itself to nonstate application. Corporate entities present an example in which it has been rejected as a default rule, at least insofar as equality is as between persons; among stockholders, the usual approach is one share, one vote. In some cases common stockholders are denied voting rights altogether, as are employees. Not that such disenfranchisement is unusual in the nonstate context. Adherents of religions do not get to vote on doctrine, although democratic-type procedures may prevail at some levels, as when cardinals select a pontiff. Most NGOs do not submit policy or staffing decisions for member approval, much less give corporate targets some procedural protection against unjustified calls to boycott. Beyond associational decision making, individuals may be afforded variable status within associations. Some employees enjoy certain protections, where others do not. Academe, with its stratification between tenured and nontenured faculty, presents an excellent example. Within the tenured ranks, democracy reigns on a one-member, one-vote basis. Others lack any formal voice.

So nonstate entities are unlikely to be democratic in the sense that we think states are, or at least the way we think they should be. Though some have called for a global parliament,[20] democracy is unlikely on a global scale. But even in the absence of formal democratic decision making, accountability norms can be vindicated in the realms of nonstate governance. In addressing accountability challenges at the global level, write Ruth Grant and Robert Keohane, we should regard "strict analogies from domestic democratic politics . . . with skepticism, and we should resist the temptation to narrow the issue of accountability to that of democratic control."[21] Power-holders beyond the state can be constrained through mechanisms other than the ballot box.

Stakeholder paradigms, in which interested, discrete constituencies are afforded some collective voice in decision-making processes, appear particularly promising in this respect, as refined outside the public law context (such as the NGO-corporate negotiated codes of conduct). States themselves are experimenting with stakeholder mechanisms—for example, U.S. administrative agencies now engage in the practice of "negotiated rule making," in which administrative regulations are promulgated only after consultation with interested constituencies. But the prospects for stakeholder frameworks are greater in the sphere of global governance, in which many decision-making structures are being built from scratch. The International Labor Organization presents one long-standing example of a stakeholder approach at the international level, with employers, employees, and governments equally represented on a tripartite basis. Some have suggested a similar institution for global environmental protection policy making, in a forum bringing together representatives of corporations, environmentalist organizations, and states.[22] Activists and scholars have attacked the World Trade Organization for not providing adequate channels for stakeholder participation; the organization's future success may hinge on bringing civil society to the trade table. The WTO will never be democratic in any formal sense, but WTO process may win legitimacy among important constituency groups (including environmentalists, labor unions, human rights advocates, and others) if it affords them sufficient voice in trade governance. Meanwhile, some are questioning the accountability of the stakeholder groups themselves, with "who elected NGOs?" as a tagline. Theorists are grappling with these challenges as global governance shows itself to be a durable presence.

THE CITIZENSHIP OF GROUPS

These matters could occupy volumes of organizational theory, some already written. This book has been about how a national community can and cannot draw membership boundaries. There are lessons here, too, that go bidirectionally between state and nonstate forms of association. If the state is only another form of association, and citizenship is about membership in that organization, then the theory of citizenship should translate to nonstate communities. It is on this front that citizenship conceptions will either fade away or prove their continuing utility. The primary issues of membership in nonstate entities are the same as for the state: how one acquires membership (at birth or subsequently); how one loses it; and how members are treated differently from nonmembers. These issues are normatively consequential to the extent that affiliation sustains rights and identity. The greater the rights and (often correspondingly) the stronger the identity, the more significant the normative implications will be. The significance of membership issues outside of the state will grow in proportion to the importance of nonstate communities.

All communities set terms for membership. Where the threshold for membership is low (usually correlated to lesser benefits and tertiary identity), they are hardly worthy of note. If all it takes to join the Sierra Club is $25 in annual dues and self-identification as an environmentalist, it is difficult to frame the membership condition in any controversial way. At the other end of the nonstate scale, membership in most indigenous and racial groups may be entirely ascriptive, with no possibility of volitional accession. If you do not have the requisite bloodline, you cannot be a member. You cannot convert, to use a membership threshold in another major component of civil society; to use that of states, the approach is exclusively jus sanguinis, with no opportunity for naturalization. Unions usually require relevant employment, experience, and/or certification for membership. In professional and educational contexts, admissions issues are more obvious. Membership boundaries will pose different challenges in other realms. On matters of sexual orientation, it may be whether transsexuals qualify for the advocacy support of gay and lesbian organizations, and whether discrimination on the basis of sexual orientation (however defined) should qualify as a concern of international human rights. There will be similar boundary questions in defining such groups as the disabled (what conditions qualify) and the elderly and children (what age defines them, and for what purposes). Membership admission issues abound in the context of religion, on such issues as the terms of conversion and the status of the children of "mixed" marriages.

Membership in these groups can be valuable where members have a special status under public law, as in the case of race membership for purposes of affirmative action. But these communities are not only constructed by the state. Union membership is valuable for securing certain benefits from employers (in some industries, such as entertainment, union membership marks the line between the haves and have-nots). Religious membership provides community support, material and otherwise. For some purposes, membership may be valuable at the global level on advocacy and status questions. Membership is often valuable in its own right, insofar as it supplies an identity. Wherever the community is one in which or through which people live their lives, membership will itself be at least part of the prize. Where it is valuable, the terms of membership may be contested.

The termination of individual membership from a community is often more consequential than admission. Termination can involve the forfeiture of significant vested interests. To the extent that a life is lived within a particular community, the loss of membership can amount to the loss of everything that is meaningful. It is the equivalent of banishment. In various contexts, historical and contemporary, excommunication from a religious community presents an individual detriment far more significant than loss of citizenship, for it may mean the loss of an individual's entire social network, the loss of an identity. Likewise with respect expulsion from corporate, professional, and educational communities.

In other cases exit may be a matter of volition rather than one of imposition. Community membership carries burdens and obligations from which individuals may prefer to free themselves. Here the question is a right to exit as opposed to a right to retain membership. In some settings, the right to exit is relatively unobstructed, at least as a matter of community rules; one can leave a profession or sell one's shares without interference from the relevant community (although exit may involve other costs). But other communities restrict exit. Some religions refuse to recognize the possibility of renunciation. It is especially controversial in the context of race and ethnicity, where exit may be impeded both as an internal and external matter (that is, under community rules as well as according to broader social perceptions). It is difficult, for instance, for a person of African or Asian heritage (even partial) to avoid the racial identity.

LEARNING FROM CITIZENSHIP

To think of these issues as matters of citizenship can illuminate them. First of all, membership criteria at some level pose issues of exclusion. That has been liberalism's rallying point in the context of the state membership; as already discussed, liberal citizenship theory has taken aim above all at exclusion from the polity. To the extent that community membership affords benefits and identity, membership requirements involve deprivation and inequality, implicating justice. Of course, membership in some nonstate communities has already been confronted. At the intersection of race, education, and employment, for example, antidiscrimination rules and affirmative action along with changed social norms have taken aim at exclusion. In others, the liberal analysis does not so readily compute. To the extent membership in a racial or ethnic group carries with it status benefits, how can membership be restricted in any way without undermining equality and expressive autonomy? To the extent that membership is legitimately restrictive (that is, to the extent exclusion is acceptable), are these groups constrained by justice principles in defining membership criteria?

Consider tribal membership. One has to explain why it is legitimate for a tribe to exclude any individual who would like to enjoy the benefits of membership. These benefits can be substantial, sometimes literally paying dividends. Assuming that the prospective member is willing to take on any corresponding community obligations, it is not obvious on what basis she can be excluded. To make the case more difficult, assume the individual resides on tribal land, so that she is clearly impacted by tribal decision making. On the one hand, a liberal theorist would be hard pressed to defend the membership exclusion, which would give rise to a caste system. Those who are affected by government should have an equal voice in government.

On the other hand, tribal membership (at least in the Native American context) has been definitionally a question of blood relationships. To require the admission of individuals not sharing that relationship would be to undermine the very nature of the tribe. Intuition leads us away from extending membership, even if the resulting exclusion is consequential and in some sense clearly discriminatory. Multiculturalism may explain this intuition where liberalism comes up short. For the multiculturalist, the membership question is one of community self-determination.

Communities must be able to define themselves if they are to qualify as communities, even though that definition will inevitably leave some outside the gates.

One can also use the experience of citizenship in the state to inform termination issues. International law provides that states cannot arbitrarily deprive individuals of nationality; in the U.S. context, we have seen that nationality will never be terminated against an individual's will. As a background norm, the former seems a useful guide to community conduct. One can easily pose situations in which excommunication raises serious justice concerns. But our intuition leads us to accept termination in some cases, as when the individual acts against core community interests. Thus, the capacity to excommunicate members of religious organizations seems justifiable, at least where a member engages in conduct that would threaten fundamental tenets of the community.

As for volitional exit, the possibility is sometimes highlighted to distinguish the state from other communities, as in, you can opt out of nonstate communities where you cannot escape the state. As a practical matter, the distinction is no longer so clear. Escape from the American national community can now be accomplished with some greater ease in a world of vastly greater mobility. This has its costs, of course—one no longer enjoys, most notably, the right to enter U.S. territory (although only tax-evading former citizens are categorically barred from reentry). But there are costs to exiting nonstate communities as well, in the amount of whatever benefit is posed by membership. In some cases it may be trivial—the club's lunchroom and the conviviality of fellow members in a congenial setting. In others it can be devastating, as from an observant, insulated religious community.

In other words, there is a correspondence between the state and nonstate contexts. One has a qualified right to opt out of the state, as a matter of both U.S. law (a right essentially absolute for someone demonstrating an intent to reside outside the country) and international law (which provides that the capacity to expatriate not be unreasonably restricted).[23] That might buttress a correlate right of exit from nonstate communities, a right long asserted by liberal theorists.[24] On the other hand, who is to say that a religion, as a theological matter, cannot hold to the impossibility of renunciation? In the context of racial or cultural communities, the limitation of exit possibilities might be defensible, by way of enhancing community solidarities and community strength relative to other communities.

The terms of state and nonstate membership are also mutually informative. We have seen the trends towards the acceptance of plural citizenship, that is, concurrent membership in more than one state. That may work for some nonstate entities but not for others. Religion obviously doesn't allow for multiple affiliations. It would be hard to challenge that bar without questioning the legitimacy of sectarian divisions (although as a matter of identity and heritage, it is not uncommon for individuals to identify themselves as, for instance, "half" of one religion and "half" of another, even where their tenets may be incompatible). Most other nonstate affiliations are not so jealous. One can maintain memberships in any number of advocacy organizations, for example; Amnesty International does not ask that you forgo commitments to other human rights organizations as a condition of membership. Race, however, again presents a restrictive form of membership. At least in the United States, it has been the case that one cannot claim to be both black and white, even as product of both. That is being tested today, with the emergence of a new preference for the designation "mixed race," but it is not clear that the long-standing practice against plural membership in racial communities will erode.

Finally, as a general matter, we consider it legitimate for nonstate communities to discriminate in favor of their members. In most communities, such classifications are taken as a given. No one would question the legitimacy of Amnesty International restricting its directorate elections to dues-paying members. The American Association of Retired People does not have to offer its product discounts to nonmembers. University degrees are not anyone's for the asking, and the person on the street has no right to use the college playing field or libraries. Unions are not obligated to advocate the cause of those not on their rolls. Religions do not have to promise redemption for those of other faiths. And so on. The corporate context might present the most significant exception, one in which some recognition of nonmember interests is being dictated as a norm. The corporate social responsibility movement aims to take account of nonmembers impacted by a corporation's activities. On the other hand, that doesn't stop a corporation from discriminating in favor of its members. Corporations restrict the distribution of profits to shareholders in the form of dividends, and one would expect it to discriminate in favor of its employees over others. Likewise with respect to advocacy organizations that work on behalf of particular groups, which discriminate in favor of that group's members. A disability rights organization does not work to advance the interest of the nondisabled.

This may seem syllogistic, hardly worthy of remark. But it presents a stark contrast to our thinking about the state. We cannot say unhesitatingly any longer that the United States should be able to discriminate against nonmembers, that America should work only in the interests of Americans. That is no longer accepted as a matter of discourse, nor, as we have seen, does it in many ways reflect the practice of American citizenship.

Of course, it was once the case that such discrimination against noncitizens could be taken for granted. There was a time when multiple state memberships were thought an offense against nature, a time when one's membership in the state could be terminated involuntarily, and a time when admission to membership was restricted on a meaningful basis. In considering the parameters of nonstate membership, these practices are all still accepted in a variety of contexts where they are not accepted in the context of citizenship in the state.

THE CITIZENSHIP DILEMMA

That perhaps further illuminates the decline of the national community. A group's ability to discriminate, to demand singular membership, to set the terms of admission and for expulsion—these prerogatives may be necessary to maintaining community cohesion and identity. Michael Walzer finds it difficult even to contemplate the alternative. "Membership as a social good is constituted by our understanding," he observes, "its value is fixed by our work and conversation; and then we are in charge (*who else could be in charge?*) of its distribution."[25] Insofar as a community loses these powers, by whatever cause, it loses the ability to police its boundaries. Insofar as somebody else is in charge of membership decisions, in other words, the understanding and mutual trust that makes for a "community of character" (to use another powerful Walzerian formulation) is undermined, and with it the special bonds that support democratic citizenship. Without the power of definition, the possibility of difference slips away. Difference is what community is all about, at a constitutive level. It is what builds those bonds of loyalty, of allegiance, of a willingness to sacrifice for fellow members.

Where those qualities are increasingly out of place in describing the citizen's relationship to the state, they may now be applicable to nonstate forms of association. Because nonstate communities are free to set their own membership criteria in most respects, they are more likely to be able to sustain the intensity of community ties. This intensity is obviously contingent—stamp collectors aren't going to put their lives on the line for each other—but the upside potential for filial intensity is unlimited in the absence of imposed constraints. That may point to the migration of identity away from the state and to other forms of community.

The move will reflect and satisfy the deep longing for mutual solidarities and trusting relationships. But it will also come at a cost. These communities will be exclusionary, and their terms of exclusion may not be constrained by liberal principles. What of the exclusion by the Seminole tribe of blacks, even where they have a clear historical claim to membership? What of religious rules setting membership by descent on a matrilineal basis only, in a way that is clearly gender-discriminatory? Some of these rules, those most offensive to liberal norms, may be overcome with public law mechanisms, whether national or international. As nonstate communities increasingly span territorial boundaries, international human rights could prove instrumental in mitigating injustice in nonstate membership practices. Nonstate communities may also be constrained by norms articulated and pressed by nongovernmental organizations, so that for example an Amnesty International might press a particular religion with respect to the exclusion of homosexuals. In the short run, however, those tools will constrain such practices at the margins only (if that), and groups will remain largely free to set membership qualifications as they please. These rules and the many others that set high, sometimes insuperable, barriers to community entry are a part of what makes these communities strong.

In this case, then, it is the "citizenship" law of the nonstate community that doubles back to inform our understanding of membership in the state. Exclusion is a premise to community. Exclusion may be unappealing, even discreditable, but inclusion dilutes identity. Insofar as a state-based community defines itself in such a way as to be all-inclusive, it cannot survive as a robust form of community. That is America's dilemma, the citizenship dilemma. To the extent it realizes its aspirations of inclusiveness, it sets the scene for its demise. The more inclusive America becomes as a community, the less special it becomes as a location of identity, of differentness. For those needs, Americans and others will start looking beyond the state.

Conclusion

THROUGHOUT HEATED RECENT debates about immigration policy, reform advocates—President Bush included—played hard on the phrase "a path to citizenship." Regularizing the status of some portion of an enormous population of undocumented aliens was framed in citizenship terms. That surely was one way around touching the political third rail of any form of acknowledged amnesty for illegal immigrants. But more than avoiding political hazards, reform advocates may have been drawn to the ennobling implications of the citizenship angle. The label situated these aliens in the great tradition of assimilation and rejuvenation. It said: these people could be of us, these people want to be Americans, and after all what more is being American than a state of mind and the will to join the project? As the *New York Times* intoned along with the requisite bow to America's history as a nation of immigrants, "[c]itizenship must be the key to reform."[1]

That may serve the politics. But what is actually at stake has little directly to do with citizenship. The real prize is legal residency, not citizenship. It's all about the green card, not the naturalization certificate. As Saskia Sassen notes, claims-making by undocumented aliens surrounding the debates has been "more about the right to have rights than about the desire to become American citizens per se."[2] Undocumented aliens are looking for the greater security that would come with regularized status. (The fact that they have some security already—and political clout—is evidenced by the fact that hundreds of thousands openly took to the streets in the spring of 2006 to protest anti-immigrant legislation then before Congress.)

But citizenship itself is not really at issue here. Those whose presence in the United States might be legalized through immigration reform will have no obligation to become citizens, and indeed many of them will not, in line with declining naturalization rates.

As an incidental sop to nationalists, Bush carefully asserted in his immigration policy platform that "those who swear the oath of citizenship are doing more than completing a legal process, they are making a lifelong pledge to support the values and the laws of America." He reaffirmed the naturalization applicant's "obligation to learn the English language and the customs and values that define our nation," whatever they might consist of. The Office of Citizenship, created in 2002 along with the Department of Homeland Security, is put front and center in White House press releases. Never mind that aside from the superficial redesign of the naturalization exam, its main function appears to be hawking civics flashcards for use in preparing for the test, and even those are perpetually out of stock. And while the *Times* stressed the citizenship angle on immigration reform, the only citizenship-related action item on its editorial agenda has been to keep down naturalization application fees.

Citizenship policy has thus largely gone missing from engagement on the distinct issues of undocumented aliens and immigrant admissions. Which is not to say that the immigration reform debate is irrelevant to the future of American citizenship. On the contrary, the fact that citizenship law issues have figured hardly at all in the debate (or any other immigration policy debate over the last several decades) demonstrates its demotion. One might expect that as part of a grand bargain on immigration, the bar to citizenship would be raised and the "unity of America" (to use another line of the Bush package) restored. But none of the serious reform proposals—including those that would come down hard on immigrants—would change the requirements for citizenship. The House held desultory hearings on dual citizenship from which no serious proposal emerged. Proposals to limit birthright citizenship have drawn more serious public attention, but as in the 1990s those proposals have been complete nonstarters. And at the same time that a 2006 House-approved bill would have maintained a hard line against undocumented aliens, no one appears to have seriously suggested turning the clock back on legal immigrants by making them ineligible for federal benefits. Noncitizens, in other words, are no longer in the legislative crosshairs.

So citizenship practices have been marginal to the great debates on immigration. That may explain why the United States is having such a difficult time orienting itself as a nation on the immigration issue. If immigration were in fact a path to meaningful citizenship, the existing citizenry would have a metric for deciding whom to admit and what to expect of them. As it is, the increasingly unstable sense of identity leaves the country floundering on immigration's premises. What's left are the powerful economic forces driving increased migration and the fact that borders are no longer subject to effective control. Presence, not membership, becomes the end point, and the immigration equation is reduced to labor needs, family unity, and the modicum of resourcefulness necessary to get yourself in. Most everyone who comes has a dream, but it's no longer uniquely American.

Many among the large numbers who have managed to get themselves here (legally or illegally) will become citizens, in the face of lower barriers to naturalization. But many will maintain their homeland citizenship, and otherwise maintain at least an ambiguous and sometimes largely instrumental posture to the formal American tie. A growing population of immigrants will not bother with citizenship. These denizens are on a path to nowhere special vis-à-vis their American citizen neighbors. By persistently inhabiting the same space as the citizenry, they will undermine the sense of territorial solidarity that has been a key feature of the citizenship regime and a core tenet of the dominant American paradigm of liberal governance.

More obviously, the lack of recent attention to citizenship policy also says a lot about the place of citizenship itself. If the most important debate on immigration policy in at least a generation—arguably more important than any other such debate since the turn of the last century—doesn't center citizenship in a meaningful way, then that's pretty good evidence that it is no longer a cardinal feature of identity. A hundred years ago, the United States welcomed immigrants, but only on the sternly nationalist premise of Americanization. Lip service may still be paid to old notions of assimilation. But practice in law and on the ground tells a different story, one in which citizenship has emerged an increasingly porous boundary of human community, matching the increasingly porous boundaries of globalization's other spaces. American citizenship no longer reflects or defines a distinctive identity. That may explain the flagging national project, the sense of anomie that infects most everything about national governance. Governance without shared purpose and a robust feeling of community is unsustainable over the long run. We can see that fading solidarity play out on the terrain of citizenship practice.

Where most others across the political spectrum would use this account as a rallying call for citizenship's revival, this book is not intended to kindle correctives. Indeed, a major theme here has been the irreversibility of citizenship's decline. This has been a forensic exercise, mapping out the descent at the molecular level of citizenship law. This perspective confirms the general perception across American society that America is losing its sense of special social, cultural, and political purpose and that Americans themselves feel less bonded to each other. Those who describe this drift invariably look to restore the intensity of the national tie. Call it patriotism on the right, civic duty on the left—both point in the same direction, toward the formerly elevated place of the nation among our many forms of association. But the law of citizenship points elsewhere.

Lacking alternative foundations of ethnicity or religion, American citizenship has reflected a purer form of state-based association, a sort of control test for the modern nation-state. The result was an association with various contested criteria of membership. Race presented an ascriptive and obviously conflictual barrier to entry in various respects for much of the nation's history, but defining other boundaries of citizenship has also been notoriously difficult. Beyond the trope of civic faith, territorial presence and strong norms against dual citizenship played crucial functions in maintaining a coherent citizenry coinciding with community on the ground. Those backstops are no longer available to shore up community now breached by the global diffusion of culture and democratic governance.

None of which is to devalue the American project as a historical matter or deny the important place of the United States for both its members and the world going forward. The American experience has been remarkable, not the least because of its citizenship practices. Although it has been exclusionary, as are all forms of community, it has offered the best that the nation-state can offer. It may also be the case that the nation-state has offered more than any other form of community, in terms of security, economic and social innovation, and the vindication of individual dignity. That puts the United States at the top of the heap of human history, and it explains the nostalgia that pervades citizenship talk across the political spectrum. There is much to grieve in America's dissipation. America's greatness does not make it for all time.

This book might be difficult to justify if it were aimed only at bringing down the state in our imaginations. That would deny some possibility of human agency. There would be no way to put the thesis to work. But the suggestion here that community may be migrating beyond the state both demands and allows a shift of our energies to other platforms. More analytic capacity should be shifted to understand these alternative locations of community, as much in the popular discourse as in the academic. These new homes for citizenship are ones in which all the possibilities of the state—good and bad—might come to be replicated. If that is where community is moving, then we had better train our sights in those directions by way of attempting to correct injustices and build on virtue.

NOTES

1. *Calvin v. Smith*, 77 Eng. Rep. 377, 382 (K.B. 1608). For a discussion situating *Calvin's Case* in the history of European political and legal theory, see Polly J. Price, Natural Law and Birthright Citizenship in *Calvin's Case* (1608), 9 *Yale Journal of Law and the Humanities* 73 (1997).

2. The Constitution provides that Congress shall have the power to "establish an uniform Rule of Naturalization." U.S. Const. art 1, sec. 8, cl. 4.

3. See 1 Stat. 103 (1790).

4. See Gerald L. Neuman, *Strangers to the Constitution* 34–40 (1996).

5. See James H. Kettner, *The Development of American Citizenship, 1608–1870*, at 318 (1978). As Kettner notes, the Constitution's use of the phrase "natural-born citizen" for purposes of presidential eligibility implies a birthright citizenship principle.

6. See *Scott v. Sandford*, 60 U.S. 393 (1857).

7. I use the term intentionally, where the use of "African American" in a historical context itself poses citizenship questions. See also, for example, Rogers M. Smith, *Civic Ideals: Conflicting Visions of Citizenship in U.S. History* (1997) (using the term).

8. *United States v. Wong Kim Ark*, 169 U.S. 64 (1898).

9. *Elk v. Wilkins*, 112 U.S. 94 (1884).

10. See Act of Feb. 8, 1887, ch. 119, 24 Stat. 388 (so-called Allotment Act, under which lands were dispossessed from tribal control and assigned to individual Native Americans in fee simple); Act of June 2, 1924, ch. 232, 43 Stat. 253 (extending citizenship to all Native Americans born in U.S. territory).

11. One Native American law scholar has argued that the automatic extension of citizenship to Native Americans at birth is destructive of identity. See Robert B. Porter, The Demise of the Ongwehoweh and the Rise of the Native Americans: Redressing the Genocidal Act of Forcing American Citizenship upon Indigenous Peoples, 15 *Harvard BlackLetter Law Journal* 107 (1999). A group of Puerto Rican nationals attempted to renounce their

U.S. citizenship while remaining resident in Puerto Rico, an attempt rejected by the State Department and the courts. See *Lozada Colon v. U.S. Department of State*, 2 F. Supp. 2d 43 (D.D.C. 1998).

12. Peter H. Schuck and Rogers M. Smith, *Citizenship Without Consent: Illegal Aliens in the American Polity* (1985).

13. See, for example, Gerald L. Neuman, Back to *Dred Scott?* 24 *San Diego Law Review* 485 (1987); Joseph H. Carens, Who Belongs? Theoretical and Legal Questions About Birthright Citizenship in the United States, 37 *University of Toronto Law Journal* 413 (1987); David A. Martin, Membership and Consent: Abstract or Organic?, 11 *Yale Journal of International Law* 278 (1985–1986).

14. See, for example, H.J. Res. 64, 104th Cong. (1995).

15. See Neuman, *Strangers*, at 165.

16. See, for example, Children Without a Country, *Washington Post*, Aug. 10, 1996, at A18; Tampering with a Birthright, *Chicago Tribune*, Dec. 27, 1995, at 14; A Birthright Denied, *Boston Globe*, Aug. 22, 1993, at 72.

17. See Neuman, *Strangers*, ch. 2.

18. See Rogers Brubaker, *Citizenship and Nationhood in France and Germany* 32 (1992).

19. See Christine J. Hsieh, American Born Legal Permanent Residents? A Constitutional Amendment Proposal, 12 *Georgetown Immigration Law Journal* 511 (1997–1998) (proposing legal residency but not citizenship for children of noncitizen, nonlegal residents).

20. See Michael Walzer, *Spheres of Justice* 52–61 (1983).

21. See Helen Elizabeth Hartnell, Belonging: Citizenship and Migration in the European Union and in Germany, *Issues in Legal Scholarship: Richard Buxbaum and German Reintegration* (2006), available online at http://www.bepress.com/ils/iss9/art12.

22. See Moisés Naím, The New Diaspora, *Foreign Policy*, July–August 2002, at 96. The new characteristics of diasporas are the subject of a growing academic literature. See, for example, Arjun Appadurai, *Modernity at Large: Cultural Dimensions of Globalization* (1996); Robert C. Smith, *Mexican New York: Transnational Lives of New Immigrants* (2006); and Peggy Levitt, *The Transnational Villagers* (2001).

23. Mark Wyman, *Round-Trip to America: The Immigrants Return to Europe 1880–1930*, at 3–14 (1993) (providing statistics on immigrants in the United States who returned to Europe).

24. Graeme Hugo, Circular Migration: Keeping Development Rolling?, *Migration Information Source*, Migration Policy Institute (June 2003), available online at http://www.migrationinformation.org/Feature/display.cfm?ID=129.

25. See Ann Gorman, Affluent Cross Border to U.S. for Childbirth, *Los Angeles Times*, Apr. 17, 2003, § 2, at 1.

26. On L visas issued to multinational executives, see Ruth Ellen Wasem, Immigration Policy for Intracompany Transferees (L Visa): Issues and Legislation, *Congressional Research Service* (Jan. 26, 2006). For recent figures on the issuance of nonimmigrant visas in all

categories, see U.S. Department of State, Report of the Visa Office 2005, available online at http://www.travel.state.gov/visa/frvi/statistics/statistics_2787.html.

27. As of 2003, of an estimated 34 million foreign-born residents, 11.3 million were naturalized citizens, 12.2 million were legal permanent residents, and 9 million were undocumented, which would leave 1.5 million foreign-born on temporary visas. See Michael Fix, Jeffrey S. Passel, and Kenneth Sucher, Immigrant Families and Workers: Trends in Naturalization, Urban Institute (Sept. 2003), at 2, available online at http://www.urban.org/UploadedPDF/310847_trends_in_naturalization.pdf.

28. Fernando Riosmena, Return Versus Settlement Among Undocumented Mexican Migrants 1980–1996, in *Crossing the Border: Research from the Mexican Migration Project* 265 (Jorge Durand and Douglas S. Massey, eds., 2004); Douglas S. Massey, Five Myths About Immigration: Common Misconceptions Underlying U.S. Border-Enforcement Policy, *Immigration Policy in Focus*, American Immigration Law Foundation (Aug. 2005), available online at http://www.ailf.org/ipc/infocus/2005_fivemyths.pdf.

29. Bashir Ahmed and J. Gregory Robinson, Estimates of Emigration of the Foreign-Born Population: 1980–1990, U.S. Bureau of the Census (Dec. 1994), available online at http://www.census.gov/population/www/documentation/twps0009/twps0009.html.

30. Appadurai, *Modernity at Large*, supra, at 172.

31. See A. Dianne Schmidley and J. Gregory Robinson, Measuring the Foreign-Born Population in the United States with the Current Population Survey: 1994–2002, U.S. Bureau of the Census (Oct. 2003), available online at http://www.census.gov/population/www/documentation/twps0073.html.

32. See Larry Rohter, Island Life Not Idyllic for Youths from U.S., *New York Times*, Feb. 20, 1998, at A4.

33. See, for example, Celia W. Dugger, In India, an Arranged Marriage of 2 Worlds, *New York Times*, July 20, 1998, at A1; Paula Span, Marriage at First Sight, *Washington Post*, Feb. 23, 2003.

34. See H.J. Res 129 (103d Cong.) (1993) (extending citizenship to children of citizens and legal residents only).

35. See Act of Mar. 26, 1790, ch. 3, 1 Stat. 103.

36. See Equal Nationality Act, Pub. L. No. 73–250, 48 Stat. 797 (1934). See also Martha Gardner, *The Qualities of a Citizen: Women, Immigration and Citizenship, 1870–1965*, at ch. 9 (2005).

37. See 66 Stat. 236 (1952).

38. *Rogers v. Bellei*, 401 U.S. 815, 834 (1971).

39. The primary jus sanguinis rules for transmitting citizenship at birth are found in sec. 301(c) and (g) of the Immigration and Nationality Act, 8 U.S.C. § 1401.

40. For academic perspectives on the U.S.–Mexico border, see, for example, *The U.S.-Mexico Border: Transcending Divisions, Contesting Identities* (David Spener and Kathleen Staudt, eds., 1998); *The Late Great Mexican Border: Reports from a Disappearing Line* (Bobby Byrd and Susannah M. Byrd, eds., 1996).

41. See Texas Education Code § 54.060(b) and (c) (providing for in-state tuition at certain state universities for residents "of a nation situated adjacent to Texas"). This provision is distinct from that granting in-state tuition to undocumented alien residents of Texas; the break here is for residents of Mexico. More than 10 percent of the students enrolled at the University of Texas at El Paso are Mexican residents.

42. Ronnie D. Lipschutz, Constituting Political Community: Globalization, Citizenship, and Human Rights, in *People Out of Place: Globalization, Human Rights, and the Citizenship Gap* 29, 32 (Alison Brysk and Gershon Shafir, eds., 2004)

CHAPTER 2

1. See Peter Riesenberg, *A History of Citizenship: Sparta to Washington* 20–23 (2002).

2. On the history of English naturalization, see James J. Kettner, *The Development of American Citizenship 1608–1870*, at 65–78 (1978).

3. Philip Gleason, American Identity and Americanization, in *Concepts of Ethnicity* 57, 62 (William Petersen et al., eds., 1982).

4. See Act of Mar. 26, 1790, ch. 3, 1 Stat. 103.

5. See Rogers M. Smith, *Civic Ideals: Conflicting Visions of Citizenship in U.S. History* (1997).

6. For a description of cases prompting legislation waiving the oath requirement on disability grounds, see Hector Becerra, She's One Step Closer to Citizenship; House Oks a Bill That'll Let Vijai Rajan, a Disabled Anaheim Woman, Obtain Her Goal Despite Being Unable to Say or Comprehend the Oath, *Los Angeles Times*, Oct. 11, 2000, at B1.

7. See, most notably, Georgie Anne Geyer, *Americans No More* 137–89 (1996); John J. Miller, *The Unmaking of Americans: How Multiculturalism Has Undermined the Assimilation Ethic* 147–73 (1998).

8. See 8 U.S.C. § 1427(a)(1).

9. See 8 U.S.C. § 1430(a) (three-year residency for spouses of U.S. citizens); 8 U.S.C. § 1430(b) (eliminating residency requirement for certain other classes of aliens).

10. See 8 U.S.C. § 1439 and 1440.

11. John R. Logan, et al., Immigrant Enclaves and Ethnic Communities in New York and Los Angeles, 67 *American Sociological Review* 299, 300 (2002).

12. See, for example, Kevin Sack, Far from Mexico, Making a Place Like Home, *New York Times*, July 30, 2001, at A1; Patrick J. McDonnell, Mexican Arrivals Seek New Frontiers: Far-Flung Regions Like Maine and Alaska Join in Witnessing Largest Sustained Mass Migration to U.S., *Los Angeles Times*, Jan. 1, 1998, at A1.

13. See 8 U.S.C. § 1423.

14. See 8 U.S.C. § 1423(b)(2).

15. As many as 30 percent of naturalization applicants in some areas seek disability waivers from the language and civics tests. See Patrick J. McDonnell, INS Struggles with Waivers for Disability, *Los Angeles Times*, July 31, 1998, at B1.

16. Gerald L. Neuman, Justifying U.S. Naturalization Policies, 35 *Virginia Journal of International Law* 237, 267 (1994).

17. According the 2000 census data, almost 30 million residents identify themselves as Spanish speakers, of which just under 8 million speak English "not well" or not at all. Overall, 47 million speak a language other than English at home. More than 20 million residents of the United States speak English less than very well. See Hyon B. Shin and Rosalind Bruno, Language Use and English-Speaking Ability: Census 2000 Brief (October 2003) (available on U.S. Census Web site).

18. See David Crystal, *English as a Global Language* (2d ed., 2003); The Coming Global Tongue, *The Economist*, Dec. 21, 1996.

19. See Ted Anthony, The English Conquest; Nearly a Quarter of the Human Population—Whether They Like It or Not—Are Using What Is Fast Becoming the World's First Global Language, *Chicago Tribune*, Apr. 24, 2000, at N1.

20. See John Tagliabue, In Europe, Going Global Means, Alas, English, *New York Times*, May 19, 2002, § 1, at 15.

21. Joseph Berger, Wave of Foreign TV Becomes "Emotional Outlet" for Immigrants, *New York Times*, Feb. 23, 2004, at B1; Celia W. Dugger, A Tower of Babel, in Wood Pulp, *New York Times*, Jan. 19, 1997, § 1, at 25.

22. The sample questions are available in *A Guide to Naturalization* issued by the Bureau of U.S. Citizenship and Immigration Services of the Department of Homeland Security, on its Web site at http://www.uscis.gov/natzguide.

23. See Miller, supra, at 159.

24. See August Gribbin, Stir in the Melting Pot, *Washington Times*, Nov. 26, 2000, at C1.

25. See Peter J. Spiro, Questioning Barriers to Naturalization, 13 *Georgetown Immigration Law Journal* 479, 486–87 (1999).

26. See Noah M. J. Pickus, Becoming American/America Becoming: Final Report of the Duke University Workshop on Immigration and Citizenship 28 (1997), available online at http://kenan.ethics.duke.edu/PDF/BecomingAmerican–AmericaBecoming.pdf.

27. Thomas L. Friedman, Global Village Idiocy, *New York Times*, May 12, 2002, § 4, at 15; Press Release, McDonald's and MTV Launch Global Music Partnership to Strengthen Connection with Young Adult Audience, 2/10/2005, available online at http://www.mcdonalds.com/usa/news/2005/conpr_02102005.html.

28. McAtlas Shrugged, *Foreign Policy*, May–June 2001, at 26, 32. See also James L. Watson, China's Big Mac Attack, *Foreign Affairs*, May–June 2000, at 120.

29. Robert W. McChesney, The New Global Media, in *The Global Transformations Reader* 266 (David Held and Anthony McGrew, eds., 2000).

30. See, for example, Kevin R. Johnson, "Aliens" and the U.S. Immigration Laws: The Social and Legal Construction of Nonpersons, 28 *University of Miami Inter-American Law Review* 263 (1996–97).

31. See U.S. Commission on Immigration Reform, *Becoming an American: Immigration and Immigrant Policy* 26 (1997).

32. Citations for legislative source materials included in this chapter can be found in Spiro, supra.

33. See Barry Newman, Foreign Legions: Lots of Noncitizens Feel Right at Home in U.S. Political Races, *Wall Street Journal*, Oct. 31, 1997, at A1.

34. See Neuman, supra, at 258.

35. See 42 U.S.C. § 1973aa–1a.

36. National Commission on Federal Election Reform, *To Assure Pride and Confidence in the Electoral Process* 28 (Aug. 2001); Remarks by the President on Federal Election Reform, July 31, 2001, available online at http://www.whitehouse.gov/news/releases/2001/07/200107 31-1.html.

37. *Dunn v. Blumstein*, 405 U.S. 330 (1972).

38. Linda Bosniak, The Citizenship of Aliens, 56 *Social Text* 29 (1998).

39. See *Boddie v. Connecticut*, 401 U.S. 371 (1971).

40. Noncitizens are not entitled to the spousal exemption from estate taxes. Thus, when a U.S. citizen dies, her noncitizen spouse will be required to pay estate taxes where a citizen spouse would not.

41. Naturalization applications reached a peak of more than 1.4 million in 1997. Receding to fewer than 500,000 by 2000, applications saw a short spike in 2002 (to over 700,000), most likely explained by 9/11. In 2003 fewer than 525,000 aliens applied for citizenship. See Department of Homeland Security, *Yearbook of Immigration Statistics: 2003*, at 137 (2004).

42. See U.S. Census Bureau, *Profile of the Foreign-Born Population in the United States: 2000*, at 20 (2001).

CHAPTER 3

1. Quoted in Peter J. Spiro, Dual Nationality and the Meaning of Citizenship, 46 *Emory Law Journal* 1411 (1997).

2. 9 Opinions of the Attorney General 356, 361 (1859).

3. Act of January 29, 1795, ch. 20, § 1, 1 Stat. 414.

4. 3 John B. Moore, *A Digest of International Law* 713 (1906) (annual message of President Grant, Dec. 7, 1874).

5. Act of March 2, 1907, ch. 2534, § 2, 34 Stat. 1228.

6. Id. The law was upheld by the Supreme Court in *Mackenzie v. Hare*, 239 U.S. 299 (1915).

7. See Act Relative to the Naturalization and Citizenship of Married Women (Cable Act), Pub. L. No. 67–346, § 3, 42 Stat. 1021 (1922) (law continued to strip U.S. citizenship from "any woman citizen who marrie[d] an alien ineligible to [U.S.] citizenship"); Act of Mar. 3, 1931, ch. 442, § 4(a), 46 Stat. 1511–1512 (1931) (repealing remaining termination provision).

8. See Naturalization Act, 1870, 33 and 34 Vict. 168, ch. 14, § 6.

9. Thomas Sowell, *Migrations and Cultures: A World View* 25 (1996).

10. See Richard W. Flournoy Jr., Dual Nationality and Election, 30 *Yale Law Journal* 693 (1921).

11. See Nationality Act of 1940, ch. 876, § 401(c), 54 Stat. 1137, 1169.

12. See Nationality Act of 1952, ch. 477, § 350, 66 Stat. 163, 269.

13. 356 U.S. 44 (1958).

14. Hague Convention on Certain Questions Relating to the Conflict of Nationality Laws, Apr. 12, 1930, 179 L.N.T.S. 89, 101.

15. Report of the International Law Commission to the General Assembly on Multiple Nationality, U.N. Doc. A/CN.4/83 (1954), at 19.

16. Nissim Bar-Yaacov, *Dual Nationality* 4, 266 (1961).

17. John P. Roche, The Loss of American Nationality—The Development of Statutory Expatriation, 99 *University of Pennsylvania Law Review* 25, 32 (1950) (birthright dual nationals can now "carry such dual nationality with them from birth to the grave").

18. 387 U.S. 253 (1967).

19. For a history of the *Afroyim* case and its aftermath, see Peter J. Spiro, *Afroyim*: Vaunting Citizenship, Presaging Transnationality, in *Immigration Law Stories* (David A. Martin and Peter H. Schuck, eds., 2005).

20. See Thomas M. Franck, Clan and Superclan: Loyalty, Identity and Community in Law and Practice, 90 *American Journal of International Law* 359, 379 (1996); Stephen Kinzer, Yugoslav-American in Belgrade Leads Serbs Who Don't Follow, *New York Times*, Aug. 24, 1992, at A1.

21. See U.S. Department of State, Advice About Possible Loss of U.S. Citizenship and Dual Nationality, reprinted in 67 *Interpreter Releases* 1092, 1093 (1990).

22. See Stanley A. Renshon, *The 50% American: Immigration and National Identity in an Age of Terror* 9 (2005).

23. Frances Stead Sellers, A World Wishing to Cast a Vote, *Washington Post*, Nov. 21, 2004, at B1.

24. On the political status of external citizens, see Peter J. Spiro, Perfecting Political Diaspora, 81 *New York University Law Review* 207 (2006).

25. See Hannah Arendt, *The Origins of Totalitarianism* 292 (1951) (2d ed., 1966) (noting that for stateless persons, "the loss of national rights was identical with the loss of human rights").

26. See Convention on Reduction of Cases of Multiple Nationality and Military Obligations in Cases of Multiple Nationality, May 6, 1963, 634 U.N. Treaty Series 221; Council of Europe, European Convention on Nationality, arts. 14–17, ETS No. 166, Nov. 6, 1997, 37 *International Legal Materials* 44.

27. See Enforcement First Immigration Reform Act of 2005, H.R. 3938, 109th Cong. § 703.

28. See, for example, Renshon, *The 50% American*, supra; Georgie Anne Geyer, *Americans No More* (1997); John Fonte, Dual Allegiance: A Challenge to Immigration Reform and Patriotic Assimilation (Center for Immigration Studies Backgrounder, Nov. 2005), available online at http://www.cis.org/articles/2005/back1205.html.

29. See Linda Bosniak, Multiple Nationality and the Postnational Transformation of Citizenship, 42 *Virginia Journal of International Law* 979 (2002).

30. See Peter H. Schuck, *Citizens, Strangers, and In-Betweens: Essays on Immigration and Citizenship* 231 (1998).

31. See Ruth Rubio-Marín, *Immigration as a Democratic Challenge: Citizenship and Inclusion in Germany and the United States* (2000).

32. See Schuck, supra, at 228.

33. Greta Gilbertson and Audrey Singer, Naturalization Under Changing Conditions of Membership: Dominican Immigrants in New York City, in *Immigration Research for a New Century* 157 (Nancy Foner et al., eds., 2000).

CHAPTER 4

1. *Perez v. Brownell*, 356 U.S. 44, 64 (1957). Although Warren's pronouncement was delivered in his dissent in *Perez*, the case upholding the deprivation of citizenship on grounds of voting in a foreign political election, his reasoning was adopted in the Court's subsequent decision in *Afroyim v. Rusk*, which limited the government's power to terminate an American's nationality against his will. See *Afroyim v. Rusk*, 387 U.S. 253 (1967).

2. See Alexander M. Bickel, *The Morality of Consent* 53–54 (1975).

3. *Wong Wing v. United States*, 163 U.S. 228, 237 (1896).

4. See *In re Ross*, 140 U.S. 453 (1891).

5. See *Yick Wo v. Hopkins*, 118 U.S. 356 (1886).

6. See Peter J. Spiro, The States and Immigration in an Era of Demi-Sovereignties, 35 *Virginia Journal of International Law* 121 (1994).

7. See Homestead Act of 1862, 12 Stat. 392, ch. 75, §1 (repealed 1976); see also Polly J. Price, Alien Land Restrictions in the American Common Law: Exploring the Relative Autonomy Paradigm, 43 *American Journal of Legal History* 152, 176 (1999).

8. See Luis F. B. Plascencia et al., The Decline of Barriers to Immigrant Economic and Political Rights in American States, 1977–2001, 37 *International Migration Review* 5, 9 (2003).

9. See, for example, *Terrace v. Thompson*, 263 U.S. 197 (1923) (land ownership); *Patsone v. Pennsylvania*, 232 U.S. 138 (1914) (hunting licenses); *Clark v. Deckebach*, 274 U.S. 392 (1927) (pool halls).

10. See *Graham v. Richardson*, 403 U.S. 365 (1971).

11. See *Foley v. Connelie*, 435 U.S. 291 (1978) (police officers); *Ambach v. Norwick*, 441 U.S. 68 (1979) (public school teachers).

12. See *Graham v. Richardson*, supra.

13. See *Mathews v. Diaz*, 426 US 67 (1976) (federal welfare measure discriminating against aliens); *Hampton v. Mow Sun Wong*, 426 U.S. 88 (1976) (citizenship as eligibility criterion for federal civil service).

14. See, for instance, Deborah Sontag, In a Homeland Far from Home, *New York Times Magazine*, Nov. 16, 2003, at 48, recounting the case of a Cambodian native deported for an adolescent crime after having spent most of his life in the United States.

15. *Trop v. Dulles*, 356 U.S. 86, 102 (1958).

16. See 8 U.S.C. §§ 1101, 1151 (1994) (no cap for children, parents, or spouses of U.S. citizens); 8 U.S.C. § 1153(a)(2) (quotas apply to spouses and children of permanent resident aliens).

17. 8 U.S.C. § 1229(c)(3)(A).

18. See 3 Stanley Gordon, Charles Mailman, and Stephen Yale-Loehr, *Immigration Law and Procedure* § 35.02 (2007).

19. See Congressional Research Service, Immigration Enforcement Within the United States (Apr. 6, 2006), at 17–18, 58.

20. See Douglas S. Massey, Backfire at the Border: Why Enforcement without Legalization Cannot Stop Illegal Immigration (Center for Trade Policy Studies, Cato Institute, June 2005), at 6–7, available online at http://www.freetrade.org/pubs/pas/tpa-029.pdf.

21. See, for example, Danna Harman, Illegal Migrants Persist Despite Fences, Danger; Mexicans Try Many Routes to Get into USA, *USA Today*, Mar. 30, 2006, at 6A.

22. See Personal Responsibility and Work Opportunity Reconciliation Act of 1996, Pub. L. 104–193, § 402, 110 Stat. 2105, 2264.

23. See, for example, Kevin R. Johnson, Public Benefits and Immigration: The Intersection of Immigration Status, Ethnicity, Gender, and Class, 42 *UCLA Law Review* 1509 (1995).

24. See Ann Morse et al., America's Newcomers: Mending the Safety Net: for Immigrants (National Conference of State Legislatures, 1998), executive summary available online at http://www.ncsl.org/statefed/execsumm.htm.

25. Steven Greenhouse, Immigrant Workers Find Support in a Growing Network of Assistance Centers, *New York Times*, Apr. 23, 2006, § 1, at 22.

26. *Plyler v. Doe*, 457 U.S. 202 (1982); Dana Canedy, Hospitals Feeling Strain from Illegal Immigrants, *New York Times*, Aug. 25, 2005, § 1, at 16.

27. See, for example, Patrick McGee, Being Illegal Doesn't Hinder Privileges, *Fort Worth Star-Telegram*, May 10, 2006.

28. See Rachel Swairns, Old ID Card Gives New Status to Mexicans in U.S., *New York Times*, Aug. 25, 2003, at A1.

29. See Jamin B. Raskin, Legal Aliens, Local Citizens: The Historical, Constitutional and Theoretical Meanings of Alien Suffrage, 141 *University of Pennsylvania Law Review* 1391 (1993).

30. Hiroshi Motomura, *Americans in Waiting: The Lost Story of Immigration and Citizenship in the United States* 122 (2006).

31. See 2 U.S.C. § 441e (prohibiting contributions by foreign nationals, but excluding permanent residents from the bar). Permanent resident aliens are also able to make campaign donations under state law in, for example, California, New York, and Texas.

32. See Note, "Foreign" Campaign Contributions and the First Amendment, 110 *Harvard Law Review* 1886 (1997).

33. See Barry Newman, Foreign Legions: Lots of Noncitizens Feel Right at Home in U.S. Political Races, *Wall Street Journal*, Oct. 31, 1997, at A1.

34. See Heather MacDonald, Mexico's Undiplomatic Diplomats, *City Journal* (Autumn 2005).

35. See Peter J. Spiro, Realizing Constitutional and International Norms in the Wake of September 11, in *The Constitution in Wartime* (Mark Tushnet, ed., 2004).

36. *Hamdi v. Rumsfeld*, 542 U.S. 507 (2004); Eric Lichtblau, In Legal Shift, U.S. Charges Detainee in Terrorism Case, *New York Times*, Nov. 23, 2005, at A1.

37. See 8 U.S.C. §§ 1425, 1426.

38. Act of June 19, 1951, ch. 144, 65 Stat. 75, amending ch. 625, 62 Stat. 604 (1948).

39. William W. Fitzhugh Jr. and Charles Cheney Hyde, The Drafting of Neutral Aliens by the United States, 36 *American Journal of International Law* 369 (1942); Charles E. Roh Jr. and Frank K. Upham, The Status of Aliens Under United States Draft Laws, 13 *Harvard International Law Journal* 501 (1972).

40. One could, of course, abandon one's residency status by way of avoiding conscription. This option would increasingly be available to those citizens who hold alternate nationality, who could renounce U.S. citizenship if faced with the draft.

41. See Linda S. Bosniak, The Citizenship of Aliens, 56 *Social Text* 29 (1998); see also T. Alexander Aleinikoff, *Semblances of Sovereignty: The Constitution, the State, and American Citizenship* ch. 7 (2002).

42. See John B. Moore, *A Digest of International Law* § 502 (1906).

43. See, for example, Craig S. Smith, Two Chinese Residents of U.S. Sentenced to Prison by Beijing, *New York Times*, July 25, 2001, at A1.

44. See, for example, Mary Jordan, Unknown and Alone in Mexico, Missing American Got Lost in Bureaucracy, *Washington Post*, Aug. 9, 2003, at A1 (reporting how Americans can languish for months in Mexican prison before receiving consular attention).

45. *United States v. Verdugo-Urquidez*, 494 U.S. 259 (1990).

46. *Rasul v. Bush*, 542 U.S. 466 (2004).

47. See Uniformed and Overseas Citizens Absentee Voting Act, 42 U.S.C. §§ 1973 ff et seq.

48. See David Barstow and Don Van Natta, Jr., How Bush Took Florida: Mining the Overseas Absentee Vote, *New York Times*, July 15, 2001, § 1, at 1.

CHAPTER 5

1. Peter Brimelow, *Alien Nation: Common Sense about America's Immigration Disaster* 10 (1996).

2. Rogers M. Smith, *Civic Ideals: Conflicting Visions of Citizenship in U.S. History* (1997).

3. See Georgie Anne Geyer, *Americans No More* 43 (1996), describing a call on the part of a militia leader to "live without citizenship."

4. Id. at 53.

5. John J. Miller, *The Unmaking of Americans: How Multiculturalism Has Undermined America's Assimilation Ethic* 7 (1998).

6. Samuel P. Huntington, *Who Are We? The Challenges to America's National Identity* 365 (2004).

7. See Stanley A. Renshon, *The 50% American: Immigration and National Identity in an Age of Terror* 145 (2005). For an earlier articulation of the "psychological conflict" argument, at a time when the observation had more force, see Nissim Bar-Yaacov, *Dual Nationality* 159 (1961). See also Huntington, supra, at 204–213.

8. Miller, supra, at 149.

9. See Scott Veale, Snoop Doggy Roosevelt, *New York Times*, July 2, 2000, §4, at 7.

10. Smith, supra, at 506.

11. Bonnie Honig, *Democracy and the Foreigner* 109 (2001).

12. Michael Walzer, *What It Means to Be an American* 29 (1996).

13. Kenneth L. Karst, *Belonging to America: Equal Citizenship and the Constitution* 41 (1989).

14. Quoted in David A. Hollinger, *Postethnic America: Beyond Multiculturalism* 134 (1995).

15. Jürgen Habermas, Citizenship and National Identity: Some Reflections on the Future of Europe, 12 *Praxis International* 1 (1992).

16. Michael Walzer, most notably, in *Spheres of Justice* 52–63 (1983).

17. For example, an immigrant concentration in one California congressional district (the 33rd) allowed the election of a representative with fewer than 50,000 votes, the lowest of any in the country. See Dudley L. Poston Jr., et al., Remaking the Political Landscape: The Impact of Illegal and Legal Immigration on Congressional Apportionment, Center for Immigration Studies Backgrounder (October 2003), available online at http://www.cis.org/articles/2003/back1403.pdf.

18. Honig, supra, at 93.

19. Ruth Rubio-Marín, *Immigration as a Democratic Challenge: Citizenship and Inclusion in Germany and the United States* (2000).

20. Kenneth L. Karst, The Bonds of American Nationhood, 21 *Cardozo Law Review* 1141, 1179 (2000); Hans Kohn, *American Nationalism: An Interpretive Essay* 144 (1961).

21. John Rawls, *Political Liberalism* 12 (1993).

22. Quoted in Walzer, *Spheres of Justice*, supra, at 50.

23. Walzer, *Spheres of Justice*, supra, at 33.

24. Id. at 44.

25. Seyla Benhabib, *The Rights of Others: Aliens, Residents, and Citizens* 219 (2004).

26. Walzer, *Spheres of Justice*, supra, at 59.

27. Karst, *Cardozo Law Review*, supra, at 1160.

28. See Barry Newman, Foreign Legions: Lots of Noncitizens Feel Right at Home in U.S. Political Races, *Wall Street Journal*, Oct. 31, 1997, at A1.

29. See John Stuart Mill, Considerations on Representative Government, in *On Liberty and Other Essays* 203, 427 (1991) (observing that strongest national roots are found in the "identity of political antecedents; the possession of a national history, and consequent community of recollections; collective pride and humiliation, pleasure and regret, connected with incidents of the past").

30. Arthur M. Schlesinger Jr., *The Disuniting of America: Reflections on a Multicultural Society* 146 (1998).

31. See David A. Martin, New Rules on Dual Nationality for a Democratizing Globe: Between Rejection and Embrace, 14 *Georgetown Immigration Law Journal* 1 (1999); T. Alexander Aleinikoff, *Between Principles and Politics: The Direction of U.S. Citizenship Policy* 36 (1998).

32. See, for example, Peter H. Schuck, Plural Citizenships, in *Immigration and Citizenship in the 21st Century* 149, 178 (Noah M.J. Pickus, ed., 1998).

33. Noah M. J. Pickus, *True Faith and Allegiance: Immigration and American Civic Nationalism* 182 (2005).

34. Hollinger, supra, at 140.

35. Michael Walzer, *Obligations: Essays on Disobedience, War, and Citizenship* 218 (1970).

36. Robert Reich, *The Work of Nations* 119 (1991).

37. Iris Marion Young, *Justice and the Politics of Difference* 190 (1990).

38. David Miller, *On Nationality* 139 (1995).

39. Joseph Raz, Multiculturalism: A Liberal Perspective, *Dissent*, Winter 1994, at 67.

40. Schlesinger, supra, at 141.

41. Young, supra, at 172.

42. Walzer, *Spheres of Justice*, supra, at 34, 39.

43. Benjamin R. Barber, The Rights of We the People Are All the Rights There Are, in *A Passion for Democracy* 60, 72 (1998).

44. Walzer, *Spheres of Justice*, supra, at 32.

45. See, for example, Jack L. Goldsmith and Eric A. Posner, *The Limits of International Law* (2005).

46. Yasemin Soysal, *Limits of Citizenship: Migrants and Postnational Membership in Europe* 142 (1994).

47. Keith Faulks, *Citizenship* 37 (2000).

48. Arjun Appadurai, *Modernity at Large: Cultural Dimensions of Globalization* 171 (1996).

CHAPTER 6

1. Arjun Appadurai, *Modernity at Large: Cultural Dimensions of Globalization* 158 (1996).

2. Peter W. Singer, *Corporate Warriors: The Rise of the Privatized Military Industry* (2004); Laura A. Dickinson, Government for Hire: Privatizing Foreign Affairs and the

Problem of Accountability Under International Law, 47 *William and Mary Law Review* 135 (2005).

3. See Steven R. Ratner, Corporations and Human Rights: A Theory of Legal Responsibility, 111 *Yale Law Journal* 443 (2001).

4. Anthony R. Benedetto, The Impact on "The Vanishing Trial" if People of Faith Were Faithful to Religious Principles of Settling Disputes without Litigation, 6 *Pepperdine Dispute Resolution Law Journal* 253 (2006).

5. See, for example, Edward J. Blakely and Mary Gail Sndyer, *Fortress America: Gated Communities in the United States* (1997)

6. See Timothy C. Shiell, *Campus Hate Speech on Trial* (1998).

7. See James A. R. Nafziger, International Sports Law: A Replay of Characteristics and Trends, 86 *American Journal of International Law* 489 (1992); Brendan I. Koerner, Where Do Athletes Go to Court? *Slate*, July 1, 2004.

8. See Neil Weinsock Netanel, Cyberspace Self-Governance: A Skeptical View from Liberal Democratic Theory, 88 *California Law Review* 395 (2000).

9. Will Kymlicka and Wayne Norman, Return of the Citizen: A Survey of Recent Work on Citizenship Theory, 104 *Ethics* 352, 363 (1994).

10. See Laurence R. Helfer, Whither the UDRP: Autonomous, Americanized, or Cosmopolitan?, 12 *Cardozo Journal of International and Comparative Law* 493, 495 (2004).

11. T. H. Marshall, *Citizenship and Social Class, and Other Essays* (1950).

12. On the institutional logic of such relative generosity at the state level, see Peter J. Spiro, Learning to Live with Immigration Federalism, 29 *Connecticut Law Review* 1627 (1997).

13. Index of Global Philanthrophy 2006; Richard Boudreaux, The New Foreign Aid, *Los Angeles Times*, Apr. 16, 2006, at A1.

14. See Ginger Thompson, Mexico's Migrants Profit from Dollars Sent Home, *New York Times*, Feb. 23, 2005, at A1.

15. See Lan Cao, Looking at Communities and Markets, 74 *Notre Dame Law Review* 841 (1999).

16. See Gordon B. Dahl and Michael R. Ransom, The 10% Flat Tax: Tithing and the Definition of Income, 40 *Economic Inquiry* 120 (2002); Dean R. Hoge, *Money Matters: Personal Giving in American Churches* (1996); U.S. General Accounting Office, Taxpayer Compliance: Analyzing the Nature of the Income Tax Gap (Jan. 9, 1997). Taxpayer compliance falls to 68 percent where income is not subject to third-party reporting or withholding.

17. See Jessi Hempel and Lauren Gard, The Corporate Givers: U.S. Companies Have Discovered That Global Philanthropy Can Reap Big Dividends, *Business Week*, Nov. 29, 2004, at 100.

18. See, for example, Peter J. Spiro, New Global Potentates? Nongovernmental Organizations and the "Unregulated" Marketplace, 18 *Cardozo Law Review* 957 (1996); Elliot J. Shrage, *Promoting International Worker Rights through Private Voluntary Initiatives: Public*

Relations or Public Policy? (2004); Gary Gereffi et al., The NGO-Industrial Complex, *Foreign Policy*, July–Aug. 2001, at 56.

19. See Naomi Roht-Arriaza, Shifting the Point of Regulation: The International Organization for Standardization and Global Lawmaking on Trade and the Environment, 22 *Ecology Law Quarterly* 479 (1995).

20. Richard Falk and Andrew Strauss, Toward Global Parliament, *Foreign Affairs*, Jan.–Feb. 2001, at 212.

21. Ruth W. Grant and Robert O. Keohane, Accountability and Abuses of Power in World Politics, 99 *American Political Science Review* 29, 42 (2005).

22. See Steve Charnovitz, A World Environment Organization, 27 *Columbia Journal of Environmental Law* 323 (2002); Geoffrey Palmer, New Ways to Make International Environmental Law, 86 *American Journal of International Law* 259 (1992).

23. The Hostage Act of 1868 declared expatriation "a natural and inherent right of all people." Act of July 27, 1868, 15 Stat. 223 (codified at 22 U.S.C. § 1732). The International Covenant on Civil and Political Rights provides that "everyone shall be free to leave any country, including his own."

24. See, for example, Joseph Raz, Multiculturalism: A Liberal Perspective, in *Ethics in the Public Domain* 170, 187 (1994); Leslie Green, Rights of Exit, 4 *Legal Theory* 165 (1998).

25. Michael Walzer, *Spheres of Justice* 32 (1983) (emphasis supplied).

CONCLUSION

1. See They Are America, *New York Times*, Feb. 18, 2007, § 4, at 11 (editorial).

2. Saskia Sassen, The Bits of a New Immigration Reality: A Bad Fit with Current Policy, in *Social Science Research Council, Border Battles: The U.S. Immigration Debates*, available online at borderbattles.ssrc.org (2006).

SELECTED BIBLIOGRAPHY

Aleinikoff, Thomas Alexander. *Semblances of Sovereignty: The Constitution, the State, and American Citizenship.* Cambridge, Mass., Harvard University Press (2002).

Aleinikoff, Thomas Alexander. *Between Principles and Politics: The Direction of U.S. Citizenship Policy.* Washington, D.C., Carnegie Endowment for International Peace (1998).

Aleinikoff, Thomas Alexander, and Douglas B. Klusmeyer (eds.). *Citizenship Policies for an Age of Migration.* Washington, D.C., Carnegie Endowment for International Peace (2002).

Aleinikoff, Thomas Alexander, et al. (eds.). *Citizenship Today: Global Perspectives and Practices.* Washington, D.C., Carnegie Endowment for International Peace (2001).

Appadurai, Arjun. *Modernity at Large: Cultural Dimensions of Globalization.* Minneapolis, University of Minnesota Press (1996).

Bauböck, Rainer. *Transnational Citizenship: Membership and Rights in International Migration.* Aldershot, U.K., Edward Elgar (1994).

Benhabib, Seyla. *The Rights of Others: Aliens, Residents and Citizens.* Cambridge, U.K., Cambridge University Press (2004).

Benhabib, Seyla. *The Claims of Culture: Equality and Diversity in the Global Era.* Princeton, N.J., Princeton University Press (2002).

Bloemraad, Irene. *Becoming a Citizen: Incorporating Immigrants and Refugees in the United States and Canada.* Berkeley, University of California Press (2006).

Bosniak, Linda. *The Citizen and the Alien: Dilemmas of Contemporary Membership.* Princeton, N.J., Princeton University Press (2006).

Bosniak, Linda. Constitutional Citizenship through the Prism of Alienage, 63 *Ohio State Law Journal* 1285–1325 (2002).

Bosniak, Linda. Multiple Nationality and the Postnational Transformation of Citizenship, 42 *Virginia Journal of International Law* 979–1004 (2002).

Bosniak, Linda. Citizenship Denationalized, 7 *Indiana Journal of Global Legal Studies* 447–509 (2000).

Brimelow, Peter. *Alien Nation: Common Sense about America's Immigration Disaster.* New York, Random House (1995).

Brubaker, Rogers. *Citizenship and Nationhood in France and Germany*. Cambridge, Mass., Harvard University Press (1992).

Carens, Joseph H. *Culture, Citizenship, and Community: A Contextual Exploration of Justice as Evenhandedness*. New York, Oxford University Press (2000).

Faulks, Keith. *Citizenship*. New York, Routledge (2000).

Geyer, Georgie Anne. *Americans No More*. New York, Atlantic Monthly Press (1996).

Gordon, Jennifer. *Suburban Sweatshops: The Fight for Immigrant Rights*. Cambridge, Mass., Harvard University Press (2005).

Hansen, Randall, and Patrick Weil (eds.). *Dual Nationality, Social Rights, and Federal Citizenship in the U.S. and Europe: The Reinvention of Citizenship*. New York, Berghahn Books (2002).

Hollinger, David A. *Postethnic America: Beyond Multiculturalism*. New York, Basic Books (1995).

Honig, Bonnie. *Democracy and the Foreigner*. Princeton, N.J., Princeton University Press (2001).

Huntington, Samuel P. *Who Are We? The Challenges to America's National Identity*. New York, Simon and Schuster (2004).

Jacobson, David. *Rights across Borders: Immigration and the Decline of Citizenship*. Baltimore, Johns Hopkins University Press (1996).

Karst, Kenneth L. The Bonds of American Nationhood, 21 *Cardozo Law Review* 1141–1182 (2000).

Karst, Kenneth L. *Belonging to America: Equal Citizenship and the Constitution*. New Haven, Conn., Yale University Press (1989).

Kettner, James H. *The Development of American Citizenship, 1608–1870*. Chapel Hill, N.C., University of North Carolina Press (1978).

Koslowski, Rey. *Migrants and Citizens: Demographic Change in the European State System*. Ithaca, N.Y., Cornell University Press (2000).

Kymlicka, Will. *Multicultural Citizenship: A Liberal Theory of Minority Rights*. New York, Oxford University Press (1995).

Marshall, T. H. *Citizenship and Social Class, and Other Essays*. Cambridge, U.K., Cambridge University Press (1950).

Martin, David A. New Rules on Dual Nationality for a Democratizing Globe: Between Rejection and Embrace, 14 *Georgetown Immigration Law Journal* 1–34 (1999).

Martin, David, and Kay Hailbronner (eds.). *Rights and Duties of Dual Nationals: Evolution and Prospects*. New York, Kluwer Law International (2003).

Miller, David. *On Nationality*. New York, Oxford University Press (1995).

Miller, John J. *The Unmaking of Americans: How Multiculturalism Has Undermined the Assimilation Ethic*. New York, Free Press (1998).

Motomura, Hiroshi. *Americans in Waiting: The Lost Story of Immigration and Citizenship in the United States*. New York, Oxford University Press (2006).

Neuman, Gerald L. *Strangers to the Constitution: Immigrants, Borders, and Fundamental Law*. Princeton, N.J., Princeton University Press (1996).

Neuman, Gerald L. Justifying U.S. Naturalization Policies, 35 *Virginia Journal of International Law* 237–278 (1994).

Pickus, Noah M. J. *True Faith and Allegiance: Immigration and American Civic Nationalism*. Princeton, N.J., Princeton University Press (2005).

Pickus, Noah M. J. (ed.). *Immigration and Citizenship in the Twenty-First Century*. Lanham, Md., Rowman and Littlefield (1998).

Raskin, Jamin B. Legal Aliens, Local Citizens: The Historical, Constitutional and Theoretical Meanings of Alien Suffrage, 141 *University of Pennsylvania Law Review* 1391–1470 (1993).

Renshon, Stanley Allen. *The 50% American: Immigration and National Identity in an Age of Terror*. Washington, D.C., Georgetown University Press (2005).

Rubio-Marín, Ruth. *Immigration as a Democratic Challenge: Citizenship and Inclusion in Germany and the United States*. New York, Cambridge University Press (2000).

Sassen, Saskia. *Guests and Aliens*. New York, New Press (1999).

Sassen, Saskia. *Losing Control? Sovereignty in an Age of Globalization*. New York, Columbia University Press (1996).

Schlesinger, Arthur M., Jr. *The Disuniting of America*. New York, W.W. Norton (1998).

Schuck, Peter H. *Citizens, Strangers, and In-Betweens: Essays on Immigration and Citizenship*. Boulder, Colo., Westview Press (1998).

Schuck, Peter H., and Rogers M. Smith. *Citizenship Without Consent: Illegal Aliens in the American Polity*. New Haven, Conn., Yale University Press (1985).

Smith, Robert C. *Mexican New York: Transnational Lives of New Immigrants*. Berkeley, University of California Press (2006).

Smith, Rogers M. *Civic Ideals: Conflicting Visions of Citizenship in U.S. History*. New Haven, Conn., Yale University Press (1997).

Soysal, Yasemin Nuhoğlu. *Limits of Citizenship: Migrants and Postnational Membership in Europe*. Chicago, University of Chicago Press (1994).

Spiro, Peter J. Perfecting Political Diaspora, 81 *New York University Law Review* 207–233 (2006).

Spiro, Peter J. The Impossibility of Citizenship, 101 *Michigan Law Review* 1492–1511 (2003).

Spiro, Peter J. The Citizenship Dilemma, 51 *Stanford Law Review* 597–639 (1999).

Spiro, Peter J. Questioning Barriers to Naturalization, 13 *Georgetown Immigration Law Journal* 479–519 (1999).

Spiro, Peter J. Dual Nationality and the Meaning of Citizenship, 46 *Emory Law Journal* 1411–1485 (1997).

Walzer, Michael. *What It Means to Be an American*. New York, Marsilio (1992).

Walzer, Michael. *Spheres of Justice: A Defense of Pluralism and Equality*. New York, Basic Books (1983).

Walzer, Michael. *Obligations: Essays on Disobedience, War, and Citizenship*. Cambridge, Mass., Harvard University Press (1970).

Young, Iris Marion. *Justice and the Politics of Difference*. Princeton, N.J., Princeton University Press (1990).

INDEX

Ackerman, Bruce, 119–120
affirmative action, 129, 153
African American
    citizenship, 12–13, 165n7
    and multiculturalism, 128
    Seminole tribe membership, 157
Afroyim v. Rusk, 68–69, 72, 172n1
Alien and Sedition Acts, 35
Alien Nation, 110, 112
aliens. *See* noncitizens
al-Marri, Ali Saleh Kahlah, 97
al-Qaeda, 104–105
American Association of Retired People, 155
American identity
    citizenship dilemma, 157
    as civic nation, 46–50, 52, 116
    conservative nationalism and, 114–115
    democracy incubator, 50
    dual citizenship and, 78–79
    English language and, 40–42
    and globalization, 44–45, 53
    immigration policy, 161
    liberal nationalism and, 115
    and multiculturalism, 127
    plurality, 134–135
    and popular culture, 43–44
    "second choice" problem, 76–77
    state citizenship and, 54–55
    as "universal nation," 34, 119
Amish, 147
Amnesty International
    and corporate influence, 147
    democratic process in, 149

governance standards, 142
    transnational networks, 126
animal rights, 125
anti-immigration activism
    and citizenship, 15, 91, 110–112
    impact of, 94–95
    and naturalization rates, 57–58
    Proposition 187, 15
    welfare reform, 89
Appadurai, Arjun, 22, 134–135, 138
Arendt, Hannah, 70, 132, 171n25
Ashcroft, John, 96
Asian immigrants, 13, 17, 35
assimilation
    conservative nationalism and, 109, 112,
        114–115
    diasporic immigrants and, 22–23
    and globalization, 10, 24–25, 161
    and immigration, 4–5, 17
    and naturalization, 23–24
    plural citizenship and, 74
    residency requirements, 37–39
    territorial citizenship and, 19
Australia, 23

Baltic states, 145
Bancroft, George, 61
Bancroft treaties, 64
banishment, 152
banking, 146
Barber, Benjamin R., 132
Bar-Yaacov, Nissim, 175n7
Basqueland, 145

183

Berlusconi, Silvio, 70
Bickel, Alexander M., 83
bilingualism, 112
birth tourism, 20
birthright citizenship. *See also* citizenship;
    jus sanguinis; jus soli
  assimilation and, 17
  attachments of, 30
  border zones, 28–30
  community and, 19–20
  and the Constitution, 12–15
  diasporic immigrants and, 22–23
  dual nationality, 64–65, 72
  German citizenship law, 18
  human rights and, 16
  intergenerational caste, 18–19
  limitations on, 160
  Native Americans, 165–166n11
  and parentage, 10–11, 25–27
  plural citizenship and, 73, 76
  race controversy, 12
  return immigration and, 20
  territorial citizenship, 19–20
  undocumented aliens, 13–15
  U.S. territories, 13
  Wong Kim Ark decision, 17
Black, Jeremiah Sullivan, 61
border zones, 27–30, 101
Bosniak, Linda, 54, 100
Brennan, William, 86, 103–104
Brimelow, Peter, 110, 112
Buchanan, Patrick, 111, 112
Bush, George W.
  and amnesty, 95
  enemy combatants, 104–105
  foreign-language ballots, support for, 51
  inaugural address, 3
  "path to citizenship," political use of,
    159–160

California, 85, 94–95, 172n31
Calvin's Case (*Calvin v. Smith*)
  and dual nationality, 62
  English common law, 11
  sovereign/subject relationship, 34
campaign contributions, 93, 172n31
Carens, Joseph H., 119
Cass, Lewis, 63
Catholic Church
  Chinese box paradigm, 125–126

sex abuse scandals, 143
transnational networks, 126
trial-type proceedings within, 149
chain immigration, 39–40, 86–87
China, 22, 103
"Chinese box" paradigm
  breakdown of, 126
  globalization and, 125
  liberal nationalism and, 126, 134
  and multiculturalism, 127–128
  pluralism, 123
  and state supremacy, 143–144
citizenship. *See also* birthright citizenship;
    naturalization; territorial citizenship
  African American, 12–13, 165n7
  Allotment Act, 165n10
  Baltic states, 145
  birth tourism, 20
  bonds of, 111
  "citizenship of aliens," 54, 100–101
  "common life" and, 120–121
  and community, 3–4, 81, 135, 156–157,
    163
  Constitution and, 11
  as criterion for employment, 85
  declining importance of, 30–31, 97, 106,
    112, 161–162
  definition of, 9
  denationalization, 66
  diasporic immigrants, 20–21
  dual nationality, 6, 68, 73–75, 78–79
  and due process, 105
  end of, 7–8
  future of in America, 53–56
  and human rights, 102, 132
  immigration, relationship to, 159–61
  as job qualification, 85
  liberal nationalism and, 115, 117, 119
  membership criteria, 153
  Nationality Act of 1940, 66
  and the nation-state, 137–138
  naturalization attraction and, 36–37
  nature of, 7
  and nonstate communities, 150–152
  obligations of, 82–83, 97–99, 106–108
  and parentage, 25–26
  professional associations and, 84–85
  renunciation of, 174n40
  state as unit of community, 109
  testing for, 42–44

transnational networks, 125
voting privileges, 30–31, 56, 81, 91–92
Walzer definition, 123–124
Citizenship Clause
ambiguity of, 13
citizenship of aliens, 100
Dred Scott v. Sandford, 9–10, 12
Elk v. Wilkins, 13
Native Americans and, 13
state citizenship and, 53
undocumented aliens and, 13–15
citizenship law
and citizenship, decline of, 162
dual citizenship and, 59–60
dual nationality, 65–67
Germany and, 18
and immigration reform, 160
mixed marriages and, 63–64
and national identity, 5–6
and naturalization, 40–42
"citizenship of aliens," 54, 100–101
Citizenship Without Consent (Schuck and
    Smith), 14
Ciudad Juárez, 28–29, 101, 105, 120, 121
civic nation, 46–50, 52, 116
civics requirement
conservative nationalism and,
    113–114
flashcards for, 160
liberal nationalists and, 122
naturalization and, 35–36, 40–45, 51
and political participation, 48
relevance of test, 45–46, 51
civil rights, 83–85
civil society, 134
Civil War
black naturalization after, 35
conscription of declarant aliens, 98
Dred Scott v. Sandford, 9, 12
CNN, 50
Coke, Edward, 11
cold war, 49, 52, 133
Colombia, 22
"common life," 120–121
communism, 49
Communist Party, 35
community
birthright citizenship and, 17, 19–20
border zones, 27–30
changing nature of, 137–138

and citizenship, 3–4, 27, 81, 135,
    156–157, 163
and citizenship law, 5
civic nation, 47
diasporic immigrants and, 23
and dual citizenship, 59, 68
and globalization, 132
"happenstance" Americans and, 31
membership criteria, 151–152
and naturalization, 33, 36–37, 56
need for, 131
nonstate forms of, 138
obligations of citizenship, 82–83,
    106–108
plural citizenship and, 73, 76–77
self-determination and, 153–154
size and solidarity, 145
state citizenship and, 55
conscription. *See* military service
conservative nationalism
citizenship as sacred quantity, 112
definition of, 109
immigration and, 113
and naturalization, 113–114
Constitution. *See also* Citizenship Clause
citizenship and, 11
due process, 84
First Amendment, 143
Fourth Amendment, 103–104
Fourteenth Amendment, 9–10, 12–13,
    53
hate speech and, 142
and legal aliens, 85
Naturalization Clause, 165n2
constitutional patriotism, 116
constitutional values, 47
corporations
democratic process in, 149
employee rights within, 141, 144
private security forces, 140
and redistribution, 147
shareholder voting, 141
social responsibility movement, 155
transnational networks, 125
Court of Arbitration for Sport, 142
Cuba, 95
culture wars, 43–44, 128, 135

Davos, 147
declarant aliens, 84, 92, 98–99

democracy
    America as incubator, 50
    constitutional values, 48–50
    globalization and, 4
    immigration and, 119
    in nongovernmental organizations,
        148–149
    nonstate communities and, 138, 149
    pervasiveness of, 52
democratic citizenship, 115
Denmark, 92
deportation
    after 9/11, 96
    and citizenship, 31, 58, 86
    criminal activity, basis for, 16, 85, 95
    enemy aliens, 86
    and 1996 immigration law, 85–86, 95
    minimal probability of, 86–88
diasporic immigrants
    American, 27
    and American pluralism, 135
    assimilation of, 22–23
    attachments of, 22–25, 29
    citizenship and, 20–21
    citizenship of aliens, 101
    plural citizenship and, 77
    and redistribution, 146
    remittances, 30, 71
    residency requirements and
        naturalization, 39–40
diplomatic protection
    citizenship privilege, 102–103
    corporations and, 140
    dual nationality, 62–66
    international law, 94
    Mexican prisons, 174n44
    passports, 140
disability
    as identity, 151
    waiver for naturalization, 40–41, 168n15
Dominican Republic
    American attachments of, 29–30
    diasporic immigrants, 22, 23
    dual citizenship, 70, 76
draft. *See* military service
Dred Scott v. Sandford, 9–10, 12
Driver's licenses, 91, 145
dual citizenship. *See also* naturalization
    acceptance of, 6, 59–60, 70, 73

Act Relative to the Naturalization and
        Citizenship of Married Women, 170n7
Afroyim v. Rusk, 69
    and American identity, 78–79, 162
    Bancroft treaties, 64
    birthright citizenship and, 64–65, 76–77
    citizenship, diminished nature of, 73–75, 83
    Congressional hearings on, 160
    conservative nationalism and, 113
    election requirement and, 65–66, 68–70
    and espionage, 61–62, 71
    expatriation and, 19, 64, 66, 68–70, 75, 77
    and globalization, 60, 67–70
    Hague Convention on Reduction of
        Cases of Multiple Nationality, 72
    historical disfavor for, 59–64
    immorality of, 59, 156
    and individual identity, 59
    and international law, 67, 72
    liberal nationalism and, 122–124
    "mixed" marriages and, 63–64, 68
    and national identity, 60, 76–79
    naturalization and, 31, 69–70, 74–76
    psychological conflicts, 113, 175n7
    "second choice" problem, 75–77
    as security threat, 61, 71
    and sovereignty, 61–62
    under U.S. law, 65–67, 72
    voting rights, 70, 105–106
    War of 1812, 62–63
dual nationality. *See* dual citizenship
due process, 83–85, 105
Dunn v. Blumstein, 53–54

education
    in-state tuition, 28, 91, 145
    Plyler v. Doe, 91
    Texas Education Code, 28, 168n41
    undocumented aliens and, 91, 105, 145
educational institutions, 142, 149
election requirement. *See* dual citizenship
Elk v. Wilkins, 13
El Paso, 28–29, 101
El Salvador, 22, 29–30
employment, 90, 144
enemy aliens, 86
enemy combatants, 96–97, 104–105
English common law, 11, 23, 34
English language

and American identity, 41, 112
conservative nationalism, 112
liberal nationalism and, 122
Nationality Act of 1952, 40
naturalization requirement, 6, 33, 35,
    39, 48, 51
and "path to citizenship," 160
environmentalism, 147–148, 150
ethnic neighborhoods, 39–40
ethnicity, 61
European Convention on Nationality, 72
European Union
constitutional patriotism, 116
dual citizenship, 69
nature of, 145
voting privileges, 92
excommunication, 152, 154
expatriation
Afroyim v. Rusk, 68–69, 172n1
Bellei case, 26
dual citizenship and, 64, 66, 69–70, 77
Hostage Act of 1868, 178n23
International Covenant on Civil and
    Political Rights, 178n23
international law and, 154
military service and, 69
ExxonMobil, 147

Florida, 85, 106
foreign aid, 134
foreign-language ballots, 51
foreign-language media, 42, 50–51
Fourteenth Amendment. See Citizenship
    Clause; Constitution
Fox News, 44
France, 11
Frankfurter, Felix, 66
free trade, 121

gated communities, 141–142
gender
Act Relative to the Naturalization and
    Citizenship of Married Women, 170n7
and citizenship, 26
dual nationality and, 63–64
military service and citizenship, 98
"mixed" marriages and, 170n6
Germany, 11, 18, 25
Geyer, Georgie Anne, 112, 175n3

Gilbertson, Greta, 76
Gleason, Philip, 34
globalization
and American citizenship, 53
American popular culture, 44
American universalism, 4–5
and assimilation, 10, 24–25, 161
Chinese box paradigm, 125
citizenship of aliens, 100
and community, 132
diasporic immigrants and, 20, 22
and dual citizenship, 60, 67–70
and national identity, 33
nonstate influence and, 147–148
redistribution, 146
residency requirements and
    naturalization, 39
and sovereignty, 78
territorial citizenship and, 19, 120–121
global marketplace, 132
global taxation, 134
Grant, Ruth, 150
Grant, Ulysses S., 63
Great Society, 144
Greece (ancient)
birthright citizenship, 11, 112
citizenship and parentage, 25
military service and citizenship, 97–98
naturalization as reward, 34
Greenpeace, 126, 147
Guam, 13
Guantanamo Bay, 21, 105
guest workers, 17, 18

habeas corpus, 105
Habermas, Jürgen, 116
Haiti, 22, 95
Hamdan v. Rumsfeld, 105
Hamdi, Yaser, 21–22, 97
Hampton v. Mow Sun Wong, 172n13
hate speech, 142
Hollinger, David, 123
Holocaust, 132
Holy Roman Empire, 119
home town associations, 146
homesteading, 84
homosexuality. See sexual orientation
Honig, Bonnie, 116–117
Hostage Act of 1868, 178n23

human rights
and citizenship, 16, 132
citizenship status and, 102
as constraint on U.S. action, 102–105
corporate citizenship report, 147
European Convention on Nationality, 72
individual rights, 115, 132
International Covenant on Civil and
Political Rights, 104
and international law, 70–71, 133
NGO influence on, 147
and nonstate communities, 138, 140,
157
and plural citizenship, 70–71
postnational model, 133
sexual orientation discrimination, 151
statelessness, 171n25
transnational networks, 125
Huntington, Samuel, 52, 112–113

identity politics, 130
Ignatieff, Michael, 116
illegal aliens. *See* undocumented aliens
immigration. *See also* naturalization
and American pluralism, 60–61
assimilation and, 4–5
border zones, 28
chain immigration, 39–40, 86–87
conservative nationalism and, 113
dual nationality, 62
federal power over, 84
Fourteenth Amendment and, 9–10
jus soli, 12
liberalization of, 95
and nativism, 9
open borders approach to, 119
as "path to citizenship," 159
racial restrictions on, 111
reform of, 160
regulations, early American, 15–16
remittances, 30, 71
return immigration and, 20–21, 65
"rotten boroughs," 117, 175n17
state citizenship and, 53–54
immigration law
and citizenship, 81, 159–162
deportation and, 85–86, 95
enforcement of, 88
privileging of citizen families, 86

India
arranged marriage, 23
diasporic immigrants, 22, 146
dual citizenship and, 70
individual identity, 59, 155
individual rights, 115, 132. *See also* human
rights
Inquisition, 149
interest groups, 125
intergenerational caste, 18–19
intergenerational justice, 129
International Covenant on Civil and Political
Rights, 104, 178n23
International Labor Organization, 150
international law
citizenship and border zones, 29
diplomatic protection, 94, 102–103
dual nationality and, 67
and the Holocaust, 132
and human rights, 70–71, 133
and nationality, 154
self-determination, 130
sovereign/subject relations, 62, 131
territorial citizenship, 101
unreasonable search and seizure and, 104
International Law Commission, 67
International Olympic Committee, 142, 144
International Organization for Standardization, 148
International SOS, 140
Internet
and the American political process, 51
availability of, 50
domain names, allocation of, 142, 144
privacy standards, 142
Iraq, 140
Ireland, 25, 69–70, 73
Israel
Afroyim v. Rusk, 69
bombing of Lebanon, 140
bond issuance, 146
dual citizenship, 73
Israeli-Palestinian conflict, 124
Italy, 25, 70, 73

Japanese internment, 86, 96–97
Jordan Commission, 47
jury duty, 82, 99
jus migrationis, 54

jus sanguinis
  birthright citizenship, 11, 25–27
  border zones, 29
  dual nationality, 64–65
  Germany, 18
  Immigration and Nationality Act,
    167n39
  membership criteria, 151
  and plural citizenship, 68
  and undocumented aliens, 14
jus soli
  anti-immigration activism, 15
  birthright citizenship, 11, 16
  border zones, 29
  citizenship of aliens, 100–101
  as creating "happenstance" Americans, 22
  dual nationality, 64–65
  English common law, 11
  and naturalization, 24
  and plural citizenship, 68, 76–77
  race controversy, 12
  resilience of, 14
  state citizenship and, 55

Karst, Kenneth, 116
Keohane, Robert, 150
Kettner, James H., 165n5
Know-Nothings, 110
Kohn, Hans, 119
Korea, 22
Korean War, 98
Kymlicka, Will, 143

labor rights, 147
Lafayette, 98
Laredo, 28
legal residents. *See* permanent residents
liberal nationalism
  and American citizenship, 115
  Chinese box paradigm and, 134
  citizenship, nature of, 118–120, 153
  and civil society, 134
  definition of, 109–110
  dual citizenship, 122–123
  immigration restrictions, 119–120
  John Stuart Mill, 176n29
  and multiculturalism, 126–127, 129–131
  and national identity, 120–123
  and the nation-state, 116

noncitizens and, 121–122
one-world government, 132–135
"opt-out" challenge to, 116–118
plural citizenship and, 123–124
redistribution, 132, 144–145
transnational networks and, 126
licensing, 84–85, 90
Lipschutz, Ronnie D., 29
locational security, 85–88
Lodge, Henry Cabot, 61

Mackenzie v. Hare, 170n6
Madison, James, 47
Marshall, T. H., 144
Mathews v. Diaz, 172n13
McDonald's, 44–45
Mexico
  citizens living in America, 22
  diasporic immigrants, 22
  diplomatic protection, 94, 174n44
  dual citizenship, 70, 72
  home town associations, 146
  Perez v. Brownell, 66
  remittances, 71
  return immigration and, 21
  Texas tuition fees, 168n41
Mickey Mouse, 44
military service
  aliens and, 98, 174n40
  conscription, 98, 139
  and expatriation, 69
  Nationality Act of 1940, 66
  and naturalization, 38
  as obligation of citizenship, 82, 97–98
military tribunals, 96
Mill, John Stuart, 122, 176n29
Miller, David, 127
Miller, John J., 112
mixed marriages, 63–64, 170nn6–7
mixed race, 155
mobility
  globalization and dual citizenship, 68
  and "happenstance" Americans, 22
  membership termination, 154
  residency requirements and, 33, 40
  territorial citizenship and, 19–20
Mormon Church, 141, 146–147
Motomura, Hiroshi, 92
Moussaoui, Zacarias, 96

MTV, 44
multiculturalism
  "affinity groups", 129–130
  and American pluralism, 134–135
  Balkanizers, 131
  Chinese box paradigm, 127–128
  and conservative nationalism, 114
  end of, 126–129
  identity politics, 130
  liberal nationalism and, 129–131
  and nationalism, 110
  redistribution, 127–128, 144
  self-determination and, 130
  and sovereignty, 129–131
  tribal membership and, 153–154

national defense, 132
national identity
  American universalism, 7
  birth and, 32
  and citizenship law, 5
  and globalization, 33
  liberal nationalism and, 115, 120–123
  and multiculturalism, 129, 131
  and naturalization, 5–6, 33–34, 56, 75
  and plural citizenship, 60, 73–74,
    77–79
nationalism
  and American identity, 109
  Bush and amnesty, 160
  and multiculturalism, 131
  nonstate entities, 143–144
  and one-world government, 132
  territorial presence and, 145
nationality. See citizenship
Nationality Act of 1940, 66
Nationality Act of 1952, 40, 98
nation-state. See also nonstate entities
  as affinity group, 129–130
  American citizenship and, 162
  conservative nationalism, 113
  and human rights, 132
  and identity, 125
  justification for, 129
  liberal nationalism and, 115–116
  nature of, 137
  plural citizenship and, 74
  redistribution and, 144
  regulation, efficacy of, 143

territorial citizenship and the political
    process, 120–121
  and terrorism, 133–134
  transnational networks and, 126
  as unit of community, 109
Native Americans, 13, 165n10, 165–
    166n11
nativism, 9, 109–112
naturalization. See also civics requirement;
    oath (naturalization); residency
    requirements
  after 9/11, 58, 170n41
  after permanent residency, 21
  after the Civil War, 35
  and assimilation, 23–24
  automatic, 118
  Bancroft treaties, 64
  citizenship, attraction of, 36–37
  and citizenship law, 40–42
  common usage in America, 34–37
  conservative nationalism and, 113
  Constitution and, 11
  constitutional values, 48–49
  declarant aliens, 92
  declining application for, 58, 74, 81,
    160
  and dual citizenship, 62–63, 70
  eligibility for, 117
  English language requirement, 41–42
  expatriation and, 66
  fees for, 56–57, 160
  homesteading rights, 84
  Jordan Commission report, 47
  jury duty and, 99
  liberal nationalism and, 117
  military service and, 38
  and national identity, 5–6, 32–34, 56
  Nationality Act of 1952, 40
  Naturalization Act of 1795, 63
  numbers of citizens, 167n27
  and plural citizenship, 73, 76, 83
  and race, 34–35, 85
  return immigration and, 21
  second choice problem, 75–77
  Spanish language services, 51
  test, 40–41, 42–44, 169n22
  undocumented aliens and, 16
  waivers from requirements, 40–41, 51,
    56–57, 168n6, 168n15

Neuman, Gerald, 15, 41, 51
New York, 172n31
New York City, 42, 92
New York Times, 50, 160
New Zealand, 92
NGOs (nongovernmental organizations)
   corporate influence, 147
   democratic process, 148–149
   and human rights, 157
   political power of, 106, 150
9/11. *See also* terrorism
   deprivation of rights after, 105
   and the draft, 139
   immigration after, 20
   naturalization after, 58, 170n41
   rights of aliens after, 95–97
   security after, 133–134
noncitizens
   citizenship education, 140–141
   foreign tax credits, 99
   Hampton v. Mow Sun Wong, 172n13
   and inheritance, 84
   liberal nationalism and, 121–122
   Mathews v. Diaz, 172n13
   military service and, 98
   political activism, 93–94
   property rights, 84
   rights after 9/11, 95–97
   rights of, 87
   social safety net, 89–91
   Social Security benefits, 105
nongovernmental organizations (NGOs).
   See NGOs
nonimmigrants, 23–24, 90, 166–167n26
   birthright citizenship and, 23, 24
   H-1B visa, 20–21, 90, 100–101
   J visa, 21
   L visa, 21, 166–167n26
   population of, 20–21, 167n27
   public benefits and, 90
   student visas, 90
   tourist visas, 20
nonresident noncitizens, 103–104, 106, 118
nonstate communities. *See also* corporations;
   educational institutions; NGOs; race;
   religions; sexual orientation
   and democracy, 138, 149
   and free speech, 143
   family as form of, 145–46

and globalization, 147–148
   group membership criteria, 150–152
   human rights and, 140
   membership, termination of, 154
   membership criteria, 156–157
   plural citizenship, 155
   redistribution, 144–148
   security and, 138–140
   sovereignty, 144
Norman, Wayne, 143
Nuevo Laredo, 28

oath (naturalization). *See also* naturalization
   and conscription, 98
   conservative nationalism and, 113
   constitutional values, 49–50
   dual citizenship, 69
   enforcement of, 72
   expatriation and, 66
   justification for, 51
   Naturalization Act of 1795, 63
   requirement, 35–36
   waiver for disabilities, 51, 168n6
obligations of citizenship
   history of, 82
   nature of, 97–99, 106–108
   and nonstate communities, 139
Occupational Safety and Health
   Administration (OSHA), 142
Office of Citizenship, 160
one-world government, 132–135
"opt-out" challenge, 116–118

Padilla, Jose, 97
Palestine, 124
Palmer Raids, 96–97
Palmerston, 61
parentage, 10, 25–27
particularism, 4
passports
   and customs lines, 87
   and diplomatic protection, 102–103, 140
   dual citizenship and, 76
Peace of Westphalia, 130
Perez v. Brownell, 66, 172n1
permanent residents. *See also* noncitizens
   abandonment of status, 87
   campaign contributions by, 93, 172n31
   deportation of, 86–87

permanent residents (*cont.*)
historical treatment of, 83–85
military service and, 98, 174n40
numbers of, 167n27
political influence of, 93–95
public benefits and, 89
return migration by, 21
value of status, 91, 159
voting by, 92
Philippines
American attachments of, 29–30
diasporic immigrants, 22, 71
dual citizenship, 70
Pickus, Noah M. J., 123
plural citizenship. *See* dual citizenship
pluralism, 60–61, 123, 135
Plyler v. Doe, 91
Poland, 70
policy making, 137–138
political activism
immigrants and, 113
NGOs, 106, 150
noncitizen, 93–94
resident aliens, 94, 106
undocumented aliens, 94, 159
popular culture, 43–44
postnational model, 133
private security forces, 140
professional associations, 84–85, 142
property rights, 84
Proposition 187, 15
public benefits
eligibility for, 95
in-state tuition, 91, 145
Mathews v. Diaz, 172n13
Medicare, 89
noncitizens and, 89–91
territorial citizenship, 101
territorial presence, 105
1996 welfare reform act, 81, 89,
94–95
Puerto Rico, 13, 165–166n11

Quebec, 145
"queer nation," 130

Race. *See also* slavery
American citizenship and, 162
American naturalization, 34–35, 85

birthright citizenship, 12
as identity, 152, 155
and multiculturalism, 127
state citizenship and, 53
racism, 111
Rawls, John, 119, 124
Raz, Joseph, 127
redistribution
and citizenship, 111
globalization and, 146
liberal nationalism and, 132
and multiculturalism, 127–128, 130
and nonstate communities, 144–148
religions and, 146–147
Reich, Robert, 125
Reid, Richard, 96
Religions
membership criteria for, 151–152, 157
as nonstate communities, 141
Peace of Westphalia, 130
plural membership, 155
and redistribution, 146–147
remittances, 30, 71, 146
Renaissance Era, 34, 119
residency requirements
citizenship by descent, 26–27
election requirement and, 65–66
English language requirement and, 42
naturalization and, 33, 35, 37–38
political assimiliation and, 47
relevance of, 46, 51–52, 97, 159
state citizenship and, 53–54
time period for, 37–38
residency status
citizenship and, 26–27
naturalization test and, 43
undocumented aliens and, 16
resident aliens
chain immigration, 86
civil rights of, 83–85
deportation of, 95
diplomatic protection for, 103
jury duty, 99
liberal nationalism and, 117–118
and naturalization, 37, 57, 117
obligations of citizenship, 82
political power of, 94, 106
public benefits and, 89
restrictions on, 87

rights of, 81, 86
and taxation, 99
voting privileges, 92
return immigration, 21, 65
Revolutionary War, 98
Rogers v. Bellei, 26
Rome (ancient), 11, 34, 54
Roosevelt, Theodore, 61
"rotten boroughs," 117, 175n17
Rubio-Marín, Ruth, 118

San Diego, 28
Sassen, Saskia, 159
Schlesinger, Arthur M., Jr., 122, 128
Schuck, Peter H., 14–15, 23, 76
Scotland, 145
secessionist movements, 145
"second choice" problem, 75–77
security
    after 9/11, 133–134
    and American nation, 162
    Department of Homeland Security, 160,
        169n22, 170n41
    locational security, 85–88
    nonstate entities, 138–140
    private security forces, 140
self-determination, 130, 153–154
Sellers, Frances Stead, 106
Seminole tribe, 157
separatists, 112, 175n3
Seward, William H., 64
sexual orientation
    gays, 125, 130
    identity criteria, 151
    and multiculturalism, 127
Sierra Club, 149, 151
Singer, Audrey, 76
slavery
    birthright citizenship and, 11, 64
    jus soli, 12
    reparations for, 128–129
Smith, Rogers M.
    on birthright citizenship, 14–15, 23
    on historical exclusions of
        citizenship, 111
    on the nation-state and liberalism, 116
Snoop Dogg, 115
social responsibility movement, 155
Social Security, 89, 105, 144

sovereignty
    and dual citizenship, 61–62
    English common law, 11
    and globalization, 78
    international law and, 101, 131
    and multiculturalism, 129–131
    and nonstate entities, 144
    sovereign/subject relationship, 34
Soysal, Yasemin, 133
Spanish language, 41, 51, 169n17
state. *See* nation-state
state citizenship, 53–56
statelessness
    danger of, 132
    and human rights, 133, 171n25
    jus sanguinis, 14
suffragette movement, 64

Taiwan, 71
Takoma Park, 92
Taney, Roger, 12
TANF (Temporary Assistance for Needy
        Families), 89
taxes
    estate taxes, 57, 170n40
    global taxation, 134
    and noncitizens, 82, 98–99
Temporary Assistance for Needy Families
        (TANF), 89
territorial citizenship
    and assimilation, 25
    Citizenship Clause, 12, 100
    "citizenship of aliens," 100–101
    and community, 19–20, 27–28
    conservative nationalism and, 113
    and globalization, 19, 120–121
    importance of, 32
    justification for, 15–16
    liberal nationalism and, 117–118, 161
    public benefits, 101
    residency status, 26–27
    roots of, 10–13
    transnational networks and, 20
territorial presence, 100–101, 105, 145
terrorism. *See also* 9/11
    extraterritorial enforcement after,
        104–105
    and local police, 139–140
    and nonstate actors, 139–140

terrorism (*cont.*)
  rights of aliens, 96
  security after, 133–134
Texas
  citizenship and employment, 85
  Education Code, 28, 168n41
  resident alien campaign contributions,
    172n31
  as state identity, 55
Thirty Years' War, 130
Tijuana, 28
Tocqueville, Alexis de, 134
transnational networks
  citizenship and, 20, 125
  corporate redistribution, 147
  dual citizenship, 76
  liberal nationalism and, 116
  mobility and residency requirements, 33
  nation-state, 126
tribal membership, 153
Turkey, 18, 71

undocumented aliens
  amnesty for, 94, 95, 159
  "assistance centers" for, 90
  birthright citizenship and, 13–15, 23, 30
  civil rights of, 83
  definition of, 13–14
  driver's licenses for, 91, 145
  education for, 90–91, 105
  estimated population of, 21
  intergenerational caste, danger of, 17–19
  liberal nationalism and, 117
  political power of, 94, 59
  public benefits and, 90–91
  Proposition 187, 15
  return immigration and, 21
  and risk of deportation, 87–88
  state assistance for, 145
  unions and, 90
  voting privileges, 92
unions, 90, 148–149, 151–152
United States v. Verdugo-Urquidez, 103–104
Universalism
  citizenship and, 4
  liberal nationalism and, 132
  and national identity, 7
  and naturalization, 34
USA PATRIOT Act, 96

U.S. Constitution. *See* Constitution
U.S. territories, 13

Vietnam War, 98
visas. *See* nonimmigrants
voting
  Afroyim v. Rusk, 68–69
  and citizenship, 30–31, 56, 81, 91–92
  corporate shareholders, 141, 149
  denationalization and, 66
  Dunn ruling, 54
  in foreign elections, 70, 172n1
  liberal nationalism and, 117, 122
  plural citizenship and, 105–106
  U.S. territories, 13
  Voting Rights Act, 51

waivers
  fees for naturalization, 56–57
  mental disability, 51
  naturalization, 40–41, 168n6, 168n15
Walzer, Michael
  American nationality, 116
  birthright citizenship, 17
  citizenship definition, 123–124
  community of character, 156
  national identity, 120–121
  nation-states and identity, 125
  one-world government, 132
  on statelessness, 132
War of 1812, 62–63
Warren, Earl
  citizenship, nature of, 83, 172n1
  Perez v. Brownell, 66
  right to travel, 120
welfare benefits, 134, 145, 160
welfare reform, 81, 89, 94–95
welfare state
  and citizenship, 31, 56
  family, 145
  and illegal aliens, 14
  and nonstate communities, 144
Wilson, Woodrow, 119
Wong Kim Ark v. United States, 13, 17
World Trade Organization (WTO), 150
World War I, 96–98
World War II, 86, 96–97, 132

Young, Iris Marion, 127, 129–130

CPSIA information can be obtained at www.ICGtesting.com
Printed in the USA
BVOW04*2010090816

458465BV00002B/16/P